The Christian's Guide to Designing a Loving Trust Plan

The Christian's Guide to Designing a Loving Trust Plan

Revised and Expanded Edition of *Loving Trust*

The Smart Alternative to Wills and Probate

Robert A. Esperti
Renno L. Peterson

ZondervanPublishingHouse
Grand Rapids, Michigan

A Division of HarperCollinsPublishers

The Christian's Guide to Designing a Loving Trust Plan
Revised and Expanded Edition of *Loving Trust*
Copyright © Robert A. Esperti and Renno L. Peterson, 1988, 1991, 1995
This edition printed by arrangement with Viking Penguin, a division of Penguin Books USA Inc.
All rights reserved.

A note to the reader.

The authors are not engaged in rendering legal, tax, accounting, or similar professional services. While legal, tax, and accounting issues covered in this book have been checked with sources believed to be reliable, some material may be affected by changes in the laws or in the interpretations of such laws since the manuscript for this book was completed. For that reason the accuracy and completeness of such information and the opinions based thereon are not guaranteed. In addition, state or local tax laws or procedural rules may have a material impact on the general recommendations made by the authors, and the strategies outlined in this book may not be suitable for every individual. If legal, accounting, tax, investment, or other expert advice is required, obtain the services of a competent practitioner.

Loving Trust® and Loving® are registered trademarks and service marks of Robert A. Esperti and Renno L. Peterson for their specific type of estate planning and estate-planning documents. Their specific estate planning includes love—an ingredient that has too significantly been missing from traditional estate planning.

To improve the readability of the text, rather than inserting ® after the words "Loving Trust" or "Loving," the first letter of "Loving Trust" and "Loving" is capitalized to indicate that they are registered trademarks or service marks that are normally followed by the appropriate noun defining the book or service.

Library of Congress Cataloging-in-Publication Data

Esperti, Robert A.
   The Christian's guide to designing a loving trust plan : the smart alternative to wills and probate / Robert A. Esperti and Renno L. Peterson.
      p. cm
   Originally published: Loving trust. New York : Viking, 1988.
   Includes indes.
   ISBN 0-310-46161-8
   1. Living trusts—United States—Popular works. 2. Estate planning—United States—Popular works. I. Peterson, Renno L. II. Title.
KF734.Z9E867 1995
346.7305'2—dc20   94-44261
[347.30653]   CIP

All Scripture quotations, unless otherwise indicated, are taken from the Holy Bible, *New International Version®. NIV®*. Copyright © 1988, 1991, 1984 by International Bible Society. Used by permission of Zondervan Publishing House. All rights reserved.

Edited by Mary McCormick and James Ruark
Printed in the United States of America

95 96 97 98 99 00 / ❖ DH / 10 9 8 7 6 5 4 3 2 1

For the joys of our lives:
Our wives, Liz and Karen,
and our sons, Rob, James, Andy, and Eric,
With Loving Trust

God did not give us a spirit of timidity,
but a spirit of power, of love
and of self-discipline.
2 Timothy 1:7

Contents

PART THREE

How to Get Your Loving Trust Plan Done

Preface:
Loving Trust—for Richer
or for Poorer

In sharing our Loving Trust knowledge in the classroom with our professional colleagues—lawyers, accountants, life insurance agents—we have often heard, " 'Loving Trust' is a wonderful concept, but I don't have that many wealthy clients." This response is exasperating, because Loving Trust planning is for almost everyone, rich or not.

If you have life insurance, your family needs Loving Trust protection. If your employer provides you with retirement benefits or disability insurance, or if you own your home or other assets, you and your family need Loving Trust protection.

We all need to be good stewards of whatever we have; that's where Loving Trust planning comes in. It is planning for ourselves and our loved ones that can grow and change with us throughout our lives.

Ninety-seven percent of us will not pay a dime of federal death tax, yet many of us will become disabled, and all of us will die; we will leave loved ones behind. We all want our life insurance and our other possessions—regardless of how modest or grand they may be—to be used to care for our loved ones, just as we would have done if we were there.

In our law practice, we routinely helped our clients with their Loving Trust plans. Our Loving Trust clients came from all walks of life. They were school-teachers, office workers, salespeople, waiters, and small-business owners; they were executives, tradespeople, professional athletes, retired couples, and tycoons. Our Loving Trust clients were single and married; many were parents and grandparents, others had no children. No matter what their race, economic background, or religion, they all had one common trait: They were people who cared enough about themselves and their loved ones to create their Loving Trust planning.

If you have little ones, teenagers, or mature children, your Loving Trust planning will convey your love and guiding hand. If you love your spouse, your Loving Trust planning will carry your marital vows beyond "Till death us do part."

If your dreams include charitable giving, your Loving Trust plan will help those dreams come true.

Your Loving Trust planning will allow you to give what you have to whom you want, when and in the way you want; to plan for yourself in your mature years or in case you become infirm; to provide joy to your children and grandchildren alike. It will save legal costs and, if necessary, federal death tax.

We are often asked, "At what age should I start my Loving Trust planning?" Our reply is, "If you have loved ones and insurance or other property, there is no better time than now!"

Acknowledgments

We thank Pamela Heim for her efforts in crafting the first drafts of chapters 1 and 14, and Jim Groen for his spiritual leadership and support over the past two decades.

All Scripture is God-breathed and is useful for teaching, rebuking, correcting and training in righteousness.

2 Timothy 3:16

Introduction to the Second Edition

Loving Trust was originally published in 1988. In writing it, we made the assumption that lawyers and other estate-planning professionals clearly recognized that will planning/probate was not nearly as effective as living trust-centered estate planning. Based on this assumption, we wrote *Loving Trust* as a *how-to-plan* book that would assist responsible readers in preparing for meetings with their lawyer and other planning professionals through a well-conceived estate-planning approach that we call "Loving Trust."

Loving Trust was not intended to be a book about *why* the revocable living trust is the best estate-planning vehicle. We assumed that almost every professional already knew how effective the living trust is; we saw no reason to dwell on it. Unfortunately, our assumption was just plain wrong!

Loving Trust created an immediate and unintended controversy among estate-planning professionals. For many professionals, it was a wonderful affirmation of how they viewed the proper estate-planning process. It confirmed their expertise and gave them a good feeling that "the proper estate-planning message" was finally getting out to the public. For others—particularly will-planning/probate lawyers—the opposite was true. Because *Loving Trust* debunked wills, probate, joint tenancy, and other commonly used but misunderstood planning techniques, they reacted with fear and anger.

Loving Trust generated a host of living trust-planning books, some of which were responsible attempts to educate the public. Many of them, however, were vague efforts that made mostly unsubstantiated attacks on wills, probate, and lawyers without offering any real explanations about why living trusts are superior planning vehicles.

The popularity of *Loving Trust*, coupled with the entire living trust movement, encouraged enterprising entrepreneurs to start living trust businesses whose sole aim was to make a fast dollar by selling living trust forms directly to the public while neatly sidestepping practicing attorneys and other estate-planning professionals. These companies used scare tactics to coerce people, particularly senior citizens, to buy their bare-bones, one-size-fits-all living trust forms. The public has been fleeced by these hucksters from coast to coast.

Some of these companies sell living trusts through salespeople who represent themselves as estate planners. These salespeople, who are inadequately trained and who are not lawyers, fill in a form and send it back to the home office where a boilerplate living trust is prepared. The salesperson then delivers the trust to the unsuspecting customer, who pays for the trust in the belief that some real planning has been done. In some instances, a lawyer is involved. This lawyer rubber-stamps the boilerplate living trust as "legal" in that particular state. Just because a document is legal does not make it effective. These lawyers rarely, if ever, meet the customers to make even a cursory determination of whether or not the boilerplate that the attorney reviewed fits the needs and desires of the customer. In several states, this type of behavior by an attorney has been held to be unethical.

The reputation of the living trust, and that of many highly trained professionals who routinely recommend it to their clients, has been damaged by these phony estate planners. Thankfully, many of these companies have been put out of business because of successful watchdog actions by various consumer-fraud agencies, and others are in the process of being put out of business.

As a result of the popularity of the Loving Trust movement, a number of old-fashioned will-planning/probate lawyers attempted to discredit living trusts in general. They attacked the living trust companies as frauds but in doing so either stated blatantly, or implied cleverly, that the living trust was the real culprit, that it was an overstated "gimmick" at the least, or a planning technique with only limited application to the rich at best. They denounced the use of the word *love* in estate planning as unprofessional and even made fun of it in their writings.

A number of so-called professional articles on living trusts that confused lawyers and laypersons alike appeared in technical journals and in magazines. These articles contained generalizations that were largely untrue, and which created doubt in the reader's mind by referencing obscure technicalities that had little relationship to planning realities. None of these authors presented an objective, well-founded comparison of living trusts as compared to will planning/probate and other planning techniques.

As we witnessed these events unfolding, we decided that enough is enough. We felt strongly that we needed to put an end to this controversy—the inaccurate innuendo, camouflage, and smoke—that was diverting public and professional attention from the more important "Loving Trust" estate-planning issues. In 1992 *The Living Trust Revolution: Why America Is Abandoning Wills and Probate* was published by Viking Penguin as our response to this false controversy. This book definitively proves that revocable living trust-centered estate plans are far superior—in virtually all instances—to will planning/probate, joint tenancy, or any other method of estate planning. This dispute can now be put to rest, and we can again return to the much more important issues of *how* each of us should plan the right way for ourselves and our loved ones.

INTRODUCTION TO THE SECOND EDITION

This new edition of *Loving Trust* allows us to expand significantly many of the planning ideas found in the original edition. It also allows us to tie together *The Living Trust Revolution* and *Loving Trust* so that practicing professionals and people who care about their affairs and loved ones will know the right way to go about their planning.

We believe more than ever that planning the Loving Trust way is a necessity for every responsible American family. Estate planning is not death planning. It is an act of love for those we love! It should further our ideals and the prosperity of our loved ones and charities.

It is our hope that this new edition of *Loving Trust* will help you to plan your estate properly and that you will share its message with your professional advisers, and with those friends and family members who also wish to properly provide for themselves and their loved ones.

Part One

WHY YOU NEED A LOVING TRUST PLAN

Chapter One

Put Love in Your Giving

This is the message you heard from the beginning: We should love one another.
1 John 3:11

Dear friends, let us love one another, for love comes from God. Everyone who loves has been born of God and knows God.
1 John 4: 7

This is a book about law, stewardship, and love. It is a book about living planning and living concerns and opportunities. It is a book that emphasizes your insights and your ability to use them to better the lives and horizons of others. It is a book that talks about loved ones and good causes and whether or not they will be cared for and espoused after you are gone.

We have tried to reduce an incredibly diverse body of law into a simple and understandable text. Our only regret is that we couldn't say it all with Scripture; It says it so much better to those who understand.

Many will read this book and walk away with the feeling that they should accomplish some estate planning with Loving Trust techniques and have every intention of doing so at a convenient time in the future. To them we would say "Therefore keep watch, because you do not know the day or the hour" (Matthew 25:13).

Paul is absolutely clear on commitment and love in a Christian marriage: "Husbands, love your wives, just as Christ loved the church and gave himself up for her" (Ephesians 5:25), and "However, each one of you also must love his wife as he loves himself, and the wife must respect her husband" (Ephesians 5:33). Does the commitment, love, and respect in a Christian marriage stop on the death or disability of a spouse? Or can it continue? This book emphasizes planning strategies that can assist your spouse after you are gone. These strategies have their roots in the everyday Christian love that Christian spouses display to one another.

Solomon teaches us that "a good man leaves an inheritance for his children's children" (Proverbs 13:22) and that "an inheritance quickly gained at the beginning will not be blessed at the end" (Proverbs 20:21). Paul spoke of our responsibility to our children when he preached to the Corinthians: "Now I am ready to visit you for the third time, and I will not be a burden to you, because what I want is not your possessions, but you. *After all, children should not have to save up for their parents, but parents for their children*" [italics added] (2 Corinthians 12:14).

Solomon tells us much about our responsibility in raising children, "Train a child in the way he should go, and when he is old he will not turn from it" (Proverbs 22:6); "Discipline your son, and he will give you peace; he will bring delight to your soul" (Proverbs 29:17); "The rod of correction imparts wisdom, but a child left to himself disgraces his mother" (Proverbs 29:15); and "Instruct a wise man and he will be wiser still; teach a righteous man and he will add to his learning" (Proverbs 9:9).

Christians clearly have an obligation to raise their children with love and attention, to go the extra yard in an effort to instruct, lead, and correct. In short, to love so much that they will be diligent with their care and instruction: ". . . but he who loves him is careful to discipline him" (Proverbs 13:24). Does this obligation stop with your disability or death, or can it continue? That your Christian love, and its hopes, fears, dreams, values, and ambitions can survive you with respect to your children and their children is a major topic of this book.

We would assert that "giving" is at the very core of love. Richard Braunstein put it well when he said, "It is possible to give without loving, but it is impossible to love without giving." Love not only prompts us to be generous in what we give but also to be responsible in *why* and *how* we give.

The scriptural principle that the motive for a gift is inextricably tied to the gift itself is of utmost importance. "All a man's ways seem right to him, but the LORD weighs the heart" (Proverbs 21:2). Yet many of us give sparingly or foolishly: others of us give grudgingly, out of a sense of obligation, or out of a dread or fear of the consequences that will result if we refuse to give.

Too many Christian parents have said in one way or another, "I know my child will be totally irresponsible with his or her inheritance, but I'll still take the easy road and just leave it to him or her outright; the fact that the money may be squandered, or worse yet, that my child's life may be ruined by mammon is not my problem." Others have said, "I make a sizable donation to my favorite charity each year. I never ask what the money is used for and I don't know the skills and character of its leaders, but I make my tithe and that's all that matters."

Then, too, there's always the good-provider husband who dominates the family's financial affairs and doesn't bother to acquaint his spouse in the basics of their household finances, much less the subtleties of their investments. This is a husband who steadfastly maintains, "I love my wife. Everything that's mine is hers.

Love not only prompts us to be generous in what we give but also to be responsible in *why* and *how* we give.

PUT LOVE IN YOUR GIVING

What she does with it is her business (even though I never took the time to teach and inform her so that she knows our business). After all, life is for the living."

The attitude of giving without loving motives or loving instructions permeates the token gifts that so many of us leave to charity after we are gone. The "I leave this token bequest to XYZ charity on my death" is a "loveless" gift that is all too common. Where is the love? Where is the joy? Where is the wisdom and instruction? Where is the generosity? Where is the stewardship, and prudence we've been taught in the Scriptures?

The Scripture gives clear and specific instructions about our responsibilities in the matter of loving and giving. The Bible instructs us to make our offerings out of love through our *cheerfulness*. "Each man should give what he has decided in his heart to give, not reluctantly or under compulsion, for God loves a cheerful giver" (2 Corinthians 9:7). We're instructed not to give to people or organizations simply because we feel pressured to do so. Rather, we are encouraged to do so out of cheerfulness with enthusiasm and even exuberance.

Most of us have false notions of what we should do as responsible persons: "A good husband *should* leave his estate outright to his wife; never mind that he does it without assistance and without instructions or prudent and loving safeguards." Or, "Even though my children have different needs and require different planning, I *should* treat them exactly the same when it comes to my finances and their inheritance. I'll give them their shares in exactly the same way, without any instructions." Or, "I want to be thought of as a charitable person, so I guess I *should* leave a token amount to charity and the Lord's work."

If we succumb to the easiest of planning paths—either doing nothing or following *should* pressure about what we give and to whom we give it—we won't, in all likelihood, give joyfully. And, if we don't give joyfully, we won't give in love. If we spend more time preparing and carefully structuring our gifts, we will enhance the value of our gifts, and our joy will be directly proportionate to those efforts. With a greater magnitude of joy will come even greater gifts, and then even greater joy, for all believers recognize that we cannot out-give God. "And God is able to make all grace abound to you, so that in all things at all times, having all that you need, you will abound in every good work" (2 Corinthians 9:8).

We need to give *freely* if we are to give lovingly. Jesus said, "Freely you have received, freely give" (Matthew 10:8). No matter how hard we've worked for what we have, we know that what we attain and possess comes from and through a gracious God. He has given us the physical strength, business acumen, and ability to learn, earn, and invest so that it is possible for us to accumulate our material possessions. "Everything comes from you, and we have given you only what comes from your hand" (1 Chronicles 29:14). As a result, we should not be so naive and prideful in ascribing our successes in the accumulation of our worldly wealth solely to our skills, hard work, and training but rather to God's blessing for which he would like His work blessed as well.

If we don't realize the importance of God and his grace in our acquiring and accumulating, we face the very real danger that we will feel annoyed at the idea of being called upon to be generous while we're alive, or take too little, if any, responsibility for what happens to our worldly goods upon our death.

If we make our gifts grudgingly or with hesitation and twinges of doubt, or with the expectation that we will gain stature among our neighbors and business associates, we have missed His joy and grace. If we give other than out of love, we do not manifest His love and the love we have for others. If we give freely by planning in love, we will freely receive far more than we give.

If we love, we give wisely. "Be very careful, then, how you live—not as unwise but as wise," Paul exhorted the church (Ephesians 5:15). Heaven puts no premium on foolishness, and yet many people have engaged in all kinds of foolishness in the way they've practiced stewardship with loved ones and their tithe and love offerings. They've given to scoundrels and to false causes. They've handed large sums over to loved ones without so much as a single instruction, content in the naive expectation that somehow it doesn't matter that the funds may soon be squandered and the lives of loved ones altered and smashed as a result. Giving "freely" doesn't mean that you give a young child a sharp knife without instruction and guidance; to do so is not an act of love or responsible parenthood; it is both hurtful and irresponsible.

Too many of us have rendered unto Caesar what we should have rendered to His work and for the benefit of our loved ones. "Then Jesus said to them, 'Give to Caesar what is Caesar's and to God what is God's.' And they were amazed at him" (Mark 12:17). Jesus didn't say that we should give everything to Caesar, but only what he was due. And yet, too many of us ignore simple and available planning opportunities that would enable us to give our wealth to loved ones and to charities that represent His work. Too often, otherwise good Christian men and women have inadvertently rendered unto Caesar—the Internal Revenue Service—that which could be better given to the Lord's work. We get mentally lazy and ignore the planning opportunities before us by claiming—or complaining of—our lack of knowledge. Jesus warned us of such behavior by giving us a straightforward and biting instruction: "Be as shrewd as snakes and as innocent as doves" (Matthew 10:16).

This book will share meaningful planning techniques that will save the reader many dollars that can be better used by loved ones and favorite charities that accomplish His, rather than government's work.

Shrewdness and innocence are not, however, a replacement for love nor are they love's equal. Christian love is the light that cannot be darkened. Mother

PUT LOVE IN YOUR GIVING

Teresa captured its light when she said, "What counts is not how much you give, but how much love you put in the giving."

Saint Paul told his protégé, Timothy, "If anyone does not provide for his relatives, and especially for his immediate family, he has denied the faith and is worse than an unbeliever" (1 Timothy 5:8).

Most Christians take Paul's statement to Timothy seriously. As best we can, we care for our spouses, children, aging parents, and grandchildren. We sacrifice our pleasures to assure that they will be taken care of by our efforts. We are the quintessential "good providers" who would judge ourselves as negligent and unloving if we didn't work hard to provide for the current needs of our loved ones. We provide for and give to our loved ones and tithe to Christian charities; we practice the scriptural "good works'" mandate of James: "As the body without the spirit is dead, so faith without deeds is dead" (James 2:26).

Many of us understand the joy that can come from giving and, in addition, give freely of our "love offerings" with exuberance while we are alive. Others of us give with a sense of obligation or duty to support the Church and other causes we deem worthy. Regardless of our motivation, however, each year, at income tax time, we have an opportunity to contemplate our gifts and recollect our joy or the sacrifices we made to fulfill our tithe.

The fact is, "living" giving is not foreign to most of us. It is an integral part of our wonderful walk with Christ.

Does our love and tithing obligations stop upon our deaths? Or, can we—in spite of our physical death—continue to care for the important people in our lives and for God's work? Can we extend our love beyond our mortal life through thoughtful planning? Can our wisdom, knowledge, beliefs, and instruction survive us as Solomon's survived him? Can we leave our loved ones and cherished causes better off because we worked and cared, loved and planned?

With Christian principles and Loving Trust estate-planning techniques we describe in this book, all of us can share our hopes, fears, dreams, values, and ambitions. Each of us can give in love what we have to whom we want, the way we want, and when we want, and we can save tax dollars and administrative costs. With responsibility for our stewardship, and with our love for Him and our family, we can continue that stewardship after we are gone.

In everything I did, I showed you that by this kind of hard work we must help the weak, remembering the words the Lord Jesus himself said, "'It is more blessed to give than to receive'" (Acts 20:35).

> "What counts is not how much you give, but how much love you put in the giving."

Chapter Two

The Truth Behind Probate

This chapter is about money—your money. It tells how expensive will planning/probate is.

Every day, lawyers are advertising their services in your daily newspapers. Most of these ads list prices for the various services they describe. A typical ad, which we found in our morning newspaper the day this chapter was written, went like this (we changed the name of the law firm):

The Law Firm of Ruff & Ready Full Legal Services

Divorce (Uncontested)	$175.00
Initial Consultation	$15.00
Bankruptcy (Personal)	$250.00
Simple Will	$25.00
Basic Corporation	$250.00

Almost every newspaper advertisement for legal services contains the price of a simple will. According to this ad, for only ten dollars more than an initial consultation, you could have your will done. What a great bargain! But have you ever wondered why wills are oftentimes such a bargain?

AARP (American Association of Retired Persons) has called the low fees charged by attorneys for wills "loss leaders." It is their theory that, by preparing a will for a very low fee, attorneys generate substantial probate fees. A number of other will-planning/probate critics agree with this theory. In fact, even the American Bar Association has recognized this problem and has voiced concern over how this method of charging may increase the cost of probate and decrease the quality of the initial work performed.

Norman F. Dacey, author of the best-seller *How to Avoid Probate!*, has taken the position that wills are cheap because they are loss leaders for most lawyers. A will means that eventually, when the client dies, there will be a probate. That's when lawyers reap the rewards.

THE TRUTH BEHIND PROBATE

In 1966 Dacey's book topped the best-seller list for months, selling more than one-and-a-half million copies. Dacey's book consisted of some thirty pages of attacks on the legal profession and more than five hundred pages of forms to be used for do-it-yourself probate avoidance. Dacey advocated not using a lawyer at all, professing that using his forms was all you needed to avoid probate. Dacey was enjoined from the unauthorized practice of law by the Connecticut Bar when he was on the lecture circuit prior to the publication of his book. He was prosecuted and convicted for the unauthorized practice of law after the publication of his book, and, after a lengthy court fight, his conviction was overturned.

Dacey was very cautious when he wrote his book, evidently trying to avoid the legal problems that the book created. Most of the comments about lawyers are quotes from other people's speeches, comments, or publications. He tried to avoid the consequences of making a head-on attack on lawyers and judges by letting others make his points for him. Dacey did, however, get in a few shots of his own. To give you an idea of the tone and content of his book, here are some quotes from the 1983 revised edition:

> It would be wrong, of course, to suggest that there are no honest lawyers, for there are—just as there are four-leaf clovers. Finding either is widely regarded as a stroke of rare good luck. If Al Capone could return to Chicago, he wouldn't bother with the beer business—he'd be a "specialist in probate practice."

As you can see, Dacey was less than laudatory about the legal profession as a whole and probate lawyers in particular.

Dacey's examples of abuses of the probate process are numerous and, if true, paint a sad picture of the whole sordid business. His premise—that probate is an antiquated process in which only the lawyers and judges profit—has been validated by the attempted reforms in the probate system that have taken place since Dacey's book was published. Unfortunately, these reforms and Dacey's solutions have not had the far-reaching effect that was hoped for. Most estates are still needlessly probated.

Twenty years after Dacey's book burst upon the scene, Barbara R. Stock wrote *It's Easy to Avoid Probate and Guardianships*. Her message was the same as Dacey's: Probate is an evil system designed only to make lawyers rich at the expense of the American public. Her book is the result of a survey done by Ms. Stock of five hundred probate files. The book relates the results of that survey and an explanation and indictment of the probate process. Like Dacey's book, the better part of Stock's book is devoted to methods for avoiding probate and how those methods work. There are forms for trusts and other probate avoidance devices. Initially Stock recommended the limited use of a lawyer. Perhaps it was her thinking that such advice would protect her from the lawsuits and legal problems faced by

Dacey in his heyday. However, Stock quickly reversed positions and began a new career as a self-proclaimed expert selling bare-bones boilerplate.

Chapter 3 of Stock's book is entitled "Probate: A System Designed by Attorneys for the Benefit of Attorneys." It is here, for the most part, that she makes her observations about the legal system and the probate lawyers in it:

> It is to the advantage of the attorneys to maintain an appearance of complexity and to find a way to drag these probate proceedings out. Fortunately, doctors are kinder with their scalpels than attorneys . . . at slicing away estate assets.

Stock's message is the same as Dacey's. They both believe that the probate system is fueled by the greed of the legal establishment.

That brings up some questions. Are more people avoiding probate now than before Dacey wrote his book? Are people still going through probate, despite the hue and cry over the last twenty years?

Howard Hughes, the man with more money than just about anyone, didn't avoid probate, and goodness knows he had the dollars to hire the best probate avoiders in the world. J. Paul Getty didn't avoid probate, and his estate attorneys' fees were twenty-seven million! How would you like to make that much for a few years of work? Presidents John F. Kennedy and Lyndon B. Johnson didn't avoid probate!

On the other hand, other well-known celebrities such as John Lennon and Bing Crosby avoided it by using a revocable living trust. We can't ascertain what their documents said because—unlike a will—they were totally private. Our law firm specialized in helping our clients avoid probate, yet other lawyers in our city were totally convinced that the probate process was necessary and protected the public.

Who is right and who is wrong?

We believe that both Dacey and Stock are right in some respects and very much wrong in others. They are right about probate. It can be needlessly expensive, needlessly time-consuming, and needlessly suffered by loved ones. Dacey and Stock make a mistake when they make lawyerly greed and bad faith the sole whipping boys for probate abuses. We believe that Dacey's and Stock's solutions and approaches to avoiding probate are oftentimes dead wrong. Their attacks on lawyers make good reading; their alternatives are as bad as those they attack.

> **[Probate] can be needlessly expensive, needlessly time-consuming, and needlessly suffered by loved ones.**

The Probate Process

The word *probate* is synonymous with the public's frustration with the legal complexities, delay, and expense associated with the death of a loved one. Probate epitomizes the differences between will planning/probate and planning using a fully funded living trust-centered plan—a plan we call a Loving Trust plan.

THE TRUTH BEHIND PROBATE

Probate occurs both when a person dies with a valid will (testate) and when a person dies without a valid will or will-substitute (intestate). Contrary to the popular opinion overwhelmingly held by the public, if a person dies owning property in his or her own name, and that owner executed a last will and testament, that property *will go through probate*. A will that is executed will inevitably be probated.

If valid will-substitutes have been used, probate is not required. Commonly used will-substitutes include living trusts, joint tenancy ownership, and beneficiary designations such as those ordinarily used for life insurance and employee benefit plans. We will talk more on these later in the book.

The reason that there is a probate when you die with or without a will, absent a proper will-substitute, is not difficult to understand. When you die, your property needs to be distributed to your heirs. You cannot sign deeds, write checks, pay bills, or transact any business. Probate is the legal process of transferring property to one's heirs.

The term "probate" has more than one meaning, which sometimes creates confusion as to what the probate really includes. Technically, probate means to prove the validity of a will in a court, a process that is very short if no one contests the will, if indeed there is one. However, probate is commonly used in a much broader sense to describe the process of passing an owner's title to property after the owner's death. The technical term for this administrative court process, which can be very lengthy, is really *administration*.

In administration, the financial affairs of a deceased person are inventoried, and creditors are identified and paid. There are a host of other administrative procedures that ensure that the estate's lawyer, executor, and various taxing authorities are paid before the balance of the estate is distributed to the heirs.

Although probate and administration are, strictly speaking, two different processes, the term "probate" is commonly used for both probate and administration. Lawyers and judges generally use the term "probate" in this broad manner. Probate has been described as "Encompassing the transfer of property on death and guardianship" and "Our court-operated system for transferring wealth at death." *Black's Law Dictionary* describes the term as ". . . a general name or term used to include all matters of which probate courts have jurisdiction."

Probate is also the name of the court that has jurisdiction over probate and administration. The names of these courts vary from state to state. Courts with jurisdiction over probate and administration are sometimes called common or surrogate courts, but in a majority of states they are referred to as simply "probate courts."

In addition to probate and administration, probate courts usually have jurisdiction over the guardianship of minors and mentally incompetent adults. Guardianships, because they are under the jurisdiction of the probate courts, are often referred to as "living probates." In Chapter Four, we will explain the living probate process in much more detail.

Property passing through the probate process acts like water traveling through a leaky pipe. Every few feet some of the water escapes, and at those spots there is always someone to collect the leakage. When it reaches the other end of the pipe—where the heirs collect—there is not always a whole lot left.

While the laws that control wills and probate vary from state to state, the first order of probate business is the preparation and filing of a petition for probate or Letters of Administration (legal terminology for the commencement of the probate process). If a person dies with a will, the executor (executrix, if female) who is named in the will files the petition as soon as possible after the decedent's death. If a person dies without a will, an heir usually files the petition.

When the petition is filed, an initial hearing date is set. The purpose of the hearing is for the court to formally approve the executor who is named in the will. In some states, the executor is called a personal representative. If a person dies without a will, the court must appoint an administrator (administratrix, if female). An administrator is usually a bank trust department or a trust company but may be a professional administrator or an heir.

No matter if called an executor, personal representative, or administrator, the functions of these court-approved or appointed agents are basically the same. We will use the term *executor* because of its familiarity to most people.

In addition to the executor, the probate process requires the services of a lawyer. The lawyer is retained by the executor to guide the estate through the complexities of the probate system by preparing the filings, speaking at hearings, drafting petitions to the court, and filling in the myriad kinds of paperwork that probate and administration require. Probate without lawyers would be a contradiction in terms.

The executor and the lawyer perform the tasks required during the probate process. It is usual for first-time executors to rely totally on the knowledge and expertise of the estate's attorney.

Sometimes the executor is a lawyer who hires himself as the estate's lawyer. Two different jobs, two different fees. All part of the same leaky pipe.

In the initial probate hearing, the validity of the will is established. Probate statutes often require that, in order to prove a last will and testament, its witnesses must testify with regard to the technical validity and niceties of its signing. This is not, however, required in all states. Under modern probate statutes, many states now allow special language in a will, called a self-proving clause, that allows a will to be admitted to probate without the testimony of its witnesses. In a self-proving clause, the witnesses sign an affidavit at the time the will is signed attesting to the will's correctness in lieu of in-person testimony down the road.

Anyone who has a beef with the will can bring a lawsuit into the probate court. This is called a will contest. Almost anyone with a relationship to the decedent who has a beef with a will can contest a will by filing an objection with the probate court. This procedure is relatively uncomplicated and simple to initiate. Wills are easy to contest and the risk of a will contest is high in a setting that is designed to give a wide variety of people easy access to a court. In our current climate of allowing plaintiffs the right to have their day in court, it is highly likely that most claims, even those that have little merit, will be heard.

Will contests come in infinite varieties. In many cases lawsuits seem to be started to intimidate the heirs into staving off unwanted litigation by settling out of court. This is an effective way for the unscrupulous to collect under a will without having much of a case. The probate process is, of course, extended if will contests arise.

The next order of probate business is for the executor to notify the creditors of the deceased person so that they have an opportunity to get paid. This entails the often time-consuming task of determining all of the dead person's liabilities.

Creditors are notified either directly by the executor or by advertisements in the local newspapers. The creditors are given a period of time to make claims against the estate. Notices are also mailed to heirs and beneficiaries. Creditors must file their claims against the estate in the precise manner and within the exact time prescribed by local statutes, which is usually two to six months after probate has begun. During this legal hiatus, distributions cannot be made from the estate except for certain family allowances prescribed by state law or approved by the court.

The process of determining the nature, value, and location of the deceased person's assets is started concurrently with the notification of creditors. Depending on the jurisdiction, appraisers are either appointed by the probate judge or by the executor. The appraiser or appraisers determine the value of the estate assets from real estate to cars to furniture and knickknacks. Everything must be assigned a value. This process is especially important to the lawyer and executor, who often base their fees on the value of the estate.

Once the period for submitting creditors' claims has ended, and assuming there are no disputes and all of the assets are found and appraised, a petition for a judgment of final distribution can be presented. Once this petition is approved, the executor can distribute the remaining property to the heirs.

If a federal estate tax return is filed, an estate may remain open until such time as the audit period expires, or until an audit is actually concluded, which can be three years or more. An estate may very well remain open for a period of up to fourteen years if it elects to pay federal estate taxes on the installment method. Litigation, whether initiated by taxing authorities, creditors, or interested parties, may delay the closing of the estate for many years or even decades.

During the entire period of administration, the estate will be under the control and supervision of the probate court. Most transactions, especially monetary ones and those dealing with the specific disposition of assets, are subject to court approval.

In states that have adopted so-called streamlined probate procedures, informal or unsupervised probate is allowed. An informal probate is not directly supervised by the court, although the usual procedures for creditor notification and other administrative procedures must be strictly adhered to.

With an informal probate administration there is far less paperwork and contact with the court. However, informal probate does not relieve the executor or the attorney from fulfilling the routine steps that characterize formal probate proceedings.

After the dust has settled and everybody associated with the probate estate is either paid or paid off, the heirs can receive their shares of whatever is left.

The probate and administration process has been, and continues to be, frequently and harshly criticized by professionals and the public alike. They feel that probate is an antiquated remnant from a bygone era that serves few, if any, useful purposes. They believe that probate is not necessary and that it creates horrendous aggravation, delays, and expense.

The Costs of Probate

It is an indisputable fact that probate creates expense, but how much expense? The probate fees that were quoted in Dacey's book ranged from 8.5 percent of large estates to almost 60 percent of some smaller ones. Dacey, of course, chose the worst examples he could find, but the examples reflect what can and does happen in the probate process. The costs of probate in Stock's survey—taken almost twenty years after Dacey's best-seller went on the market—show a startling similarity to Dacey's conclusions. Her figures show that probate fees average 22 percent on smaller estates and 6.2 percent on larger estates. Stock cited small estates where the probate fees approached 60 percent of the estate, just as Dacey did. They average, according to Stock, over 7 percent of the value of the estate, with 60 percent of the total cost going to lawyers and 40 percent going to executors and others.

In contrast, a number of articles written in the late 1980s and the early 1990s by will-planning/probate advocates argued that the probate process has been streamlined in many states. These articles have either claimed or implied that probate fees for most families are not significant and that all of the controversy surrounding the cost of probate is overblown hype that has no basis in reality.

Who is right and who is wrong? What are the real costs of probate?

Let's start by explaining that almost all probate fees are expressed in terms of a percentage of the "gross estate." When professional estate planners refer to the

After . . . everybody associated with the probate estate is either paid or paid off, the heirs can receive their shares of whatever is left.

gross estate, they are talking about the full value of all the property owned or controlled by a deceased person without any reduction for debts! This is how it works. If you die and the value of all your assets is $500,000, without reduction for any debts, then probate fees refer to a percentage of the $500,000. But what if your estate has your home in it and it has a $200,000 mortgage on it? The net value of your estate is $300,000. You would think that probate would be a percentage of your net worth, not the value of everything. Not so! If your probate fees are 5 percent, they are 5 percent of $500,000, a whopping $25,000, not 5 percent of $300,000, or $15,000.

When we talk about probate fees, we are talking a percentage of the gross, not the net. Think about this as it relates to you as you read on.

The term "probate fee" is very general and sometimes hard to understand. Generally there are four basic costs of probate:

1. Court costs, including filing and docket fees and notice and publication expenses
2. Appraisal fees
3. Attorneys' fees
4. Executors' fees

Court Costs

Actual court costs vary considerably from state to state, but are generally not very high as compared with the other costs of probate. In some states, court costs are based on the value of the estate and in others they are fixed amounts that are charged uniformly to all estates. Fixed amounts take a higher percentage of a smaller estate's value and a lower percentage of a larger estate's value. Many states have an exemption for very small estates, which eliminates virtually all of these actual court costs and filing fees. However, in the majority of states, these costs will be incurred by almost all estates regardless of size.

An additional element of court costs is fees for notice and publication. Notice must be given to potential heirs and to creditors so they can submit their claims within the prescribed statutory time periods.

Court costs, docket fees, filing fees, and costs of notice and publication can run from a few hundreds of dollars to several thousands of dollars. As a percentage of overall probate fees, these costs are small, but they represent costs that can, in the main, be avoided by the use of a fully funded revocable living trust.

Appraisal Fees

An appraisal is clearly necessary to determine the value of assets so that creditors can be paid out of available assets. If federal or state estate and inheritance taxes might be due, an appraisal is required to determine the exact amount of those taxes. It is also necessary many times to have an appraisal so that the executor and the attorney can be paid their fees when their fees are based on a percentage of the estate.

Valuing an estate to determine attorneys' and executors' fees can create a conflict of interest. When the attorney and executor are paid more as the value of the estate goes up, they may be tempted to influence the selection of those appraisers or valuations that raise rather than lower the estate's valuation. At best, the attorney and a paid executor are not likely to fight too aggressively to obtain a lower valuation if a lower valuation may adversely affect their fees.

The cost of the appraisal itself varies based on the number and type of assets and the purpose of the appraisal. Valuation costs, like court costs, are generally not major expenses for most estates unless taxes and fees are increased as a result of the valuation.

Attorneys' Fees

The largest probate fees are taken by the attorney. State statutes and, to a much lesser extent, local court rules determine how and how much an attorney may charge for probate and administration work. There are two general methods allowed: *statutory percentage fees* and *reasonable compensation.*

Only eleven states have statutory percentage fee schedules for attorneys. These states are Arkansas, California, Delaware, Hawaii, Iowa, Missouri, Montana, New Mexico, Pennsylvania, Utah, and Wyoming. Statutory percentage fees have been disappearing because they are perceived as windfall fees for attorneys and not proportionate to the work performed by them.

Percentage fees are determined in a variety of ways. Some states calculate the fee on the gross value of the probate estate. California uses this type of statute. In some states the percentage is taken on certain assets, whether they are subject to probate or not.

Percentage fees, for the most part, are supposed to represent the maximum fee that can be taken by the executor or the attorney in most circumstances. In 1987, there was a bar-sponsored report on California probate fees charged by attorneys. According to the California study, instead of the maximum fee, the statutory fee often becomes the minimum fee with additional fees approved as a matter of course by the court. This occurs because states with percentage probate fees often allow the attorney to request additional fees for "extraordinary" services. Extraordinary services can consist of all or some of the following:

1. Sales or mortgages of real or personal property
2. Contested or litigated claims against the estate
3. Preparation of estate, inheritance, income, sales, or other tax returns

4. Adjustment, litigation, or payment of any of these taxes (including audits of returns)
5. Litigation in regard to property of the estate
6. Carrying on the business of the decedent, including winding it up
7. Such other litigation or special services as the representative of the estate may have to prosecute, defend, or perform
8. Suit to collect assets
9. Will contest
10. Appeal to protect creditors
11. Petition for instructions
12. Preparation of agreement between estate and person contending adversely to the estate
13. Construction of the will
14. Cancellation of lease
15. Defense of account filed by executor
16. Assistance in lease negotiations
17. Determination of title holdings, evaluation procedures for valuation of property, tax decisions for death tax returns, and income tax returns

It is common practice in many statutory fee jurisdictions for the courts to approve extraordinary fees. There are attorneys in these states who claim that they seldom, if ever, charge extraordinary fees. However, based on the studies of attorneys' fees, these attorneys are in the minority.

Lawyers sometimes take a lesser fee when a prior agreement has been made with the will maker, or when the services rendered do not warrant the full fee. The restraint shown by attorneys who forgo extraordinary fees is to be commended, but should not be viewed as charitable in light of what are generous statutory fees.

A lawyer can charge for services with regard to non-probate property as well. Thus, any title work on joint tenancy property such as filing a death certificate and preparing a new deed, and any services performed with regard to property received by beneficiary designation can also be charged for in addition to the statutory percentage fee. This means that the probate-free assets may not be cost-free.

Statutory percentage fees increase the attorney appraisal conflict that we touched on earlier. If an attorney is paid based on the value of an estate, then the attorney has a vested interest in a higher valuation.

The American Bar Association has taken a strong position against the use of percentage fees in any form. It condemns "[r]igid adherence to statutory or recommended commission or fee schedules" as a frequently unfair method of determining attorneys' probate fees.

While statutory percentage fees appear to be arbitrary and inequitable, they cannot be assessed properly without understanding the alternative method of determining how attorneys charge probate fees. It is called "reasonable compensation."

The majority of states allow attorneys to take a fee based on reasonable compensation. One of the major difficulties of this method is defining what is "reasonable." The reasonableness of attorneys' fees can be viewed from several perspectives. The heirs of an estate may view "reasonable" to mean a few hours of necessary legal work, while an attorney may view his or her services to be of a very high caliber that have generated particularly good results for the estate. This elusive "reasonable" standard leaves great latitude for judicial interpretation and makes the process of defining probate fees uncertain.

AARP (American Association of Retired Persons) did a study of probate fees in three states: California, Wisconsin, and Delaware. Of these three states, California and Delaware use statutory fee schedules. *The overall conclusion of the AARP study is that attorneys' fees, no matter how they are determined, are usually 3 percent or more of the estate's gross value.* This is consistent with other studies, including a study that we did for our book *The Living Trust Revolution*, and offers mounting evidence that attorneys' probate fees are not as low as probate advocates would like the public to think.

Attorneys' fees are consistently the same regardless of what type of fee schedule is in effect and notwithstanding the type of probate statute under which they were calculated. Our research shows that fees are about the same even between formal probate states and informal, unsupervised probate states. This point is important because, in states that have adopted so-called modern probate statutes, will-planning/probate advocates use as a major argument the fact that probate has been modernized and that it is inexpensive and uncomplicated and is still the most effective estate planning method.

All of the available evidence suggests that the costs of probate are not going dramatically downward. It also indicates that, when read in conjunction with all of the other studies, attorneys' fees are generally the same regardless of what method is employed to calculate them.

Attorneys' probate fees are hovering around 3 percent of a gross estate, with the range extending from 1.5 percent to 4.5 percent.

Executors' Fees

By law, the executor of an estate is the person or institution who is charged with the probate and administration of an estate. In practice, however, much of the probate and administration burden is left to an attorney. The services performed by an executor and the services performed by an attorney are not easy to differentiate. Yet, even to the most uninformed critic, it seems fairly obvious that the attorney and the executor represent two people, or two fees, on a single shovel.

Sometimes, an attorney serves both as the executor *and* the attorney for the same estate. When this occurs, the attorney often collects two fees for essentially one function. While taking a full fee for each function is not allowed in some states, an attorney functioning in both capacities still receives a higher fee than if serving in a single capacity.

Executors' fees are controlled by statute in most states. While there is less information available on executors' fees than for attorneys' fees, the amount of executors' fees in general can be estimated from recent reports.

The American College of Trust and Estate Counsel, an influential group of estate planning attorneys, conducted a survey that provides the executors' statutory percentage fees, or, where there were none, examples of customary local executors' fees. For many states, it was possible to calculate approximate ranges of executors' fees for certain sizes of estates and to compare them to the ranges of attorneys' fees. For estates ranging from $100,000 to $1,000,000, executors' fees were in the range of 1 to 5 percent, with the average being 3 percent.

Two Probate Fees for One Generation of Property

Advocates of the will-planning/probate process neglect to address an issue that is critical in the discussion of probate fees. For a married couple, there are potentially two probates for the same property; one on the death of each spouse.

Many Americans have simple wills that we call "I love you" wills. These commonly used wills say that when a spouse dies, all of the deceased spouse's property passes to the surviving spouse. Any property that is controlled by this type of will must go through probate.

In a simple will, it is highly likely that the surviving spouse will serve as the executor. If so, the surviving spouse doesn't usually take an executor's fee—he or she waives it. Even if this occurs, the attorney's fee, appraisal costs, and court costs remain. On the surviving spouse's subsequent death, there will be another probate. On this second probate, many of the same assets that passed to the surviving spouse through the original probate will be subjected to probate a second time. There will be attorneys' fees and, in all likelihood, executors' fees for the same property. This property is not property that has passed to a second generation; it is property of the same generation being subjected to a double dose of probate and a double payment of its attendant fees.

So What Is the Real Cost of Probate?

On the basis of all of the evidence that now exists, it would appear that the real cost of probate, where there is a paid executor and attorney, is approximately 5 to 6 percent of the gross estate. These costs are true regardless of how a state regulates its fees. If an estate does not have a paid executor, the cost of probate is generally 2 to 3 percent of the gross estate.

The studies show conclusively that the smaller the estate, the more probate takes as a percentage of the value of the estate. This is true for two reasons. First of all, many of the functions of probate are constant. These functions must be done in all estates, regardless of size, and the costs are consistent no matter how much the estate is worth. Second, people in smaller estates are more likely to have debts so that the net estate is smaller although the gross estate is used to express the costs of probate.

Advocates of will planning and probate also do not always mention that for a married couple, assets may be subject to two probates before these assets pass to children or grandchildren. These two probate fees may be incurred even if both spouses die at the same time or within a short time of each other. In reality, the cost of probate on the same assets in the same generation may be double what is anticipated.

Probate is expensive, there is no doubt about it. This leads to the conclusion that, many times, wills are cheap for one reason: There's a great deal of money to be made at the other end of the line—exorbitant probate fees paid by your heirs with your money.

Probate Takes Time

According to Stock, the average probate takes sixteen months. The average estate surveyed was valued at $110,000. An estate that size is not particularly complicated. The estates in the survey apparently were not plagued by lawsuits or other problems. They just dragged on. According to Stock, the main "dragger" is the lawyer, who likes to rack up those fees.

In our practice, we were asked with some regularity to review probates that seemed to the heirs to be taking much too long. The longest probate we saw was twenty-eight years in duration. The second longest was twenty-three years. In both cases, we were able to close the estate within months. Someone was sandbagging. What really amazed us was that the heirs would tolerate this for so long. The lawyer and the executor would have to be pretty convincing to be able to pull the wool over someone's eyes for that many years. It is frightening how the legal system can intimidate people to the extent that they really believe probate must take this long.

The studies available that have looked into the length of probate show that probate usually takes at least one year but can take much longer. It is not normally less than one year, but a family should be prepared for at least a two-year duration, just so they won't be disappointed if it takes longer than expected, because it often does.

> . . . the real cost of probate, . . . is approximately 5 to 6 percent of the gross estate.

Probate Is Public

We represented a lot of contractors in our practice. One day, a good contractor client contacted us about one of his competitors who had recently died. Our client, Ed, wanted to buy some equipment from the widow and wanted us to make an offer on his behalf. Ed figured that the equipment he needed was worth about $250,000.

Since we were paid to represent our client to the best of our ability, we recommended that we research the competitor's probate file to get an idea as to what he owned and how it was valued. We sent a paralegal to the probate court and in a few hours we had the complete probate file. We had his will, a list of all of his assets and liabilities, including litigation his business was in, promissory notes, and mortgages. We had the "private" financial statement of his business.

Our review showed that the estate badly needed cash to pay debts. The widow had petitioned the court for money, stating that she was destitute without aid from the estate. There was no doubt that the estate had to sell assets—and fast—to make ends meet. We told our client to offer fifty cents on the dollar, $125,000 cash for the equipment. The offer was accepted without negotiation.

Frankly, we are embarrassed to relate this story. It is, in retrospect, a sad commentary on lawyers and the probate system. We can only justify our action by rationalizing that we did our job and did it well. Our job was to do the best for our client, and we did. Incidentally, our client, when he dies, will not go through probate. This little lesson scared him to death.

Probate is public. Anyone can go to the probate court and look up an estate. Would you like to know about a deceased famous man in your town? Go to the probate court. If he didn't avoid probate, you will be able to find out a great deal about him.

You may think that you have nothing to hide when you die. "Who cares if someone sees what I have? I'm not ashamed." It is not a matter of being ashamed, it is a matter of being wise. Some stockbrokers, some lawyers, and some pretty shady salespeople read obituaries and death notices and prey upon the heirs. Widows and children are easy marks for con men and women. We suspect that one of the first places these crooks go is to the public probate files to find their marks.

Even if only a limited number of people look at court records, these are precisely the people that may be of concern. Presumably, the majority of people who peruse the public records are potential litigants or people who have only their own self-interest in mind.

Not only is a will a matter of public record, in most jurisdictions the complete inventory of the estate is a part of the public record as well. It, too, can be examined and copied. Petitions by heirs, creditors, and others, and all of the details of a deceased person's estate planning and financial affairs are typically part of the public record. Probate statutes require that public notices appear in newspapers, putting heirs and creditors on notice of pending probate proceedings. These legal announcements can have the unfortunate effect of creating significant public awareness and interest.

In the United States, there is a deep and abiding appreciation for keeping one's affairs private. Very few people willingly disclose their financial information to anyone except for their most trusted advisers and close family members. Very few people are willing to broadcast what they own and to whom they are going to leave it upon their death, or to advertise the state of their health and the amount of their property if they become disabled. Yet, if a person's estate goes through probate or if a person is declared by a court to be incompetent, this disclosure is exactly what occurs. People who rely on will-planning/probate are guaranteeing that their personal affairs will be placed in the public records when they die or are declared mentally incompetent. This public disclosure is something they would not do, given a choice.

If you play cards, most of the games you play are played with your cards hidden from the other players. You don't expose your hand to your opponents because doing so gives them the upper hand. There is one game in which one player is required to expose his or her hand, and that game is bridge. The person who has to expose his hand is called, appropriately enough, the dummy. Do you want your family to be the dummy?

First, Let's Kill All the Lawyers

"The first thing we do, let's kill all the lawyers" is a commonly quoted Shakespearean line. It is indicative of the feelings expressed by Dacey and Stock and subscribed to by a great proportion of the general populace. Dacey even quotes the Bible to emphasize that lawyers have been the source of mankind's problems almost since the beginning of recorded history.

We are lawyers. We still have active practices, and we are members of the fraternity that Dacey and Stock have taken on. One of our ex-partners, Milton E. "Bob" Meyer, Jr., is quoted by Dacey in his book. As a matter of fact, Bob's writings are probably the source that Dacey used to "reinvent" his solution to probate avoidance. Barbara Stock has continually recommended our book *Protect Your Estate* (formerly titled *The Handbook of Estate Planning*) in her book. Our law firm specialized in probate avoidance.

We share this autobiographical information with you to demonstrate that we are members of both camps—the good guys and the bad guys, depending on what or whom you believe. We work with and, more importantly, teach many of those "dirty," "nasty," "greedy," "uncaring" lawyers whom Dacey and Stock talk

> **People who rely on will-planning/ probate are guaranteeing that their personal affairs will be placed in the public records when they die or are declared mentally incompetent.**

about. Our firm did a great deal of probate clean-up work, although it was a small part of our overall billings. We know both sides of the probate issue.

Sure, there are corrupt and dishonest lawyers, just as there are less-than-honorable members in all other professions. There are lawyers who do not have professional motives and practice law just to make a buck. However, in our experience, these types of lawyers are in the minority. Honest lawyers are not as rare as four-leaf clovers. They represent the majority. Neither Stock nor Dacey is a lawyer. They have only been on one side of the fence. They do not have all of the answers.

We recently gave a seminar to a group of lawyers in Lake of the Ozarks, Missouri, underwritten by a major life insurance company. The seminar was about Loving Trust planning. It was supposed to be a relatively technical discussion, with the main thrust being the review of our *Loving Trust Compendium*, a technical practice book for lawyers.

The lawyers in our class were from throughout the country. They ranged from general practitioners who did very little will or trust work, to practitioners who only did simple wills, to planning specialists with many years in the practice. All the lawyers in the room derived some of their income from probate.

The seminar began exactly like this book. We attacked wills and probate as outdated. We chastised the lawyers for subjecting their clients to these two superfluous legal dinosaurs. Wow, did we get a reaction!

Our audience apparently believed in wills and probate. If we didn't know better, we'd have assumed that their motivation was solely the money created by probate. We had attacked their professionalism, and they reacted defensively and aggressively. The more they defended the system and insisted that probate is good, the more we responded with our feeling that probate is a cancer; that even a little bit is too much. There was a real confrontation.

The first day of the three-day seminar was to end at five o'clock, but most of the group stayed on for several additional hours to vent their concerns about our critique. That in itself was incredible because we were at a beautiful resort and most of the lawyers had made plans to share in the activities. Golf, tennis, and swimming were forgotten as our talks continued.

One of the most vocal critics of our point of view was a Pittsburgh lawyer named Dick. Dick is a warm, caring fellow in his late forties who, at that time, believed that probate is a necessary process that is not harmful to his clients. He did not generate a great deal of his revenue from his probate practice, because he charged hourly and evidently was very efficient. He did, however, believe in the probate process.

The session ended well into the evening, with no one, especially Dick, having changed his mind. The next two days, however, were magic. As the doubting Thomases learned about Loving Trust planning, how it worked, and the many positive things it did, they turned around. Dick and his classmates turned out to be big supporters of Loving Trust planning.

None of these lawyers appeared to be greedy or dishonest. They were a product of their education. In most law schools, there is no course in how trusts are used to help clients. The courses given are on the technical aspects of wills and trusts; they emphasize legalese. The material is purely theoretical; no practical applications or loving plans are alluded to.

Imagine, if you will, a huge gymnasium. It is empty, except for one table that is four feet long and three feet wide. Assuming that the gymnasium represents all of the types of law that lawyers practice, the table represents trust law. Trust law is a tiny part of our legal system. There is no time for our law schools to teach aspiring lawyers how to do bare-bones planning with trusts, much less with Loving Trust plans. Most lawyers do not have the opportunity to use even their limited knowledge on a regular basis when it comes to planning for their clients' loved ones.

Loving Trust planning is overlooked, not from the bar's greed or avarice but from a simple lack of knowledge! Lawyers, for the most part, do not understand that probate is bad. They are so close to the process, they cannot see past it. Probate, like shaving every morning, appears to be a necessary evil until lawyers really understand that it can be so easily and skillfully avoided.

We have repeated our Lake of the Ozarks seminar in other places. It was not an isolated incident. Our seminar experiences have taught us that lawyers know they are unpopular and that they are losing credibility with the public. They know there are too many of them; they read their press and are not insensitive or stupid. Most lawyers want to be liked and respected; they want to do a good job, a job that is best for the client, and they want to charge a fair and reasonable price for their services.

Dacey and Stock play the demagogues, secure in their own ignorance, by picking on lawyers. They sought cases of extreme abuse within the process and assumed bad motives or bad law on the part of all lawyers. We know that once most lawyers are educated in the Loving Trust planning process, they are usually more than happy to abandon simple wills and probate and enthusiastically plan for their clients' loved ones. They, like all of us, just need to learn the ropes.

No Solutions at All

Dacey's solution to avoiding probate was to publish an enormous set of forms. Law is complicated. No matter how good the forms, and Dacey's are mediocre at best, it is hard to select the right form for the right job and to fill it in properly. Here are some of the problems that we have seen occur with the Dacey forms:

The forms are not signed correctly.

The Dacey trusts are not operable because nothing is ever put into them.

They are not written in understandable English, so people have no idea what they are doing.

There are so many forms, people pick the wrong form for the wrong reason or purpose.

The forms are so concerned about avoiding probate they *totally forget to take care of loved ones!*

Like it or not, you need to have a lawyer to help you avoid probate. If you do not, you will be the classic case of the armed citizen who shot himself or herself in the foot. A little knowledge is dangerous. An incorrect Dacey form is as expensive, or more expensive, than a will. When someone messes up a Dacey form, the heirs have to hire a lawyer to clean up the mess. The odds are very high that a Dacey form will be incorrect, or the heirs will not understand what to do with it after the maker dies. A lawyer will then have to be involved, and your loved ones will begin at probate square one. If you attempt to do all your own legal work by using a Dacey form, you will get exactly what you paid for.

Despite the do-it-yourself mentality of the Dacey forms, that is not their most glaring and harmful consequence. Dacey forgot about loved ones! Out of a book of almost six hundred pages, he devotes only a few pages to taking care of spouses, children, and other loved ones. Dacey is so caught up in his probate avoidance crusade that he blithely dismisses most of the problems of leaving property outright to spouses or children. He suffers from the same ailment he accuses the legal establishment of having: a lack of compassion for people. Dacey's trusts forget love. They are money trusts. They throw out the baby with the bath water, all in the name of probate avoidance. Avoiding probate is important. Caring for loved ones is more important.

Barbara Stock's motto appears to be that probate avoidance is not everything, it is the only thing. According to Stock, at least 50 percent of all Americans need only put all of their property into joint tenancy to avoid probate and all the problems associated with it. How wrong she is. We have already addressed how joint property is the worst possible probate avoidance method. It offers loss of control, the real possibility of unintended heirs, it creates gift taxes among non-spouses, it is great for creditors, and it creates death tax problems. Joint tenancy has been around for a long time, and probate fees and lawyer fees have not gone down. Joint tenancy won't avoid probate when the last joint tenant dies. It never avoids probate on disability. As for saving fees, in many states lawyers can and do charge a probate fee on joint property.

Like Dacey, Stock forgets about loved ones. In her opinion, a trust or other probate-avoiding device that is over a few pages long is totally unnecessary, except for rich Americans. What bunk! You spend your whole life building up what you

Like it or not, you need to have a lawyer to help you avoid probate.

have. Countless hours are spent carefully nurturing your property, keeping taxes down, saving, agonizing over how to live comfortably. It seems kind of sad that all that work, time, and effort can be reduced to a few pages.

Stock is right when she claims that it is easy to avoid probate. The hard part is to pass on your wisdom, your hopes, your dreams, and your aspirations to those you love. Stock thinks that passing love is reserved for the rich. Only they can afford to have elaborate trusts, which avoid probate, avoid taxes, and provide for loved ones. How wrong she is.

Our solution to probate avoidance and to providing for loved ones is over a thousand years old—it is Loving Trust planning.

Chapter Three

Shattering Will-Myths

A financial planner friend of ours believes that the myths surrounding wills ought to be shattered. He asks each of his clients, "Do you have a will?" and if the answer is a proud "yes," his response is a very sympathetic, "I'm sorry." We're sorry, too, because wills are expensive, mostly misleading documents that often create false expectations, which are only discovered at the death of their makers.

Most people have the mistaken belief that by making a will they are prudently fulfilling their duty to those they love. They walk around with a comfortable feeling, believing their loved ones to be safe and secure, assured that if something happens to them, all will be taken care of. Nothing could be further from the truth.

We have given presentations to lawyers, accountants, financial planners, and life insurance professionals all over the country. In each of our seminars, we start by shattering the commonly held will-myths. We believe that wills, in many ways, are obsolete. They are antiquated holdovers from a bygone era. They can be expensive and may result in thwarting the very purposes for which they were made.

Your Will Doesn't Provide for You

Your will does absolutely nothing for *you*. You have to die to make it live. What good is your will if you become disabled because of accident, illness, or old age? Insurance company underwriters will tell you that you have a greater probability of suffering at least one long-term disability before you die than you do of dying without having an intervening disability. Your will is no good to you or your loved ones if you become disabled.

Your Will Doesn't Provide for Your Loved Ones

Wills are supposed to allow you to leave your property to loved ones efficiently. They seldom do. An overwhelming majority of the wills we see say the same thing. If you are married, it says, "I leave everything I have to my spouse when I die. If my spouse is deceased, then I leave everything to my children, in equal shares." If you are single, your will may leave all your property outright to children, grandchildren, or others.

Leaving property outright to loved ones through a will is like pouring a pitcher of water into cupped palms to take a drink. Most of the water falls on the floor, except for a few drops that you may be able to sip or lick off your fingers. Most of it disappears before it can be properly used.

Your Will Takes Your Family Public

Wills guarantee probate. It never ceases to amaze me how many people think that if they have a will, their property will avoid probate—when just the opposite is the case.

Probate is a public process. All your family and personal records are available to public scrutiny anytime anyone wants to take a look. What property you own, whom you owe, whom you leave your property to—all are part of the probate court's public record.

Probate is time-consuming and expensive. Some lawyers make a lot of money probating will-created estates. They collect their fees from each estate's property and money. Lawyers, by law, are the primary creditors of every estate. They will be paid first. Taxes, other creditors, and your loved ones will be paid—in that order—but only after the lawyer is paid.

You cannot always properly provide for your loved ones if you expose them to the probate process.

Wills guarantee probate.

Your Will May Not Work

The term "simple will" is a misnomer. There is no such thing. Whether a will is one page or one hundred pages, it is fraught with complex legal rules, almost all of which have been around for close to five hundred years.

If you don't sign your will exactly as the rules of your state dictate, it may be worthless. There are many rules and requirements to fulfill in order to make a will valid. Disgruntled and greedy heirs find it easy to go to court to take shots at getting a larger inheritance. These "will contests" are a frequent occurrence in the probate courts. Probate courts are a perfect place for lawsuits. Add an unhappy heir to the complexity of signing a will, and you have all the ingredients for a will contest. Who loses? Your loved ones or those greedy heirs. Who wins? Nobody.

If your will can't be found at your death, obviously the entire exercise will have been worthless. If you sign more than one will—duplicate originals—and all of them cannot be found on your death, the exercise again will have been worthless. A good many people think that if one will is good, lots of them are better.

SHATTERING WILL-MYTHS

Howard Hughes evidently thought that. His estate is still being litigated because of the many wills he allegedly left.

Try moving from one state to another with your will. If you die in your new state without changing your will to fit your new state's law, your loved ones might have significant problems. A will that is valid in one state may not work very well in another.

What are your options if a will is so bad to have? Many of us turn to so-called will substitutes or will alternatives, such as life-insurance beneficiary designations, joint tenancy, retirement-plan beneficiary designations, and "bare-bones" living trusts. Most alternatives to wills don't work very well, either. They suffer from the same congenital defects as a will. They do not take care of you while you are alive. They do not provide for your loved ones. They create lawyer's fees and court costs. They take your family public. They may not work at all! Yet, these will substitutes are used to provide for loved ones as frequently or perhaps even more frequently than simple wills.

In our experience, more people have property in joint tenancy than have wills. Given the significant pitfalls of jointly held property, this poses no small problem.

Working with many clients, giving seminars to fellow professionals, and dealing with media exposure has helped us learn how to spread the word about a better way to plan for loved ones through Loving Trust planning.

The best way to expose the myths surrounding wills and most will substitutes is for us to share our experiences, both good and bad, with our audiences; to tell real stories about real people we have worked with. This book will teach you to plan for your loved ones just as we teach the professionals. Our story is not esoteric or complicated. It is based on the simple premise that providing for loved ones is nine parts of love to every one part of legal technicality. We believe that legal technicalities can, and should be, reduced to very simple and understandable concepts.

Dr. Joyce Brothers was on the Johnny Carson show many years ago. One particular night, Johnny was being pretty hard on Dr. Brothers because she made difficult concepts seem so simple. After several minutes of enduring Johnny's sharp tongue, Dr. Brothers responded something like this, "Listen, Carson. I've spent years in colleges and universities. I have graduate and doctoral degrees. I have spent years gathering experience in my field. I've done most of this so I can take incredibly complicated material and make it simple enough so people like you can understand it."

The audience applauded, and so did we as viewers. It is to the spirit of making extremely complicated concepts simple that we have devoted our teaching careers. This is a book about basic concepts. Basic concepts can be made to look complicated or simple based upon how well the teacher grasps them and whether or not the teacher wishes the student to attain the teacher's understanding. Beware of those who attempt to make basic premises difficult. They may be camouflaging ulterior motives or a lack of knowledge.

There Is a Better Way

We have reviewed thousands of planning attempts by sincere people who were attempting unsuccessfully to provide for their loved ones. We have experienced firsthand how badly most of these loving attempts have failed. We have observed the abuses of probate, the unexpected and often tragic results of joint tenancy property, and the effect of "bare-bones legal boilerplate." Most of the planning attempts we have reviewed were lifeless and devoid of love.

This book spells out the planning opportunities that we shared with our clients, and those that they shared with us, over the years.

Loving Trust planning is our solution to providing for your care and well-being and that of your loved ones. It is our belief that everyone needs, and can easily have, a Loving Trust. The myth that you have to be rich to plan for your loved ones is a cruel deception. Loving Trust planning is for everyone.

The myth that you have to be rich to plan for your loved ones is a cruel deception.

This book is divided into three parts. In Part One, we show you why wills and other techniques used to provide for loved ones simply do not work very well. We show you what goes wrong with them, and why. We teach you about Loving Trust planning and show you how it can overcome the problems with wills and traditional will-substitute approaches, such as the typical living trust routinely prepared in most law offices.

Part 2 will teach you how to design your Loving Trust to meet your desires for your well-being and that of your loved ones. It will describe in plain language the loving motives we commonly used in our practice. It will give you practical solutions and ideas as to how you can provide for yourself and your loved ones in the way you want, and it will give you a step-by-step checklist format that will allow you to easily design your Loving Trust blueprint.

In part 3 we will show you how you can get your Loving Trust planning done quickly and inexpensively by almost any lawyer. By using our system, you will be able to find and work with a lawyer without fear or hassle. We will prepare you to deal with your lawyer efficiently so that your Loving Trust meeting time can be kept to just a few hours. We will also show you how to use other people to help you keep your time and expense to an absolute minimum.

Loving Trust planning is for all who care about their well-being and that of their loved ones. It is designed to enable you to communicate your ideas with respect to your hopes, fears, dreams, and ambitions for yourself and your loved ones.

Chapter Four

Trust Betrayed

The life insurance agent who sold you your insurance policies, the real estate agent who sold you your house, the bank officers and clerks who set up your accounts and made loans to you, the clerk in the personnel office where you work who filled in the information with respect to your retirement plans, and the stockbroker who sold you your investments have already provided for the future of your loved ones.

You have never controlled—or even had a chance to control—the bulk of what you own. Worse yet, when you did try to exercise control over your property by writing a will or trust, you probably once again assigned real control to the lawyer who prepared it.

Surprised? Don't be. You are in the same boat as most Americans. In our experience, the property of the majority of people consists of a home, life insurance, retirement benefits, and various types of savings accounts. With each of these types of property as you will soon see, someone other than the property owner has made the decision about where that property is going to pass.

If, by chance, you were allowed to make that decision, you probably had no idea what the real consequences of your decision would be. It is very likely that you are another innocent victim who believes in people who don't know what they are talking about.

Life Insurance

We recently gave a seminar on the campus of the University of Maryland to a group of top life insurance agents. The session began with a caustic exposé of how most life insurance agents determine where their clients' life insurance proceeds will pass at their deaths. "How can you, without any discussion or thought, unilaterally take control of the largest chunk of cash a person usually leaves to loved ones?" we asked them. "Who gave you the authority to plan for the families of your clients?"

They were shocked. Their indignant response was, "What do you mean? All we do is sell the right product to our clients based on their needs. We don't decide who gets the insurance proceeds. Our clients do." To that our answer was, "Want to bet?"

Do you know where to find the beneficiary designation for each of your life insurance policies? Get your policies out right now and look for your beneficiary choices. See if you can wade through all of the fine print, or even the big print, and determine where your life insurance benefits go on your death.

Do you have a group life insurance policy from work? We challenge you to find the beneficiary designation for that policy. Do you really know who your beneficiaries are? We suspect that you think you know, but are you sure? If you can't find each of your beneficiary designations, you ought to be worried. You may not even *have* a loved one as a beneficiary!

When a life insurance agent sells you a policy, an application has to be filled out and submitted to the home office of the life insurance company. Lost among all of the "vital" application information, you will see a small box entitled "Beneficiaries." It is within that box that you will find—most likely in your life insurance agent's handwriting—who will receive your insurance cash. That is the only place your beneficiaries are designated!

If you are married, you will probably see that the proceeds are payable to your spouse as first or primary beneficiary. It will then name your children, share and share alike, or in equal shares, as second or contingent beneficiaries.

For reasons we shall soon share with you, leaving your insurance proceeds *directly* to loved ones is absolutely *not* the way to leave your life insurance cash.

When we got through with our indictment of how "that little box" is really filled in, our Maryland seminar students were in an uproar. They were the pros of their field, exceptional men and women who took great pride in their professionalism and in their sensitivity to their clients. They did not like being criticized. However, they agreed with us when we told them their clients would probably have a difficult time finding their beneficiaries in all of the policy paperwork. You should have seen their reactions when we told them that they, not their clients or attorneys, were unknowingly providing the planning for most of their clients' estates.

They responded with, "We always ask our clients whom they want as their beneficiaries. We never make those decisions for our clients! If the estate is named, it's because the lawyer said to name the estate, or there was no one else to leave it to!" On and on they went; we just listened.

After the initial reaction finally died down, we asked another question, purposefully but politely ignoring all they had to say in their defense. "How many clients asked you how you thought the beneficiary designation should be filled in?" In most cases, the agents routinely fill in that box without a great deal of

> **Leaving your insurance proceeds *directly* to loved ones is absolutely *not* the way to leave your life insurance cash.**

thought, discussion, or controversy. They responded, "Most people name their spouse as primary beneficiary and their children as contingent beneficiaries." But, from the looks on our faces, they sensed that their collective answer wasn't as right as they had always thought it was. Many of them muttered, "So, what's wrong with naming your surviving spouse and children share and share alike?"

Naming a spouse and children as the beneficiaries of your life insurance policies *appears* to reflect good thinking. It sounds so loving on its face. It reflects a satisfactory discharge of one's duty and seems like the appropriate thing to do.

The fact of the matter is, it is not good. Expecting your life insurance cash to successfully care for your loved ones when naming them as outright beneficiaries is a pipe dream. It is merely wishful thinking and nothing more. Under Murphy's Law, everything that can go wrong, will. When it comes to providing for loved ones, Murphy's Law is always operational.

Too many people plan for the best. Planning for the best is not planning; it's wishful thinking. We have always told our clients, "We must plan for the worst; if we do, no one will ever be unpleasantly surprised. If you plan for the best, you won't need us—or anyone else—to charge you good money to participate in your wishful thinking." Wishful thinking is the quickest way to disaster that we know.

If you leave your life insurance, or anything else for that matter, directly to loved ones, you assume that they will actually receive the use and benefit of what you left to them. There is no guarantee—without using a Loving Trust plan—that this will occur. A beneficiary designation that directly names a person or group of people (children that share and share alike) results in your losing control over your property. Worse yet, oftentimes beneficiaries never gain control over their parents' or grandparents' property, and when they do they frequently lose it.

Can you imagine the looks on the faces of the insurance professionals as we made these allegations? We had just shattered a few cornerstones of our group's professional knowledge. They were not happy about it. It was at this point that we reassured them that we would demonstrate what really happens when life insurance is left outright to spouses, children, and estates.

Minor Children As Your Beneficiaries

Minor children cannot own property—at least not in their own names. Property that is left or given to minor children is really held and controlled by someone else for their benefit.

Have you ever attempted to open a savings account for your minor children or grandchildren? If you have, you will remember that the bank or savings officer wouldn't let you put the account just in the name of the child. He or she told you that it would be impossible to do that—that the new account would have to be a custodial account. Its caption would read something like "Eric Johnson, a minor, by Karen Johnson or Louis Johnson," or a variation, like "Karen Johnson or Louis Johnson, custodians for Andrew Johnson, a minor."

"Custodian" is the legal name for the adult person, or institution, that has custody of a minor child's money or property. Minor children cannot withdraw money from their custodial accounts; only their custodians can. Parents are their children's custodians by law and therefore are required to be signatories on their children's accounts. The same is true for all other types of property.

Custodial issues usually do not arise when a child owns toys or other personal property, because they are usually of little value. But try putting real estate in your child's name and then attempt to sell it. There is no way you can accomplish this without your or another legal guardian's signature.

Has your teenage child or grandchild tried to purchase his or her first car directly from the local dealer? If so, the chances are excellent that he or she didn't get very far without your signature.

Severe problems arise when you and your spouse are not around to act as your children's legal custodians. What if you both die in a car accident? What if one of you survives the accident but is in a coma? By law there is always someone around to take care of your children. That someone is the local probate (surrogate, common, or district) court judge representing your local government.

Minor children without parents or with mentally disabled parents are placed under the custody of a probate judge; the judge has total power over them. The judge will name two different sets of court-appointed agents who will act for the children. The first set will be the guardians of the children. Guardians are legally appointed substitute parents. They have no control of the children's money, but they do have the responsibility to care for and raise the children with whatever funds are provided them.

The probate judge will also name custodians for the children who may or may not be the same as the guardians. The custodians will be the financial guardians of the children. They will control the children's purse strings on behalf of that local judge.

The guardians will raise the children. They are the folks who will run beside that first two-wheeler and bandage those scraped knees. The custodians will count the money and account for all of the children's income and expenses. They will hold the purse strings. You can see that the court effectively divides the parental roles into two distinct functions.

The guardians and custodians will be represented by separate lawyers who will act as their legal liasions with the judge.

How do all of these different players come together on behalf of an orphaned minor? Let's assume that a little boy, Jimmy, needs to have orthodontic work done. Jimmy needs to get braces from the local dentist, and it is going to cost a great deal of money over a long period of time. Once the guardians ascertain

Jimmy's need for braces, they will either tell their lawyer who will tell the custodians' lawyer or they will directly tell Jimmy's custodians whose lawyer will in turn tell the guardians' lawyer.

If Jimmy has adequate money, in his custodians' opinion, a recommendation will be made to the judge through the custodians' lawyer to approve the expenditure. The judge will either decide the matter in chambers or in open court. The judge may or may not grant the request. Jimmy's bevy of advisers will, however, take their fees just as the local court will assess its charges.

It is at this point that we must remind you of Murphy's Law. Will Jimmy get his braces? Will the cost of making the decision be greater than that of the orthodontist? Only the judge knows—and he's on vacation. Ah, Murphy's Law!

We are sure that Jimmy's mother and father never intended the courts, court-appointed conservators, guardians and lawyers to become co-beneficiaries of their life insurance program. Did the family life insurance agent or lawyer warn Jimmy's parents of the pitfalls of leaving their life insurance directly to their children, share and share alike? We doubt it. Loving parents, in their right minds, would never knowingly place their children in such a legal quagmire. As we reflect on the situation, Jimmy's parents really never had control. The little beneficiary box on the insurance application controlled their life insurance cash, and it was filled in by an agent they hardly knew, who was just following the "usual procedures."

We each have two boys and have learned that children develop different interests and needs. For example, one son may elect to play football. We know from experience that it costs an arm and a leg to outfit a boy in helmet and pads. If the other son selects soccer, it can save a bank loan. The price of soccer shoes, shorts, and jersey does not approach the cost of the football-playing brother's helmet. The cost of the football uniform can literally be in the hundreds of dollars, while a soccer player's gear will likely be in the tens of dollars.

If you are like most people, you wouldn't give your soccer player son extra money to balance the ledger between the boys because of the comparative costs of outfitting them. Most of us love our children equally but take care of them based upon their needs. We buy our children the things they need without worrying about an exact monetary division between them. In our seminars, we use a phrase to sum up this concept of equal love, but unequal treatment: "There is nothing so unequal as the equal treatment of unequals."

Over the years we have planned for only two clients who kept, with meticulous detail, a ledger on every cent they spent on behalf of their respective children. John and Wayne were brothers. They emulated their very European parents when it came to balancing their respective children's ledgers at the end of every year.

Under our example, each of their soccer-playing sons would receive a ledger credit. They were astounded when we told them that most parents didn't provide for their children in this manner. But, undaunted, they nevertheless instructed us

> **Most of us love our children equally but take care of them based upon their needs.**

to draw their Loving Trust plans to continue this "common sense" family tradition with respect to their children and grandchildren.

Every person who leaves his or her life insurance cash in equal shares ("share and share alike," "to my children equally," or "per stirpes") to loved ones is mandating a John and Wayne balance-the-ledger master plan for their loved ones.

What has astounded us for years is that we have worked with so many people who believed strongly in loving their children equally—caring for them without this ledger mentality. How parents can so meticulously follow one course of action all of their lives, then suddenly abandon it at death for an opposite course of action can only be attributed to the fact that they do not understand the meanings and results of the legal beneficiary jargon. They, like most of us, never really have control.

If you do not believe in ledger planning, reexamine your insurance policy beneficiary designations. Do they provide for your loved ones just as John and Wayne provided for theirs?

Ledger-mentality beneficiary designations frequently result in inequitable and disastrous consequences for little ones. One such instance involved three children whose parents left them an inheritance that included a substantial sum of life insurance "share and share alike." The local bank trust department was named as the custodian of the children's insurance money. This is not a unique occurrence; bank trust departments are often named as custodians of minor children's funds by probate courts when children are directly left property by their unknowing parents.

In this case, the children were nineteen, twelve, and two years of age at the time of their parents' death. The nineteen-year-old was in college and doing quite well; the twelve-year-old had a learning disability; and the two-year-old was very healthy and had no apparent problems.

Because of medical difficulties and other complications that arose, the twelve-year-old son ran out of money and was made a ward of the state. He was placed in a state home for the mentally retarded. The nineteen-year-old never touched her money. She went through both college and graduate school on academic and service club scholarships. Following graduation she did equally well in a merchandising career that paid her handsomely. Her two-year-old brother, a surprise change-of-life baby, was not left quite as well off. Since he was so young, the bank couldn't spend too much of his money to take care of his basic needs for fear that his money would be depleted too soon. His money had to last until he was twenty-one years old, and with nineteen years to go, it had to be managed tightly and had to be carefully preserved.

Had the parents lived, we suspect that they would have allocated their resources so that the twelve-year-old and two-year-old boys would have been well taken care of. The nineteen-year-old daughter obviously needed less, so less would have been used for her benefit, leaving that much more for her brothers' well-being.

Unfortunately, the parents' life insurance designations created an iron curtain between the children. The boys could not share in their sister's windfall. Her one-third was hers to do with as she pleased. In this case, there was nothing fair about leaving the insurance money "equally" to the children. When the children were placed "in equal shares" in that little box, their parents doubtless gave little thought as to what it would really mean to everyone's well-being and life. Mom and Dad were obviously confused by the jargon, and obviously—for an instant in time—didn't consider the differing and relative needs of their children. They weren't in control; that's for sure!

If you leave minor or disadvantaged children, this sort of thing can easily happen to them. We would agree that it's not likely something will happen to you and your spouse in the near future. But, match an untimely illness or accident with poorly thought-out beneficiary designations, add to that minor or disadvantaged children, and there you—or should we say there your loved ones—are visiting with Mr. Murphy.

Terrible things can happen to your children because you provided for them with legal jargon you did not understand in a little box on an insurance application. The problems with that little box do not end with minor children—they only *begin* there.

Adult Children As Your Beneficiaries

Many of you are thinking that you don't need to worry about Mr. Murphy and that little insurance application box. Your children are grown, and you are not planning on having more. You are comfortable that there is no reason for you to get excited about equal treatment of unequals or iron curtains. In fact, this is exactly what our insurance professionals brought up to us after we shook them up so badly about directly leaving property to minor children.

Our class needed to feel that at least some of their traditional operating methods did not have Murphy's Law consequences. They were snug in their belief that leaving insurance proceeds directly to healthy adult children reflected sound planning. That was before we told them Luke's story, and then immediately followed it up with Diane's story.

Luke was married and had two children. He was a high school teacher and coach. He had always lived modestly and was happy living within his economic means; he liked his job and enjoyed his family. Luke's grandfather was wealthy. He had always loved Luke but wisely refrained from interfering in his life by lavishing too much money or too many things on him. He wanted Luke to stand on his own two feet and to be successful as a result of his self-reliance.

Luke's grandfather came to us for planning advice, but his mind was made up before he came. Nothing we said could convince him not to leave everything he owned, including a substantial amount of life insurance, directly to Luke.

When Luke's granddad died, Luke got everything in one lump sum. For the first time in his life, Luke had "real" money. He bought a big car for himself and a sports car for his wife. He bought a huge house in an exclusive area and joined the local country club so he could rub shoulders with others equally well-off.

Luke also got into deals. It became well-known around the club that if you needed money to do a deal, Luke would probably be good for it. Luke was a soft touch, and everyone knew it. He no longer had time for teaching high school; the time was quickly taken up with a daily regimen of golf, cards, and a few drinks with the "boys down at the club."

The money left as fast as it came. In fewer than three years Luke lost everything. All of those surefire deals backfired. Luke was left destitute. He had acquired a taste for gambling and drinking. He lost his money, his wife, and his children. To this day, we believe that Luke's ex-wife is still attempting to collect child support and alimony.

Luke's story is not about a bad person getting his just desserts. It is a story of someone who was overwhelmed by wealth. Luke's grandfather had the wisdom not to spoil Luke while he was alive. Yet, for some inexplicable reason, he felt he could satisfactorily do just the opposite after his death. You cannot take an Eskimo from the North Pole and a Polynesian from the South Seas and, without any warning, change their places in the dead of a northern hemisphere winter. Both will die of exposure, one to the heat, the other to the cold. Drastic change brings on drastic results.

Luke was not prepared for what occurred, and he paid the consequences of his grandfather's lack of judgment. Had Luke been given two or even three chances at wealth, he may well have learned how to handle it. If Luke's granddad had provided that Luke gradually get used to having money, Luke might be happy and prosperous today. He was never given the opportunity to learn. When property is left outright to adult children, there is no room for error. Loving Trust planning can provide that room.

Diane's story is different. She was raised in wealth, went to the best schools, and had the best training that money could buy. She was levelheaded and not likely to squander wealth.

Her parents died when she was in her early twenties. They left her inheritance to her in trust, with the exception of one large insurance policy that was left to her directly.

Soon after her parents' deaths, Diane married a young entrepreneur who was looking for a fast way to the top. Diane was his ticket. After they were married, her husband, Jeff, decided to build a racquetball facility and health spa. Jeff had

When property is left outright to adult children, there is no room for error.

nothing. To approve his loan, the bank insisted that Diane co-sign the note, pledging her money as collateral. Diane was a loving and giving wife; she signed the note, trusting that Jeff would not let her down.

Jeff turned out to be both a disloyal husband and a business failure. The project went bankrupt; Jeff left Diane pregnant and with all of his bank debt. Diane quickly lost all of her parents' insurance money to Jeff's creditors. However, the property and money left to her in trust was saved, and as a result, Diane and her baby were not left destitute.

Age does not make a person wise—experience does. And unfortunately experience usually comes from making mistakes. Some mistakes are obviously more costly than others. When loved ones receive property but don't have the knowledge or experience to manage it, the necessary experience may be gained at a cost that is simply too great to bear.

There are many Loving Trust ways to protect adult children from their inexperience and naïveté. None of these methods entails leaving the outright distributions of life insurance proceeds. We know that Murphy's Law applies to the inexperienced regardless of their age.

For many years we have asked our seminar participants if any of them have children who have learning disabilities or who are disadvantaged in some way. About one in ten participants will answer in the affirmative. In the Maryland seminar, the ratio was a little higher. As soon as we mentioned disadvantaged children, that group of men and women reacted much like any of our other classes: "Oh, no, here we go again. We can see it coming, that little box on the life insurance application is going to make for terrible messes later on!" Most of them were beginning to understand just how important that little box is.

We knew from experience that many of these honorable and excellent insurance professionals had too often filled in that little box without knowing, or even asking, whether a loved one had some form of disability.

There is no greater injustice than leaving life insurance, or any property for that matter, outright to a disadvantaged loved one.

Early in our practice, we ran into a situation where insurance proceeds and other properties were left outright to a disadvantaged child. The "child" was middle-aged, but because of his disability he functioned at approximately a four-year-old level. He had been protected and sheltered from the real world all of his life by his parents. Unfortunately, they died within a few months of one another without leaving Loving Trust instructions.

By happenstance, a relative came to us with this man-child's problems. We had to initiate a probate court proceeding that resulted in his being declared mentally incompetent. The court treated him just as it would treat a minor child. A guardian and a custodian were appointed. All of his parents' property went to the custodian to be held on his behalf. The court chose an institution for him,

> **When loved ones receive property but don't have the knowledge or experience to manage it, the necessary experience may be gained at a cost that is simply too great to bear.**

where to the best of our knowledge he still resides. His life is subject, of course, to the court's and Mr. Murphy's approval. Unfortunately, this sad story is not unique; it happens every day.

Oftentimes a child is not sufficiently "disadvantaged" to need court supervision but still needs help with money and finances. Some examples come readily to mind: an emotionally disturbed child; the child who just isn't very intelligent, or a child who is a genius but who never adapted to the real world; and the child who is downright irresponsible.

Unprotected from themselves and the many hucksters of the world, too many "well-heeled orphans" are at the mercy of anyone who has the inclination to prey on them. If you have a child with special needs and problems, would you give him or her a large lump of cash without supervision while you are alive? We believe your response would be, "Absolutely not!" We wonder why so many people do that very thing on their death!

It is a travesty that so many otherwise prudent people attempt to leave their money directly to loved ones. You now know that it often goes to a court and to court-appointed guardians, conservators, and lawyers. Every parent who leaves life insurance proceeds without Loving Trust instructions for the care of his or her loved ones is leaving only half a loaf; the money is there—absent the protection, instructions, and guidelines for its use. The results of leaving half-a-loaf insurance proceeds are not pleasant. These proceeds also end up—all too often—in the hands of creditors, fast-talking strangers, and distant relatives with a good story.

People can inherit money and property when their parents or grandparents die, but they can't inherit any more brains, experience, or emotional stability. A simple and poorly thought-out beneficiary designation simply cannot pass any of these nonmonetary qualities to loved ones. Yet, it never ceases to amaze us that this is precisely the assumption so many people make. As we told our life insurance students, "Your profession is just as guilty of poorly planning for your clients' loved ones as our profession."

Your Spouse As Your Beneficiary

Naming your spouse as the primary beneficiary of your life insurance would seem like the right thing to do. Most people want their spouse to have their life insurance proceeds, and they would like whatever is left to go to their children on their spouses' deaths. We have met very few clients who didn't want exactly this result.

Unfortunately, using a simple beneficiary designation to accomplish loving goals doesn't always work. If you leave your insurance proceeds and other property outright to your spouse, you can hurt rather than help your mate.

Let's assume, however, that everything goes exactly as you planned upon your death. Your spouse is well and receives your insurance proceeds. Your spouse is frugal and is bound and determined to leave all of those insurance dollars not used during his or her lifetime to the children. Then your spouse remarries.

You can imagine, at this point, all of the clumsy, unfortunate, and catastrophic situations we have seen as a result of nice, but poorly informed, people attempting to cope with their money and a new spouse's demands.

Keep in mind that your spouse can change his or her beneficiary designations at any time. He or she can easily name that new spouse as beneficiary after your death. In fact, under many state laws, if your spouse remarries after your death and doesn't have a signed premarital contract, your "replacement" will have significant rights to your spouse's—or should we say your—property.

We have met too many clients who found themselves in this situation over the years. A typical situation goes something like this: Dad died leaving everything to Mom either by beneficiary designation or by will. Mom, after several lonely years, finally remarried. She didn't change her will, which left everything to the children, just as her new husband didn't change his. Mom died before her new husband. Under her state's law a spouse gets one-half of the estate of the spouse who dies first, unless, either prior to marriage or during marriage, they made a contract agreeing to some other arrangement. There was no contract between our clients' mother and their stepfather.

The stepfather went to court and took his share of the estate as allowed under state law. Our clients wanted us to stop their stepfather from getting "their" money and property. There was nothing we could do. In total violation of their parents' wishes, the stepfather got one-half of their parents' property.

A beneficiary designation that leaves all of your property outright to your spouse means that you have lost control over the proceeds. Using an outright, uncontrolled beneficiary designation is like leaning out of a window on the fifteenth floor of a building and throwing dollar bills out, hoping that one or two of the folks you are attempting to throw them to will somehow catch some of them. A lot can happen to those dollar bills between the time you let go of them and their ultimate arrival.

In more cases than we care to admit, one spouse has had total control of the family purse strings throughout the marriage, and, whether by design or happenstance, the other spouse is in the dark when it comes to the family's finances. The financial spouse handles everything, from investments to balancing the checkbook. The financially unsophisticated spouse generally can't even pretend to play a good game when it comes to money, business, and finance.

Shirley came to us several months after Carl, her husband of thirty-three years, died. She had been referred by an insurance agent. Carl's life insurance was—as with most Americans—his major asset. Shirley was the beneficiary. Carl's insurance was paid to her ten days after Carl's death.

When Shirley came to us, she showed us her joint checking account. Carl was still on the account. There was over $100,000 in cash in it! It wasn't drawing interest; it was just sitting in the account making some bank officers extremely happy.

Shirley had absolutely no idea what to do with that money. Carl, for all of the years of their marriage, had taken care of their finances. Shirley received an allowance that she used to run the household and buy the personal things she needed. If she needed additional funds, she would talk to Carl. "Carl wanted me to do more," she said, "but I never wanted to. I had certain things that I did and enjoyed, and our finances were not among them. It never occurred to me that one day Carl's responsibilities would fall on my shoulders whether I liked it or not."

Shirley was fortunate that Carl's life insurance agent was both professional and caring enough to discern her problem and to offer his help. When we related Shirley's experience to our seminar class at the University of Maryland, they visibly brightened. "See," one of them said, "a beneficiary designation isn't so bad. Shirley got help from her agent; he did his job!"

Helping Shirley was not his job, though. Carl's agent was exceptional. She was very lucky that he pointed her in the right direction. If he hadn't, someone would have pointed her in another direction. Shirley and her money would have soon parted. It is not too difficult for crooks and overzealous business types to take advantage of widows and widowers who have considerable grief and newfound wealth.

There are many people who are willing to marry for money. Leaving life insurance outright to a spouse is like leaving food out on a picnic table; sooner or later, unwanted guests are going to come along to share a free lunch. When you leave large sums of money directly to a naive spouse, you are inviting others to freeload.

The problems that we have been considering get even worse if your spouse is incapacitated following your death. What happens to your spouse and to your life insurance proceeds if your spouse is in a coma from the same car accident that took your life?

Minor children, disabled children, and disabled adults have one thing in common—they cannot own property! If your spouse is plugged into all kinds of machines in an intensive care unit, loved ones will not be allowed to cash the life insurance check, let alone to spend it taking care of your spouse.

There is always someone around to help. The local probate judge, with all of the judicial machinery provided by the state legislature, is always there. A disabled spouse goes through the same court-oriented legal process as a minor child or any other disabled person. In this situation, the process goes something like this: First there is the court proceeding to declare your spouse incompetent. Then come the guardian and the conservator and the lawyers. The life insurance pro-

Leaving life insurance outright to a spouse is like leaving food out on a picnic table; sooner or later, unwanted guests are going to come along to share a free lunch.

ceeds are controlled by the court, which makes sure that all of the court-appointed agents are paid. The court makes sure that all of the family's creditors are paid, leaving the balance to be used—at the judge's, conservator's, and guardian's discretion—for the benefit of your spouse.

Can matters get worse? If you have minor children, they certainly can! Your children will have to endure the same probate process. The local probate judge is going to be plenty busy naming multiple guardians, conservators, and lawyers and then reviewing all of the red-tape paperwork they generate.

Recently we had reason to be in the Probate Court in Denver, Colorado. The court docket for the week, which is the judge's calendar of what he will be doing, was posted outside the courtroom door on a bulletin board. For five days there was not one death probate—every single trial or hearing scheduled, and there were a lot of them, was for an incompetency hearing for a minor child or disabled adult.

We live in a world where physicians can keep patients alive for a long time using sophisticated medical techniques. The result is that most of us are living longer, even though we may need the help of others to handle our affairs. The probate courts and attorneys are doing a booming business thanks to modern medicine. It's too bad that more of us aren't avoiding them by using Loving Trust planning.

Naming Your Estate As Beneficiary of Your Life Insurance

All of the bad, nasty, and evil things that can happen if you name your spouse or children as outright beneficiaries of your life insurance policies are not as bad as the consequences of naming your "estate." At every seminar we give, whether to life insurance agents, lawyers, accountants, financial planners, or the general public, we emphasize this point: "Naming your estate as beneficiary of your life insurance policies is crazy and definitely someone's malpractice."

You should see the panic on the faces in our audience—this is especially true of law and insurance groups—when we attack this practice in "malpractice" terms. Everyone wants to talk at once. "How can you say such a thing?" "You're exaggerating!" "Prove it!" We're used to the reaction, and when the uproar dies down, we patiently go about proving our point.

All insurance policies have what is known as a spendthrift clause. This clause, which is safeguarded by the laws of all states, protects your insurance proceeds and your beneficiaries from the claims of your creditors. Let's assume you have an insurance policy that pays $100,000 on your death. Let's further assume that you owe various creditors more than $100,000 and don't have a cent to your name. If, on your death, you have named anyone other than your "estate" as a beneficiary of your life insurance, your creditors cannot get the money that you owe them out of your life insurance proceeds. Your life insurance proceeds are absolutely free from the claims of your creditors.

Your life insurance proceeds can only be successfully attacked and seized by your creditors if you leave it to them. You leave your life insurance proceeds to your creditors when you leave it to your "estate"!

Why anyone, especially a professional life insurance agent or lawyer, would take a creditor-free asset and subject it to the claims of creditors is a great mystery to us. When you look at your beneficiary designations, look for "estate" type language in those little boxes. If you see it, immediately call your agent and get it changed! Remember, life insurance proceeds payable to a beneficiary other than your estate avoid probate. Making absolutely sure that you regain control of your insurance program is one of the functions of the Loving Trust planning.

The "box" controls one of the most significant assets that you own. You did not intend to lose control of your life insurance proceeds, but when your insurance agent filled in that box you probably did just that.

Jointly Held Real Estate

If you are like most people, you lost control of your real estate at your first house closing. Think back to that day; you were probably excited and equally nervous. When you completed signing the reams of closing paperwork, the house was automatically put in both your name and your spouse's name. It was then that you first lost control of your real estate.

We very much doubt that your real estate agent asked you, "Whose name does the deed to your new house go in?" Can you recall your real estate agent asking you this question? If your closing was like most others, the real estate company's secretary simply typed whatever names the agent placed on your purchase offer on the deed to your home.

If perchance your real estate agent asked you how you would like to own your home, you probably answered without much thought or hesitation, "Put it in both of our names." If you weren't asked, it is highly likely that you and your mate were named as the joint purchasers anyway.

Married couples purchasing a home almost universally take ownership as joint tenants. In a few states they own their home as tenants by the entirety. This is a special kind of ownership that's almost identical to joint tenancy. If, for some reason, you recall asking the agent why he or she was putting the deed in joint tenancy, you'll recall that the answer was "You have a good marriage, don't you?" or "We've always done it that way."

"Jointly held" has a nice ring to it. It captures the essence of "the two of us" or "our marital partnership." It is psychologically pleasing. The fact is, both you and your spouse absolutely lose the ability to control your real estate the instant you put both of your names on the deed.

Much has been written to warn the public about the pitfalls and the traps of joint tenancy. *Reader's Digest* has repeatedly written about its Murphy-like traps. Nevertheless, almost all couples keep acquiring their property "jointly." Even most of the professionals we teach, including practicing lawyers, do not have a grasp of how joint tenancy plays into Murphy's hands.

Joint tenancy does *not* mean that each spouse owns one-half of the marriage's property. When each owns half, it is either called tenancy in common or community property, an ownership method unique to eight states (Arizona, California, Idaho, Louisiana, Nevada, New Mexico, Texas, Washington). Wisconsin also has a community property type of ownership, and is classified as a community property state for purposes of a spouse's owning half. If you think that you are a half owner with your spouse of your joint property, you are dead wrong!

Imagine two birds sitting on a tree limb. You might say they both own the whole limb since both have an equal right to alight, sit, and take off from any part of it. Now imagine that one of the birds is shot by a boy's pellet gun and falls off the limb, dead. Its mate still sits on the branch. The surviving mate now owns the whole limb. Our lovebirds' situation is the essence of joint tenancy.

The proper title for joint tenancy is joint tenancy, with right of survivorship. It is the right of survivorship—which bird ends up alone on the limb—that really defines how joint tenancy works. The surviving spouse ultimately owns and controls all of the joint property because of the survivorship feature. Joint tenancy is a discreet but devastating, version of the economic game, "winner takes and controls all."

It is precisely at this point that many of our seminar students respond with, "So what's the big deal? I want my husband (or my wife) to have the house when I die." And we reply, "Sure you do, just like you want your spouse to have life insurance proceeds outright when you die, right?" Joint tenancy is another marvelous testing ground for Murphy's Law.

Residences are only part of the joint tenancy tangle. When you bought your cars, your friendly car salesperson put "joint tenancy" on the title application. With such precedents behind you, and being fast learners, you and your spouse began putting everything in joint tenancy. It was easy to do. It avoided any disputes as to who owned what, because both you and your mate thought you owned everything equally.

You may even recall one of your friends mentioning that joint property avoided probate. Your friend's information was partially correct. Jointly owned property avoids probate when a joint owner dies. That is a fact, or at least half of a fact. When the bird falls off the limb, the courts do not have to decide who owns the property. The law makes it clear that the remaining bird owns the property. Presto! An easy way to avoid the expense, aggravation, and delay of probate—maybe! For now, we'll assume that joint tenancy does avoid probate and all of its related horrors. Now it's time again to test Murphy's Law.

Ginnie and Don owned all their property jointly. It was a second marriage for both of them. Don had three children from his prior marriage. They lived with their mother, who had remarried, and Don really didn't have much contact with any of them. Don's first family was kept mostly out of his thoughts and life. Ginnie had no children from her first marriage, but she and Don had two young children. Ginnie and Don assumed that when one of them died, the other would take care of their children. Neither of them wanted to leave anything to Don's children by his first wife.

Ginnie and Don were flying in a private airplane that crashed on landing. Ginnie died instantly, but Don survived. As the survivor, he automatically received all the property, because it was all in joint tenancy. Don was the bird left on the limb. Don, however, was rushed to a hospital with multiple critical injuries.

All of Ginnie's and Don's affairs came to a halt. Friends of the family contacted a lawyer. He proceeded to get a guardian and a conservator appointed for Don. Next, the court appointed a guardian and a conservator for Don and Ginnie's two children. Luckily, a relative agreed to take both of them; otherwise, they would have been split up or sent to a state facility.

Don died soon thereafter. A probate was opened for him since he was now the sole owner of the joint property. There were no more birds on the limb, so the court had to decide where Don's property would go at his death. Don had no will or trust. Under Don's state's law, his children received equal shares of his property. Don and Ginnie's children each got 20 percent of their parents' property. Don's other children also got 20 percent each.

Don and Ginnie wanted their children to have everything when they were gone. They expected that would be the case. They never knew that their little ones would get only 40 percent of their property. They never intended that Don's older children get anything, much less 60 percent! Why did this happen? Whose fault was it? When it comes to joint property, Mr. Murphy is all smiles.

Jointly owned property between spouses and poorly thought-out beneficiary designations are two sides of the same coin. If it can go wrong, it will, and Murphy is doing the flipping! Mountain cabins, lakeshore cottages, and seaside retreats owned jointly among brothers, sisters, and their parents or in-laws are fertile breeding grounds for jointly owned catastrophes. These ownership combinations have led to many nasty and expensive lawsuits.

Our clients, Jack and Art, were brothers who were very close to one another. Their pride and joy was a mountain cabin that they had built together over the years. The cabin, which was on beautiful land near Rocky Mountain National

Park, was owned by Jack and Art as joint tenants with right of survivorship. Everyone in their families loved that cabin. It represented good times, and Jack and Art wanted it to stay in their families for a long time. Just like everybody else, they assumed that they each owned half of the cabin.

Jack and Art were shocked to hear that they each didn't own half. They were even more shocked when we told them what would happen when the first one of them died.

We explained that the survivor would own the cabin. We also explained that the dead brother's family would have no ownership or right to the cabin, even though he put up half the cost of building it. We stressed that even if the dead brother put up all the money, the cabin would still belong to the surviving brother.

They were silent with disbelief, and we weren't through yet! We stressed that one-half of the value of the cabin would be subject to federal estate tax in the deceased brother's estate. This was the classic double whammy—tax without property! Joint tenancy with right of survivorship is not designed to be fair.

One of the brothers, after listening to our explanation, then observed, "There's nothing to worry about. Whoever survives will just give half back to the other's family." We answered that his conclusion was a really bad idea. The gift could very well generate state and federal gift taxes in addition to existing death taxes. We also cautioned him that there was absolutely no guarantee that the gift would be made. We posed several additional questions: "What if the living brother were angry with a member of the deceased brother's family and decided to keep it for his family? What if the surviving brother were sick or disabled and couldn't make the gift? What if the surviving brother got greedy?"

We told them that they were certainly welcome to plan for the best, but in our opinion that wouldn't be planning, just wishful thinking. We invited them to ask Murphy if their dreams would come true. We all knew what his answer would be! They certainly got the message that joint tenancy with right of survivorship was not a prudent way for them to own their cabin.

Jointly owned property held between elderly parents and their children is another fertile testing ground for Murphy. A close friend's younger sister took care of their mother after their father died. To facilitate the undertaking, all the mother's property was put in joint tenancy with the sister. This undertaking certainly gave the sister the right to sign everything on behalf of their infirm mother. Their mother had a will leaving 40 percent of her estate to our friend and 60 percent to her sister. The extra 20 percent that was going to the sister was in recognition of the care she was giving Mother.

When our friend's mother died, the sister received all Mother's property. Joint tenancy passed the property to our friend's sister because she was the only bird left sitting on that limb. Mother's will was meaningless because joint property passes automatically to the survivor. It does not pass through the first deceased owner's estate, and therefore it is not subject to the terms of a will.

When our friend asked her sister for her share, the sister responded something like this. "Where were you when I was taking care of Mom? Who spent days and nights, year after year, caring for her? Do you know what I sacrificed? I deserve it all." Once our friend's sister discovered the property was all hers, she conveniently forgot Mother's wishes and the deal she had struck with her sister. Everything went wrong—or right, depending on one's point of view—because joint ownership was used to facilitate taking care of Mother rather than a Loving Trust plan.

It might hearten you to know that the Internal Revenue Service took away some of the sister's ill-gotten gains. When property is put into joint tenancy and the joint tenants are not husband and wife, a gift is made. The gift is from the original owner to the other joint tenant. In this case, the IRS found out about Mother's joint transfers to her daughter and charged the daughter gift tax and compounded interest for all the years it wasn't paid. The gift tax aspect of joint tenancy is almost always overlooked by everyone except the IRS and Murphy. It is one more reason that joint tenancy is a dangerously poor way to own property.

You lose control of your property when you put it in joint tenancy.

You lose control of your property when you put it in joint tenancy. It can pass to unintended heirs when you die. While it is used by many as a method to avoid probate, it *never* avoids probate on the surviving tenant's death. It is also often subject to probate expenses on the first death. It can even create death taxes without ownership and gift taxes between everyone except spouses!

With few, if any, exceptions you should not own your property in joint tenancy with anybody! If you do, you should continue reading before making changes in your ownership habits.

Joint Property and Your Bank

Bankers are very smart. They understand what joint tenancy can do for them. They endorse and encourage it because it is good for the bank, not necessarily the borrower.

Even if your realtor counseled you not to purchase your property in joint tenancy, the bank handling your mortgage would have done its best to put your house in joint tenancy anyway. When two names are on a deed, your friendly banker can easily get two names on the mortgage. Two people responsible for the payment of a mortgage are always better than just one, because if there is a default on the payment, the bank can sue two people rather than one.

Bankers also encourage joint tenancy because it saves them time and paperwork. People do not usually object to it, and it is important from the bank's point of view to accustom their customers to two signatures.

We do not have our houses in joint tenancy. Neither do our clients, or at least those who took and remembered our advice. You do not pull a fast one on your bank, or any other creditor for that matter, if you keep your home ownership out of joint tenancy. Rather, you simply avoid all of the joint tenancy problems we have been discussing.

Even though our houses are in one name, the bank has insisted that both spouses sign on the dotted lines of our respective mortgages. Most of our clients and students over the years have been shocked at the notion that the title to a residence or any other property can be in one spouse's name while the mortgage is in both. We continue to tell our students that this is not a problem, and never has been one. If you give your bank a mortgage on your house, you do not give the bank control or ownership, you only give them the house as collateral for your promise to pay back the money you borrowed; if you default on your promise, the bank can sell your house—foreclose on your mortgage—to get the money you still owe them.

You do not have to put your home in joint tenancy in order to get a mortgage on it. Whose name or names you put your residence in is your business. Who signs the mortgage is the bank's business. The bank does not have the right to tell you how to title your real estate. You have no right to tell the bank who is—or is not—going to sign their mortgage. Bankers want to make sure that they can sue as many people as possible if the sale of the property doesn't raise enough money to cover what they are owed. As a result, we rarely see mortgages that are signed by only one spouse.

Bankers have other ways of encouraging their customers to place their property in joint tenancy. Do you remember when you and your spouse opened up your first checking or savings account? You met with their new accounts person, who helped you select the proper account, checkbook cover style, and the color of your checks. That person also gave you an account signature card to sign. That signature card is the legal document that tells the world who is the owner of the account.

Banks have several printed forms of signature cards. When married couples come in, the new accounts person usually automatically presents them with the joint tenancy card. We have often been asked why bankers do this. The response we always give is, "We do not know."

At any rate, you and your spouse signed the account card as joint tenants with right of survivorship. That's the way it's done. You were not presented with alternatives. The new accounts person, like your life insurance agent and your realtor, determined (with Murphy's silent help) how your loved ones would be provided for. You were never given the opportunity to do otherwise.

All the things you buy with the money in your joint accounts are considered to be joint tenancy unless you title that property differently. One hour at a bank clerk's desk has mandated many a joint tenancy marriage. From that point on, almost all of your possessions will be owned in joint property with rights of survivorship. And you never knew the consequences of that innocent account opening. You were in someone else's hands who did not know what he or she was doing.

Are all your bank accounts in both your and your spouse's names? Do you have joint accounts with people other than your spouse? Do you know whether you signed signature cards creating joint tenancy? The only way you will know for sure is to go to the bank and look at those cards. They will tell you how the account is owned.

If the account card does not say how the account is owned but has someone else's signature on it in addition to yours, then only a lawyer can tell you whether your account is in joint tenancy. In some states, property held in more than one name without any other notation as to how the property is owned is presumed to be owned in joint tenancy. Other states presume that the property is in tenancy in common—a form of ownership that works the way most people mistakenly think joint tenancy works.

Tenancy in common between spouses means that each spouse owns half of the property. However, each half cannot be specifically identified. If you own a dog in tenancy in common, you do not specifically own the half that eats or the half that wags. You own half of the whole dog.

If you own a deck of cards tenancy in common, you do not own twenty-six cards; you own half of every card. Should you desire to sell or give your interest to someone else, you can transfer your one-half interest in each and every card. The same thing occurs on your death. If you leave your tenancy in common interest to a deck of cards, your loved ones will own a part of every card in the deck.

With tenancy in common ownership you can direct your property to loved ones rather than rely on where Murphy will pass it. With joint tenancy property, the first bird to fall off the limb cannot leave anything, because on death it owned nothing. With tenancy in common property, that bird still owns 50 percent of that limb and can leave it to loved ones in a Loving Trust plan.

The Personnel Clerk Where You Work

Most of us have a retirement plan and some group life insurance at work. These are employee benefits that offer meaningful security to most employees and their families.

We had group life insurance and a profit-sharing plan in our law firm. They were put in by sophisticated advisers. We had talented insurance agents who placed our insurance with old-line reputable companies. Our bank, one of the largest in town, was the trustee of our profit-sharing plan. The costs of main-

> **With tenancy in common ownership you can direct your property to loved ones rather than rely on where Murphy will pass it.**

taining our benefit package were substantial. Our law firm restricted its practice to tax, business, and estate planning. In those areas, we were sophisticated and knowledgeable in dotting all the i's and crossing the t's.

One day, after each plan had been in force for several years, a memo went out to our bookkeeping department, requesting an update on our beneficiary designations. We waited and waited until we received a reply that said, "What beneficiary designations?"

Somewhere in the fine-print documentation of both our plans, it said that the plan's beneficiaries would be designated by the participants. Unfortunately our participants weren't told about their benefit-planning opportunities. A sad, but human commentary on us. We were no worse or better than most businesses at keeping records. It became obvious to us that we were just like our clients: We huffed and puffed about too many little things and forgot to deal with the really important ones. An insurance executive friend of ours calls this all-too-human penchant "majoring in minors."

We thought we had planned for our loved ones, but when it came to our group insurance and profit-sharing money we left the planning to Murphy. Somehow in the daily rush of things, we forgot to hitch the cart to the benefit horse. Our loved ones never had a chance. We are lucky that we discovered our mistake before one of our employees died.

Where would our firm's life insurance and retirement benefits have been paid if we hadn't caught our mistake in time? To the estates of our deceased and disabled employees. Two marvelous fringe benefits that were absolutely probate- and creditor-free would have been paid to our employees' creditors by way of our local probate court.

Let's assume that we hadn't messed up and that we had assiduously distributed beneficiary cards to our employees. Do you think that the results would have been all that much better? In looking back, we don't think they would have been.

We would have had a clerk from our personnel department write a memo telling our employees to fill in the cards and return them to our business office by such and such a date. As a result, a life-and-death, critically important planning consideration would have been relegated to ministerial status and left to the devices of one of our least-skilled employees. We strongly suspect that this is precisely what happens all too often throughout the business sector.

Company-sponsored fringe-benefit proceeds appear to represent the bulk of what most people in the American workforce leave to their loved ones. And yet extraordinarily expensive employee benefit packages are not properly going to those loved ones. Why is Murphy put in charge of their distribution? is more than a rhetorical question—it's a national disgrace.

Do you have a group life-insurance plan at work? Are you a participant in a pension plan, stock option, thrift, or profit-sharing plan? Who do you think will receive your share if something happens to you? In what manner will they receive it? Do you recall filling in beneficiary cards? Did a personnel clerk fill them in for you? Odds are that you don't have ready answers to most of these questions. If you don't, you'll certainly want to take a break from the daily grind and make some inquiries at the earliest possible moment.

Your Stockbroker

Stocks, bonds, and mutual funds certainly represent assets that are acquired by prudent savers and investors. They go into portfolios that are carefully managed either directly by the investor or through the expertise of a professional money manager. Most investors carefully monitor their investments to assure themselves that their principal is secure and that it is earning them the highest income possible. Most investors scrutinize the credentials of their financial advisers before hiring them, and then continually monitor their investment abilities. In short, those of us who are fortunate enough to put a little away are usually not careless in its management.

But most savers and investors are not so prudent when it comes to making sure that their loved ones will receive those hard-earned and carefully managed assets.

When you open an account with your stockbroker, you go through a process that is very similar to opening a bank account. There are forms to be filled in and documents to be signed. Most of these forms are not for your benefit. They are for the benefit of the IRS and the brokerage house. In the paperwork will be an input form to set up your account on the firm's computer. How that form is filled in will determine how your investments will be handled and distributed in the event of your death or incapacity.

Stockbrokers are in the business of selling securities, just as insurance agents are in the business of selling life insurance. They are not particularly interested in how you designate your beneficiaries. That is your responsibility. When your broker sets up your account, it is likely that he or she will not stress the importance of the account title.

Without belaboring the obvious, you know that married clients are going to fill in joint-tenancy account forms and single adults are usually going to have the account put in their own names.

Your broker will not ask you to fill in a beneficiary designation form. In that respect he or she is more akin to your banker than to your insurance agent or personnel clerk. If your account is placed in joint tenancy with right of survivorship, you are right back with Murphy. If it is placed in your name or in tenancy in common, your interest is going to go through probate.

If your account has more than one name on it but doesn't say anything more, your state law will determine whether you own your interest as a joint tenant or as a tenant in common. In our experience, this rarely occurs with account statements. But if it does, call your lawyer.

On stocks, bonds, and other securities that are in your possession, you need only look to the face of the certificate to find out who owns it. Please remember, if two names appear without any other notation, you need to call your lawyer to ascertain what your interest is.

All your ongoing stock, bond, and mutual-fund purchases will automatically be titled exactly the way you chose in the original paperwork.

The ownership and control over your investment portfolio is subject, just like everything else you acquire, to the "Ten-Second Response Rule": your response to the innocent question, "In whose name do you want it?" You originally sought your broker or investment adviser to facilitate the buying and selling of your securities, not to provide for your disability or your loved ones. And you probably got what you paid for. The system took control of your investments and placed their future—and that of your loved ones—with Murphy and the courts.

We have discussed your life insurance, real estate, bank accounts, retirement plans, and stocks and bonds. These assets represent the property that most of us acquire over our lifetime. In our analysis we found that each and every one of them was ultimately controlled by the clerical mistakes or ignorance of someone else. If you are like most of us, you have been the system's victim.

Every single tragedy, inadequacy, mistake, and excess that we have discussed so far can be alleviated through the use of a Loving Trust plan. By finishing this book and following our instructions, you will be able to control everything you own by designing and implementing your Loving Trust planning to meet your hopes, fears, dreams, and ambitions for your future and that of your loved ones.

Chapter Five

The Disability Dilemma

Many of our clients had severe reservations about planning for their loved ones. We're convinced that these clients were subliminally certain that signing a will would result in their death. They associated their wills with death because of the obvious absence of lifetime benefits. They correctly assessed the fact that they had to die to make their wills work.

Good planning is living planning—not death planning! Your living planning starts with providing for you and then your loved ones. It should envision loving care, good and prosperous times, and make every attempt to minimize death's aftermath.

Insurance company statistics tell us that in any given year an individual is far more likely to become permanently disabled than to keel over dead without warning. We are living longer than ever but have not adjusted our planning formulas to provide for the consequences of our longevity. As America ages, disability planning looms larger and becomes more important.

Disability is such an important issue that the American Association of Retired Persons issued an advisory booklet in 1988 that addressed disability issues. This booklet advises that planning for a person's care and resources upon disability is equally as important as the management of a person's financial assets.

It is highly unlikely that you or your advisers will plan for your disability. This is a statistical mistake that could have devastating consequences to you and your loved ones. Most professionals equate planning for loved ones with "death" planning and ignore "disability" planning. They rarely think about the likelihood of their clients' becoming disabled prior to death or what will happen to those disability insurance checks. Your will, joint property, life insurance, retirement benefits, and most probably even your disability insurance are not likely to help you if you become disabled!

> **Good planning is living planning—not death planning!**

The Groucho Marx Story

Groucho Marx is a graphic example of a man who—along with his advisers—ignored living planning for himself and his loved ones. Groucho was infirm in his old age. He spent the last three years of his life in and out of probate court hearings and was totally under the control of the court.

Groucho had a live-in friend named Erin Fleming. Miss Fleming, a constant companion of Groucho's in his later years, went to the probate court in Santa Monica, California, in 1974, to have Groucho declared mentally incompetent. Every state allows a relative or "friend" of a person to go to the courthouse for the purpose of having someone who is no longer capable of caring for himself or herself declared incompetent and placed under the "care" of the court.

A court hearing was held, and Groucho was found to be mentally incompetent. In the hearing, Erin asked that she be named as Groucho's guardian and also his custodian. As guardian, she would be Groucho's parent, like a guardian of a minor child. As custodian, she would have control of Groucho's money. Whatever the motive for her action, her success would give her control of Groucho and his money.

Erin was named Groucho's guardian, and the Bank of America and Erin were named as joint custodians. All of the court proceedings were covered by the nation's newspapers and magazines. And why not? An incompetency hearing is fully public. It is a living probate. The entire probate record, along with all documents filed with the court, is a matter of public record. Can you imagine the media interest that was created by the anticipation of looking into the inner life of a famous star?

The publicity ebbed and flowed with the testimony in Groucho's final drama. Three years after her partial initial victory, Erin went back to the court, demanding to be named Groucho's sole custodian. The bank protested. Groucho's family joined forces with the bank, taking the position that Erin was not very nice to Groucho and was greedy. Groucho's family and the bank went to court and insisted that Erin be removed as guardian and requested that certain family members be allowed to care for Groucho.

A lengthy and spectacular trial ensued. For months the trial raged. There were allegations of murder plots, sex for hire, and drugs. If the trial dragged at all, one could anticipate that the next witness would testify to even juicier bits of gossip and innuendo.

Movie clips were shown to demonstrate Groucho's state of mind. Filmed interviews were shown to the jury. A bevy of big-name stars testified as to what Erin and Groucho did and how they did it. Housekeepers, cooks, deliverymen, anyone who had contact with Groucho and Erin—all testified, basking in the media's bright lights. It had all the earmarks of a circus. Groucho held center ring, and the press made sure there was a crowd to watch the performances.

Groucho's feelings and dignity were not important. The spectacle was far greater than its leading man during those final days. Day after day, Groucho was wheeled into the courtroom. The press reported that he was in tears some of the time. On other occasions, he was withdrawn and moody. Is it any wonder? The most grisly facts about Groucho and his behavior were amplified in the court-room. We suspect that Groucho realized that no matter who won, he—and no one else—would be the real loser.

Five days after Groucho's grandson was named as Groucho's new guardian and Erin was removed as conservator, and four or five months after the living probate trial had begun, Groucho died. The saga was over.

Groucho had a will, but it hadn't done him any good. Groucho had a lot of money, but he lost control of it to a bank and to his friend Erin.

The last three years of Groucho's life were controlled by a court that didn't know or love him. Erin and the bank—the probate court's appointed agents—had to answer to the court for all aspects of Groucho's life. All but the most mundane of decisions had to be handled by the judge. Groucho became a matter of public record as he lived in the court's and media's transparent world.

The cost was enormous. Erin had lawyers, the bank had lawyers, and Groucho had money. Erin was looked upon by Groucho's family as an interloper. Erin's every action was carefully scrutinized by their respective lawyers.

None of Groucho's advisers had bothered to plan for Groucho's disability. In all respects, except for his will, he was a neglected client.

The probate court records showed that compared to most Americans, Groucho had a lot of money. All of Groucho's money didn't help him avoid the living probate circus. Having money, power, or resources cannot in and of itself protect one from the probate spectacle. Rich and poor alike need to provide for themselves with Loving Trust planning in order to avoid a Groucho-like circus. If Groucho had had Loving Trust planning, his probate extravaganza would have been totally and unequivocally avoided.

What Happens to You, Your Spouse, and Your Children If You Become Disabled?

Many people think of "disability" as the loss of an arm or leg, and ignore the very real possibility of a complete breakdown of their mental or physical well-being. When we speak of disability, we mean Groucho's kind of disability, where you can no longer care for yourself, where because of an accident or illness, you do not have either the mental or physical capacity to manage your own affairs.

If you can no longer take care of yourself, you will not be able to endorse your disability checks. You will be incapable of being a good and loving spouse or parent. You will not be able to decide with which relative or in which rest home you would like to live. Someone will have to care and act for you. It is unlikely that that "someone" will be a loved one. The odds are great that it will be your local probate court that will cash your checks and spend their proceeds. In this respect Groucho was not unique.

Can your life insurance help you or your loved ones in the event of your disability? Recently, some insurance companies have created policies that allow some of the death proceeds to be used by people who are terminally ill. But if you are disabled, how will you ask the insurance company for these proceeds? You can't; a court can.

For most of us, however, the proceeds are not available; we have to die to get those in the hands of our loved ones. Your policy's cash value would certainly be helpful in assisting your family to pay the bills, but unfortunately you'll have to sign the paperwork to get it, and you're disabled. In the absence of other planning, it will take a court order.

Can your joint tenancy property help you or your loved ones in the event of your disability? After all, since there are two names on the property, your other tenant should be able to conduct "business as usual." This is not the case. Joint accounts are absolutely frozen—by law—if one of the owners is declared legally incapacitated.

Do you remember our bird-on-a-limb analogy? You haven't fallen off the limb yet. Your signature is required, and since you are unable to sign, the law says everyone will have to wait until the court acts on your behalf. As we have told our clients for years, "So much for joint tenancy!"

Can your disability insurance help you or your loved ones in the event of your disability? This would seem to be a foolish question. Disability insurance is purchased to provide for you and your loved ones if you become disabled. Why wouldn't it help? After all, that's why we buy the stuff! It works all right—just the way gasoline works when it powers an automobile. The only requirement is that it get into your car's gas tank. If you are incapacitated, you will not be able to endorse your disability check if it is made out to you. The court will have to do that for you. Your disability insurance, just like everything else you own, will be subject to the Groucho Marx process. Are you the beneficiary of your disability insurance? If you aren't, you will be the exception that proves the usual rule.

The same problems arise with the disability payments from your retirement plan. Almost everyone is routinely made the beneficiary of his or her plan until that person dies. Those checks will be coming straight to you even though you are incapacitated.

We have seen desperate spouses resort to desperate measures when faced with their husband's or wife's disability. Ruth came to us in dire straits. Her husband had a stroke and other medical difficulties that left him incapacitated. She and her children struggled to stay free of the probate court. In her zeal she started endorsing her husband's name on his disability checks. Her forgery was picked up by a bank clerk, and she was summoned by the appropriate banking authorities. She readily confessed and came to us for help. We had no alternative but to initiate a living probate for her husband. Luckily, the bank was discreet and did not make an issue of it.

If you become disabled, it is probable that you will hold center ring in a probate circus just as Groucho did. Your trial may not be as spectacular, nor your affairs as sordid, but the process will be a facsimile of Groucho's. Your creditors will be notified of the probate hearing, an announcement will appear in your local paper, and all of your colleagues and friends will hear about it. Anyone with the inclination and the motive can go to the court and thumb through your file, picking up interesting tidbits of information with regard to your personal and economic lives.

Just like Groucho, you and your family will pay significant legal fees as an added burden. If you are as rich as Groucho was, the expense will not devastate your savings. If you are not, that could very well happen. Your legal fees may be less than Groucho's, but as a percentage of your net worth, they may be much more!

A General Power of Attorney

Let's assume that you read about Groucho and said, "That is never going to happen to me!" Let's further assume that you immediately give your spouse and other loved ones your general power of attorney.

If told about your strategy, we would compliment you on a nice try but tell you that giving out those general power of attorneys wasn't a very good idea. A general power of attorney ends at your disability. It ceases to have any legal effect the minute you or your loved ones need it! A general power of attorney doesn't "generally" work and can be extremely dangerous.

There are few legal instruments as dangerous as a general power of attorney. It comes close to giving the holder a blank check to do almost anything he or she wants with your property. The holder might even attempt to take all of your property for his or her own! The holder has the power to generally do whatever he or she wants with your property without answering to anyone. If you give a general power of attorney, you have given up substantial control over everything that you own.

Do you remember Murphy? Murphy loves general powers of attorney. People change as circumstances change. Regardless of their new motives, beliefs, aspirations, and "new" relationships with you, their power to take or dispose of your

> **A general power of attorney ends at your disability.**

property remains 100 percent within their control. If you have given someone such a power either get it back or cancel it—in writing—immediately!

General Durable Powers of Attorney

In the last few years, a new type of power of attorney has been adopted in every state's law. This new power of attorney is called a *durable power of attorney*. Since traditional powers of attorney are invalid upon the disability of their makers, the durable power of attorney was created by statute so that a power of attorney would survive the disability of its maker.

The durable power of attorney is one of the most creative legal innovations in recent memory. It has become a popular method for planning for disability. Some of its frequently mentioned advantages are as follows. It is:

- Inexpensive
- Flexible
- Simple and understandable
- All-encompassing
- Can be used for health care decisions in many jurisdictions

On its face, a durable power of attorney is an appealing concept. In fact, those professionals who embrace will planning/probate have readily advocated durable powers of attorney as prudent planning tools, and frequently recommend that they accompany their will-planning/probate efforts. By doing so, they attempt to correct the inability of a will to care for its maker.

Since will planning is death planning, whereas Loving Trust planning deals with lifetime issues, will-planning/probate advocates combine a will and a durable power of attorney, and claim that this combination can match a Loving Trust plan. By using these two instruments, probate lawyers claim that both death and disability planning can be accomplished.

Combining a will and a durable power of attorney just isn't adequate for most people. The biggest drawback of a durable power of attorney is that a vast majority of those drafted are general powers of attorney. Since general powers of attorney contain virtually no instructions, the agent just has too much discretion.

If lack of instructions was not enough, there are some other practical problems with using a general durable power of attorney. The success of a durable power of attorney is always dependent on its acceptance by other people. Despite the fact that every state has adopted some form of durable power-of-attorney statute, the concept is not universally recognized by those who have to deal with general durable powers. For example, many banks insist that in order for them to honor a durable power, it must be on their approved general power-of-attorney forms.

> The success of a durable power of attorney is always dependent on its acceptance by other people.

This problem also applies to many brokerage companies as well. They often require that the power of attorney include broad investment language that allows maintaining margin accounts, trading in options or commodities, or investing in other specific transactions. Unless the durable power specifically allows these powers, a brokerage company will almost always refuse to accept the durable power. These requirements vary from company to company, making it difficult, if not impossible, for an attorney to draft a durable power of attorney that always works.

Real estate transactions often create similar problems. A durable power of attorney that does not contain specific wording with regard to real estate may not be accepted by a title or mortgage company.

These problems are often worse for people who transact business in more than one state. A durable power of attorney prepared in one state may very well not be accepted in another even though there are laws aimed at preventing these problems. For purposes of interstate commerce, the durable power of attorney has not yet come into its own.

The age of a durable power of attorney also creates problems. The older it is, the less likelihood there is of its being accepted. A person who is given a durable power of attorney will want to make absolutely sure that the power is in effect and will want evidence of its current validity. This may be difficult or impossible to accomplish because the maker, who is the only person who can really vouch for the power's validity, is disabled. More often than not, if there is no one available who can prove that the power is still in force, the person to whom the power is presented will refuse to accept it.

Sometimes, lawyers write durable powers of attorney with lots of instructions in an attempt to show what the maker wants done with his or her property. Unfortunately, the acceptability of a durable power of attorney is likely to decrease with its complexity. At times, even a simple, straightforward durable power of attorney is difficult to use. From a practical perspective, both individuals and institutions do not readily accept these powers without a lot of inquiry, delay, and concern. It follows that the more instructions that are put in the power to protect the maker, the less effective the power will be.

When the provisions of a general durable power of attorney are inadequate or unacceptable, the agent, the maker's creditors, the maker's family, or some other interested person will have to commence a Groucho Marx guardianship proceeding. The probate court will then appoint a financial guardian to care for the maker's property. Since durable powers of attorney are designed to avoid exactly this result, they oftentimes fail in their mission.

Many states' laws make the durable power of attorney ineffective. Anytime someone, usually a disgruntled relative or creditor, does not agree with the actions of the person who is acting under the durable power, he or she can force a living probate, which has the effect of invalidating the power. This will almost invariably thwart the intentions of the maker, and will result in all of the expense, publicity, delay, and red tape that the durable power was designed to eliminate.

Another disadvantage of a durable power of attorney is that it is personal to the agent named. This means that if the agent you name in the durable power becomes disabled, dies, or just does not want to act, then the power is useless. Once your agent resigns, becomes disabled, or dies, the power is automatically revoked by operation of law. Even if you name joint agents, the death of one revokes the power. When a durable power of attorney is revoked by any of these occurrences, there is no one left to manage your financial affairs. The only alternative is the appointment of a financial guardian through a court-controlled Groucho Marx proceeding. Unfortunately, this is exactly what the durable power of attorney was created to avoid in the first place.

General durable powers of attorney are not the panacea that they have been touted to be. They have significant drawbacks when used in conjunction with will planning/probate. That is not to say that they do not have meaningful uses in estate planning; they do, but not as a substitute for proper Loving Trust disability planning.

Limited Durable Powers of Attorney

Durable powers of attorney are most effective when they are limited to specific tasks such as funding living trusts or providing for health care. A limited durable power of attorney should always be used in conjunction with a Loving Trust plan to put property into the disabled trust maker's trust. This gives the trust maker the opportunity to say, "If I forget to put any of my assets into my trust while I am healthy, I would like you to do so for me when I am disabled so that they can be controlled by the instructions in my trust."

The maker of a limited durable power of attorney can name any number of power holders without fear of losing control. The only power granted to the power holders is the right to put assets in the maker's Loving Trust plan. The disabled person's property will be controlled by the terms of his or her trust instructions. The principal does not grant an agent *carte blanche* authority with a limited durable power of attorney. The disabled person's property and wishes will be governed by well-defined instructions that are designed to give the maker and his or her family maximum protection and benefits.

Loving Trust Planning

If we had to select the greatest virtue of a Loving Trust plan, your protection upon your disability would be the likely candidate. A Loving Trust plan is far superior to any other estate-planning technique in planning for a protracted illness or mental incapacity. It gives you the invaluable ability to appoint a trustee who will be subject to the instructions in your Loving Trust plan. By leaving written instructions, you can be comfortable in the knowledge that those instructions will provide for your care and that of your family in the event of your disability.

Loving Trust planning is first and foremost designed to take care of you. It is designed to take care of you the way you want, without any interference or "help" from the probate courts. Guardians, conservators, probate lawyers, probate courts, and the fees and publicity surrounding them are totally unnecessary because by law, a revocable living trust-centered plan—done the Loving Trust way—eliminates them all!

Loving Trust planning can also be used to provide for your loved ones in exactly the manner you deem best. Loving Trust planning allows you to anticipate problems that may arise because of sickness, disability, or old age. It is yours to design as you wish for the care and protection of you and your loved ones. It is an inexpensive alternative to Groucho's story. It can ensure that you will be cared for by those you trust most.

Some of the advantages of a revocable living trust-centered plan done the Loving Trust way are:

- Its terms control the disposition and management of the property you or your limited durable power of attorney holders put into it.
- It survives the death, disability, and termination of trustees and names successor trustees.
- It offers more protection against mismanagement and abuse.
- It is easier to transact business with a trustee than with an agent or a guardian because the authority of trustees is more readily accepted.

Remember, a properly written revocable living trust contains extensive instructions that the trustees are required to follow. In addition, a properly drafted revocable living-trust document contains provisions for successor trustees, giving it continuity in the event that one or more of your original trustees are unable or unwilling to serve. A revocable living trust does not terminate on the disability, death, or other termination of a trustee. In fact, even if a successor trustee is not named, a trust remains valid; a court can name a trustee without taking jurisdiction over the agreement. This is a great advantage that a living trust has over a durable power of attorney.

The plans that most of us have made for our disability are woefully inadequate or nonexistent. If you are like most of us, you have two choices: You can trust that somehow you and your family will make it through the living probate circus, or you can plan your way around it by using Loving Trust planning.

Chapter Six

Planning with Loving Trust

We are often asked: "What does a trust look like?" "How does it operate?" "Where do you find one?"

Many people think a trust is a sophisticated legal device used only by the superrich; this is a misconception. Trusts are for people who care and who have some property or life insurance that they want to pass to loved ones. Generally, trusts are written instructions that allow their makers to give what they have to whom they want, in the way and when they want. A trust has a maker and beneficiaries who will receive property according to the maker's instructions; it also has a trustee who will follow those instructions.

Wills can create trusts. These are called death (testamentary) trusts. Trusts are also created in simple contracts (indentures) called living trusts. The instructions "I want my brother to use my property to take care of my two children until they reach the age of twenty-one" could be found in a will, and if so, would create a death trust. If they are written down outside of a will, they would create a living trust. When the maker reserves the right to change the trust at any time and for any reason, it is called a revocable living trust. When a maker wants to make an absolute gift to the trust beneficiaries—a gift with no strings attached—the trust is irrevocable; the maker cannot change the trust instructions once the trust is signed.

A death trust comes into existence only upon the death of its maker. It must go through probate to get assets in it. Unlike a death trust, a living trust can avoid probate, and it can be used to take care of its maker. Living-trust property can be immediately put in the care of a trustee, or it can be delivered at some later date. A living-trust maker can be both a trustee and a beneficiary of his or her trust.

Unfortunately, most living trusts that we have reviewed are not very thorough or explicit. They do not give the trustee meaningful instructions as to what the maker desires. These "bare-bones boilerplate" living trusts don't do much planning for either the maker or loved ones, but they can avoid probate if properly set up.

79

A Loving Trust plan gives more—much more—for much less. It does so because it can:

- Provide for you
- Provide for your loved ones
- Keep your affairs and those of your loved ones private
- Avoid probate
- Work in every state
- Avoid complex will rules

A Loving Trust plan can do everything a will can do and much more. A will merely disposes of property when you die. A Loving Trust plan does that, too. A will can create death trusts for your loved ones, but these trusts will be subject to the control of the probate court and the probate process. A Loving Trust plan can create those same trusts, free from the supervision and control of the probate court and the probate process. A will can be used to minimize federal estate taxes. So can a Loving Trust plan. A will cannot take care of you; a Loving Trust plan can. A will most likely does not control all of your property. Loving Trust planning is specifically designed to control all of your property. A will is cheap on the front end and extraordinarily expensive on the back end. A Loving Trust plan has no hidden rear-end charges and involves a reasonable front-end preparation fee. We discuss these costs in chapter 7, "The Cost of a Loving Trust Plan."

Loving Trust plans avoid probate, and the affairs they handle are not a matter of public record. The size, nature, composition, etcetera, of a trust maker's estate is not available for general public scrutiny.

The longer a Loving Trust plan has been in existence, the more impervious it is to attack. If a Loving Trust plan has been in existence for a period of time before the maker's death, it is exceedingly difficult for a court to find that the plan was invalid from its onset. This is especially true if an "independent" trustee, such as a bank trust department, trust company, or a person who is not related to the maker, has been serving as a trustee of the maker's revocable living trust.

In a will contest, the probate court is facing a totally different set of circumstances. There is no operating history to overcome, just the clear-cut legal standards that have determined the validity of wills for centuries. The probate court only has the task of applying these standards and then approving or denying the validity of the will.

It is significantly more difficult for disgruntled heirs and other parties to attack a trust when its contents are not open for inspection. There is less incentive for greedy or unhappy heirs to attack a trust whose value cannot be ascertained. Anyone who has ever played baseball knows that you cannot hit what you cannot see. The same is true for trusts. When a trust is created, its maker is not

A Loving Trust plan can do everything a will can do and much more.

required to give notice of its existence to anyone. After the maker dies, the trustee has to notify only the trust's beneficiaries.

Challenges by dissatisfied heirs are reduced because of the confidential nature of Loving Trust plans. It is hard to overestimate the value of the confidential nature of trusts in protecting the intentions of their makers and the interests of their beneficiaries. The privacy that is endemic to a trust gives it overwhelming advantages over the traditional will-planning/probate alternative.

Revocable living-trust planning does not eliminate the ability of truly wronged heirs when they have just and worthy disputes. However, the nature and confidentiality of the living trust ward off people who would hope to enhance their position at the estate's expense.

In contrast, the will-planning/probate process makes access to sensitive information extremely easy. Once the probate file is open, almost anyone can make a claim at little expense and risk.

Privacy is far easier to retain through the use of a fully funded living trust than will planning/probate. Will planning/probate is a public proceeding that often discloses personal and financial affairs to the public. Living trust-centered planning is far more successful in keeping sensitive financial and personal information confidential.

A Loving Trust plan can properly embrace all the work done by your life insurance agent, your realtor, your bank's clerks, the clerk where you work, and your stockbroker. A Loving Trust plan assures that your property will be used for you and your loved ones. It places control where it belongs—with you. It is not a pitcher that pours its water into open fingers. Loving Trust planning allows you to control your destiny as well as that of your loved ones. It takes the control of your life away from well-meaning but unknowledgeable advisers and clerks.

A Loving Trust plan is a revocable living trust that far surpasses the "bare-bones" living trusts suggested by Dacey and Stock. Used solely for the purpose of avoiding probate, their living trusts are terse sets of instructions that set out where property will pass on death. Bare-bones living trusts only do part of the job; they are the zombies of the trust world, only half alive. Their emphasis is on one benefit, probate avoidance, and that is all.

Loving Trust plans are fleshed-out living trusts that are brought fully to life with loving directions. They not only avoid probate but also allow you to provide for your loved ones in the manner that you choose. Loving Trust plans allow your hopes, dreams, and aspirations to survive you.

Bare-bones living trusts are commonly used as a panacea for will planning. Perhaps we should say that they are commonly misused, because most living trusts we have reviewed simply do not do what their makers expect them to do.

The Chairman of the Board of a major national bank asked us to review his living trust to make sure it met his objectives. When we are asked to review exist-

Loving Trust planning allows you to control your destiny as well as that of your loved ones.

ing plans, our first step is to take a page from a legal pad and fold it in half from top to bottom. We ask our clients what they think their current will or trust says. We ask them to be very specific, detailing what they think will happen to them, their spouses, and children upon their death or disability. We write their perceptions down on the left half of the page. Next, we review their will or trust and write down what it really says on the right half. We then compare the two halves to see if there is a match.

When the chairman saw the left half juxtaposed against the right half, he was astounded. What he thought his trust said and what it really said were miles, or even light-years, apart. He thought there were all sorts of provisions for him and his loved ones. There were very few, and the few there were did not say what he thought they should say.

This experience was not new to us. It repeats itself almost every time we go through this exercise. Usually the client believes that he or she has conveyed to the lawyer the essence of what is needed on death or disability. The lawyer fits the client's requests into his or her own preconceived notions of what is called for, and a miscommunication results. The reasons for such miscommunications are many. The client is usually at fault for not communicating clear planning objectives. The lawyer is usually at fault for being a poor listener and questioner, forcing the client's wishes into very restrictive legal forms. Both are guilty in that neither spent the time to educate the other. The client does not educate the lawyer as to the client's real motives. The lawyer fails to educate the client as to all of the legal options available to meet the client's motives.

Most clients end up with bare-bones legal work. The client's loved ones suffer, and so does the image of the legal profession.

In our lectures to lawyers, the most disturbing point, at least to them, is when we speak about bare-bones legal work, whether it be bare-bones (simple) wills, or bare-bones (simple) living trusts. It's as if these lawyers finally realize what has been wrong all these years, why clients have been so reluctant to do any planning, and why heirs are usually so unhappy.

Lawyers have been selling death. Death does not sell or make people happy. Bare-bones legal work does not sell, nor does it make people happy. Love sells. Love makes people happy. Providing for clients and for their loved ones makes all the difference in the world between happy clients and dissatisfied ones. No plan is good without LOVE! And no other method of providing for you and your loved ones is as effective or as satisfying as a Loving Trust plan.

A Loving Trust plan is a revocable living trust fleshed out and made truly alive by adding big doses of love. To understand how one works, you need to understand what a trust is. Explaining a trust intimidates most professionals. They want to make it a great deal more complicated than it really is. We believe that a trust's terms are similar to the instructions parents leave with their children's baby-sitter. This analogy has helped many of our clients and students to visualize just what a trust is and how it operates.

The Baby-sitter Story

Both of us have two boys. We love our boys, but once in a while we like to leave home and spend time alone with our wives. When we leave, we have baby-sitters take care of our boys. Our wives are loving and caring. They want to make sure that the baby-sitters are fully apprised as to what they need to do.

If we are going to leave for a weekend, the baby-sitter receives about twenty minutes of verbal instruction. He or she is left with a notepad of several pages detailing all that needs to be done for the boys. Any contingency that our wives (and we) can think of is added to the instructions. Little gummed stickers are stuck all over the house with notes on them, both for the boys and the baby-sitter. We will be close to a phone, and, of course, we will call at least two times a day to clarify our instructions. You can't be too careful when it comes to caring for those you love.

Does this sound familiar? We think it does, because when we share this story in our seminars, the students always start smiling, nodding, and laughing.

Loving Trust planning is your set of baby-sitter instructions for the care of your loved ones. Like those instructions, it provides for your loved ones' basic needs and care, as well as for their special needs and circumstances. The difference between the two is that with a Loving Trust plan you will ultimately not be near a telephone to clarify or add to your instructions.

If you have a will or a trust, now is the time to look at it. If it is not handy, try to remember what is in it. When we review wills and trusts, there are usually, at most, one or two paragraphs about how children are to be cared for. There may be a few more for a spouse, but not many. Most of the language in a will or trust is merely bare-bones boilerplate legalese, containing no instructions to speak of, but plenty of other very cold and sterile verbiage that no one with less than a law degree can understand.

A will or a trust is supposed to contain explicit instructions on how you want your loved ones cared for with your property. It is our experience that almost all wills and trusts do just the opposite.

Sad, isn't it? Most of our baby-sitter instructions for our loved ones are far more complete than our instructions for our final trip. Why is this the case? Because we somehow believe that short is better; that a legal document that is longer than a few pages is no good. Bare-bones legal work is supposed to tell a trustee baby-sitter what we want to have happen to our property and how we want to take care of our loved ones. But, by definition, it cannot succeed. Little can be accomplished in one or two paragraphs.

A Loving Trust plan is a complete set of legal baby-sitter instructions. The baby-sitter is called a trustee. As your baby-sitter follows your instructions, so must your trustee. Your instructions will be for yourself if you are disabled and for your spouse, children, or other people you love and wish to care for when you are gone. Those who receive the benefits of your Loving Trust instructions are called beneficiaries. When you make your Loving Trust plan, you are called a trustor, grantor, or settlor. They all mean the same thing: maker of a trust.

Your Loving Trust plan contains your instructions. By the law of every state, your trustee must follow your living trust's instructions to the letter for the benefit of your beneficiaries. That is what Loving Trust planning is all about.

The Loving Trust plan embodies far more than just probate avoidance. It emphasizes caring for loved ones and follows your instructions rather than barebones legal forms. It is a living trust format infused with your loving directions.

Lawyers can easily draft living trusts if they have the knowledge and the desire to do so. Most lawyers have access to good legal forms, books, and word processors. But, being able to draft a living trust is only one of the necessary ingredients. Someone has to take the time to listen to your instructions, to anticipate the worst, and head off Murphy's Law. Someone has to flesh out those general instructions with loving detail to make sure your trustees do just what you would do if you were there.

Criticisms of Loving Trust Planning

Loving Trust planning has its critics. They are primarily lawyers who cling to the notion that will planning/probate offers the traditional, time-honored way to plan. We believe that the age of will planning/probate has come and is on the verge of being eliminated because it does not meet the planning objectives of most Americans. There is a great deal of evidence that suggests that more people are insisting on planning that uses a living trust as its foundation and that wills and probate are becoming unacceptable methods of planning for loved ones.

We hear primarily two areas of criticism of Loving Trust planning. The first is that the term "Loving Trust" is hokey or too mushy or is too sales-oriented, that it is a gimmick rather than acceptable planning. The second is that living trusts, which are what Loving Trust planning is based on, are overrated and have some defects. Let's look at both of these areas of criticism.

Loving Trust Is Not an Appropriate Term

Unfortunately, many people associate estate planning with death planning, and as we have stated, not many of us are thrilled with the prospect of contemplating our own death. What critics of Loving Trust planning do not understand is that estate planning is *not* an act of death. On the contrary, it takes love and caring for a person to plan for loved ones if he or she becomes disabled or dies. That is the ultimate act of love.

In addition, Loving Trust estate planning is living planning. There is no better method of getting organized. Loving Trust planning allows each and every one of us to find out what we own, how we own it, and what we would like our property used for if we are disabled and when we die. A vast majority of Americans live long, useful lives. More and more of us are living so long that we face the prospect of long-term health care and perhaps even a lengthy stay at a nursing home or hospital. It is appropriate that we plan for ourselves with as much love and caring as we would plan for others—perhaps even more.

There is nothing wrong with the notion that we need to add love to our planning. If we don't, then why plan at all? What difference does it make to those who do not have love as to whether they plan or not? It is these people who generally do not plan. Those who think Loving Trust planning is a gimmick fail to understand the depth of love that it requires to take the time and effort to plan the right way using the right professionals.

Living Trusts Are Overrated

Revocable living trusts are not perfect, but they are the best overall estate planning technique available. As you have read and heard, living trusts have their critics and we are fully aware of all of their criticisms. The reason that we wrote *The Living Trust Revolution: Why America Is Abandoning Wills and Probate* was to put these criticisms to rest once and for all. Our conclusion in that book, after comparing the strengths and weaknesses of living trust-centered planning with will planning/probate, is that a living trust-centered plan is always superior to will planning/probate. Read this book for a meaningful comparison of will planning/probate to revocable living trust-centered planning.

A living trust-centered plan is an estate plan that is based on a revocable living trust. It includes a Pour-Over Will, special durable powers of attorney, health care powers of attorney, a living will, and other essential estate planning documentation. When you take this type of planning and add loving instructions and good professional advice, you have the essence of Loving Trust planning.

By using a number of different documents prepared in just the right manner, a Loving Trust plan can accomplish everything a will can and very much more.

There is one quirk that a revocable living trust has that we would like to remind you about. It is minor, but because it can be a trap for the unwary, we would like to acquaint you with it.

It is not uncommon for trust makers to want to make gifts of their property. If all of a trust maker's property is held in his or her revocable living trust, it is quite natural to make the gift directly from the living trust to whomever the

Loving Trust estate planning is living planning.

maker wants to make the gift to. This apparently harmless act may have adverse federal estate-tax consequences for people who have federal estate-tax liability. If a trust maker should die within three years from the time that a gift has been made directly from his or her living trust, the value of the gift could be included in the maker's estate for federal estate-tax purposes.

The solutions to this trap are simple. If a living trust is drafted so that trustees are prohibited from making gifts from living trusts, then even if the trustee violates the terms of the trust by making a direct gift, there will not be a three-year problem. The Internal Revenue Service is willing to look the other way even if the trustee knowingly violates the provisions of the trust. Another solution is that living trust language should contain a provision that states that any gifts made from the trust will be considered to be transfers that are first made to the trust maker and then to the person receiving the gift. One other solution is for the trust maker to take property out of the trust, title it in his or her own name, and then make the gift to the third party.

Several bills have been introduced in Congress to eliminate this aberration in the tax laws. We expect that the law will be changed in the near future, making gifts from living trusts no different from direct gifts from individuals.

As you can see, with proper knowledge and trust drafting, the potential adverse estate-tax consequences of making gifts from a trust can be eliminated. This issue highlights an even more important point. It is imperative that when you do planning that you use a qualified estate-planning attorney. Making sure seemingly ordinary transactions comply with state law, trust law, and estate and gift tax law cannot be underestimated. If you see a knowledgeable professional, these potential pitfalls can be avoided.

Picture in your mind the following scenario. You see a tall, elderly man; he is very skinny, almost a skeleton. His skull-like head is covered with a top hat. He is wearing an old-fashioned frock coat that ends just below his knees. In his hands is a snap-open coin purse. It is old and threadbare. It is so old that a tiny moth flies out when he opens it. He reaches his long, bony fingers into the coin purse and pulls out a bright, shiny nickel. In front of him is a poorly dressed widow. At her side are several obviously destitute children, looking very morose and exceedingly hungry. He smiles with a macabre grimace and hands the widow and children the nickel. It is their trust allowance for the week.

To many people this scene captures the essence of a bare-bones trust—an old, conservative banker, handing out nickels to widows and starving children. It's no wonder that when the word "trust" is mentioned, there is a silent—or sometimes not so silent—groan and a shudder of fear.

Loving Trust plans can and do present a picture exactly the opposite of the traditional banker and the widow with her starving children. They offer a portrait of a smiling and happy widow or widower with well-fed kids being taken care of with love from their parents' or spouse's Loving Trust plans.

A Loving Trust plan offers much more than a will. It offers you much more control than your advisers have ever previously given you. It offers you more than a bare-bones living trust. A Loving Trust plan offers much more than all those alternatives and does so at far less cost to you or your loved ones.

Chapter Seven

Our Loving Trust Plan

Our Loving Trust plans:
- Allow us to control our property while we are alive
- Provide for us, our spouses, and our children, without any court supervision, if we become sick, injured, or disabled
- Provide for our loved ones in exactly the way we want after we die
- Make absolutely sure we don't take our families public and make a lot of strangers richer at our expense or the expense of our loved ones

You must determine what your motives are before creating a Loving Trust plan.

You can have your own Loving Trust planning and achieve the same results as we have with ours. It is not difficult to design and build a Loving Trust plan once you know how. We would like to show you an example of what the terms of a Loving Trust plan are by sharing a summary of our Loving Trust plan with you. Our actual trust documents have a bit more legalese in them than our translation, but our translation will do them justice. We used this plain-English translation technique when we went through our clients' trusts with them. There is no reason to explain Loving Trust planning in more complicated language.

Both of us are very happily married and have been married only once. We both have two boys who are about three years apart. As you can guess, our Loving Trust plans are pretty similar, but there are differences. The Loving Trust translation that follows will blend a little of each of our actual Loving Trust plans together. For purposes of avoiding confusion, the names are fictional. The Loving Trust instructions are not.

Creating a Loving Trust plan begins with desires and motives. You must determine what your motives are before creating a Loving Trust plan. Our primary motive is to be assured that we will be well-taken-care-of if we become sick or disabled. We do not want to end up like Groucho. We want to reduce our federal estate tax, while taking care of our wives, children, and grandchildren (neither of us has grandchildren now, but we hope to have some someday). We want our wives to be able to use all our property for themselves and for our children and grandchildren. Half of our property is our wives' to do with as they please. When our wives die, we want to make sure that at least half of our property goes to our children and grandchildren.

We want our wives to have complete control over our property, but we do not want to leave it outright to them. We want our spouses to have the assistance and expertise of our friends and colleagues in administering our trusts and investing their assets. We do not want our children or grandchildren to have their trust property outright at our spouses' death. We would like to ease our children into their inheritances by providing them with two distributions.

As you read through our Loving Trust synopsis, it is likely that you will encounter paragraphs that you will not understand or that will be foreign to your experience and thinking. Do not despair. At this time we simply want to give you an understanding of what Loving Trust instructions cover. Once you have finished reading through Part Two, we would like you to read our Loving Trust instructions again. We think you will find that your understanding of its terms will be significantly increased.

With these basic motives in mind, here is our Loving Trust plan:

Introduction

My name is Rob Epson, and this is my trust. My wife's name is Lisa. My wife, Lisa, and I are the trustees of my trust. We have two children, Billy, ten, and Don, seven. Any other children we may have or adopt, I want automatically added to my trust.

My Rights

This is my trust. While I am alive I have total control over it. I can put property in it, and I can take property out of it. I will also control the income it creates. I can change my trust for any reason at any time. If I don't want my trust anymore, I can also cancel or revoke it at any time.

I Wish to Provide for Myself

If I become disabled, my trustees shall care for me according to my instructions. After I am taken care of, my trustees may use my property to care for my wife and children.

Distribution of My Personal Property

I give my personal property to my loved ones according to the written instructions on the attached memorandum. Whatever I have not listed shall go to my wife, or to my children if she is not alive. If my children fight over my personal property, my trustees are to sell it and divide the proceeds.

How I Want My Property Allocated

I want to reduce federal estate tax, give my wife whatever she needs, and make sure that at least one-half of my property goes to my children on her death.

I want my property divided into two parts. One shall be called my wife's Pocketbook Trust. The other shall be called my Family Trust.

I want my trustees to save federal estate tax by properly allocating my property between my Pocketbook and Family Trusts. If my trustees need to create two Pocketbook Trusts to achieve this goal, they are to do so.

How to Provide for My Wife

My wife's share of my property shall go to a Pocketbook Trust. It is hers. She can have any or all of it anytime she wants. If she is sick or disabled, then my trustees are to care for her in whatever she needs. She can leave her trust property to anyone she wants. If she neglects to do so, it shall automatically go to my children's trust.

If I need two Pocketbook Trusts, my wife will receive all the income and get whatever she needs from the property in her second trust.

How to Provide for My Family

My Family Trust shall be for my wife, my children, and my grandchildren. My trustees shall take care of my loved ones based on their needs, but shall always give first priority to my wife.

How to Provide for My Minor Children

My Common Trust for my sons and grandchildren will begin when my wife dies. It will have the property my wife didn't give away and my remaining Family Trust property.

It will remain in effect until my youngest son is twenty-three years of age, or finishes college, whichever happens first. Until this happens, my trustees are to take care of my sons in whatever they need. My trustees do not have to use the property in my Common Trust equally for each son. They are to care for each of my sons based on their respective needs.

My trustees may use my property to assist my sons' guardians in caring for them. They must be sure that the funds are used with my sons' welfare in mind; they are not to give the guardians a windfall.

If one of my sons would like extra money for a business, a profession, a wedding, a house, or any other extraordinary need, my trustees are to ask themselves two questions:

1. Is the extraordinary need valid?
2. If it is, will giving him the funds be financially harmful to my other son's basic financial needs?

If these tests are passed, my trustees shall give my son the money for this extraordinary need as an advancement against his ultimate inheritance. When his inheritance is ultimately paid out, they are to deduct the advancement.

If one of my sons dies while this trust is in existence, and he has children, they will then be beneficiaries of this trust.

When my youngest son reaches the age of twenty-three, or completes college, my trustees shall divide the Common Trust property into a Separate Trust for each of my sons.

How to Distribute My Sons' Property

My trustees shall take care of my boys in everything they need from their respective Separate Trusts.

I love my boys and want to give them two opportunities to receive their inheritances. When my son is twenty-five, my trustees shall give him half of his trust property. He can have the other half when he reaches thirty. If he is already over twenty-five when his trust is created, my trustees shall immediately give him half. He can have the other half in five years. In the meantime, my trustees shall provide for each of my sons from their respective trusts.

What Happens to My Property on the Premature Death of a Son

If one of my sons dies, he may leave his trust property to whomever he wants. If he fails to do so, it will stay in trust for his children. If he has no children, then his trust property will pass to his brother's trust.

How to Ultimately Distribute My Property

If I have no surviving family members, half of my property shall be distributed equally between my relatives and my wife's relatives. The other half shall be distributed to the United Way.

My Trustees and How They Can Be Terminated

My wife and I are the initial trustees of my trust. Either of us can resign at any time, as can any other trustee. I can fire a trustee at any time for any reason. After I die, or become disabled, my wife can fire a trustee for any reason. After my wife dies, a majority of my children can also fire a trustee for any reason. After I die, or become disabled, Jack Cravets and Jean Douglas shall be added as co-trustees, along with my wife. If any of these trustees resigns, or is fired, then he or she will be replaced by the following people in the order as shown:

Kiley P. Thornton

Pete Johnson

Paula Hoffman

If these trustees aren't available, then First National Bank shall serve as a co-trustee.

My Trustees' Powers

I give my trustees every power that I would have in administering my property for my loved ones.

Our actual trusts are several pages long because, like our baby-sitter instructions, we want to be sure that our instructions are clear and detailed. We won't have an opportunity to correct any mistakes once we are gone. The length and the detail are what distinguish our Loving Trust plans from a bare-bones living trust. We love our wives and children, and we have much to say as to how they should be cared for.

Some of what we said in our trust synopsis, even though it was stated in simple language, may be confusing or unclear. That's all right. The following chapters will bring all of it into perspective for you. For now, we want you to get a feel for what a Loving Trust plan does and how it is put together.

The most important aspects of our Loving Trust planning for you to remember are these:

- A Loving Trust plan contains your instructions about how you wish you and your loved ones to be cared for.
- Loving Trust instructions name trustees to operate your trust. You are a trustee while you are alive and well, but other trustees will take over when you become disabled or die.
- Your instructions can be as detailed or as terse as you want. You can do whatever you want with your Loving Trust plan as long as it is not illegal or against public policy.
- Your trust will create for your loved ones a number of separate trusts that will have specific instructions for their care.

To help you better visualize what a Loving Trust plan is, we have included a diagram of our trust. When you fill in the diagrams of your Loving Trust plan at the end of part 2, refer back to this diagram. It will help you to better understand how a Loving Trust plan really works.

Chapter Eight

The Cost of a Loving Trust Plan

We think that one reason that will planning/probate should be avoided is because of its costs. These costs can be excessively high, and, in many cases, totally unnecessary. We believe that virtually *all* costs associated with the probate process can be substantially, if not totally, eliminated with a fully funded revocable living trust done the Loving Trust way, and that any administration costs that are incurred after a person's death can be substantially reduced.

Even when the costs of creating, funding, and administering living trusts are taken into consideration, a Loving Trust plan is significantly more economical than the will-planning/probate alternative.

The Front-end Costs of Preparing Loving Trust Planning and Will Planning

The time it takes an attorney to prepare a simple will as compared to a simple trust, or to prepare a complicated will versus a complicated trust, should not differ appreciably. Except for the type of documents used, the planning that is required should be the same or similar, with the recognition that a living trust usually contains additional standard legal language that makes it both a longer and thicker document. By using computer technology, most lawyers can now create estate planning documents quickly and efficiently so that the time it takes to physically produce them is relatively insignificant. This is true both for routine boilerplate clauses and for instructions for your loved ones. The time and effort an attorney devotes to capturing your instructions for the well-being of yourself and your loved ones is not boilerplate, but it can nevertheless be produced quickly through technology once it is ascertained.

If attorneys give their clients the opportunity to select either the will-centered approach or the Loving Trust approach to planning, they will have to take the

> . . . virtually *all* costs associated with the probate process can be substantially, if not totally, eliminated with a fully funded revocable living trust done the Loving Trust way. . . .

time to explain the merits and drawbacks of each. Thus, there will be little, if any, difference in the actual time that is spent in client conferences.

Regardless of whether a will or Loving Trust plan is implemented, a practitioner must give equal time and care to determining what assets the client owns, and to determining how those assets are titled. These procedures are absolute planning necessities! Lawyers cannot accomplish responsible estate planning without them. Any attempt to short-cut these steps can be catastrophic. For example, if a client owns an investment property in joint tenancy with right of survivorship and that property is ignored by the attorney, that client's will or living trust cannot possibly control where it will go. It will not pass to loved ones or charity pursuant to the client's wishes in either a will or living trust. That property will simply pass to the surviving joint owner. A will can only control your property if the property is titled in your name or if it is payable on death to your estate. A living trust can only control your property if it is titled in the name of the trust or made payable to the trust at your death.

Except for the actual task of putting property in the name of your trust, the process of explaining wills and trusts and ascertaining the legal title to assets should not vary between will-planning/probate and living trust attorneys.

Modern practice requirements demand that practitioners augment both will and living trust plans with additional necessary estate-planning documents such as some type of durable power of attorney, a power of attorney for health care decisions, and a living will. Each of these documents serves a distinct planning function relating to sickness or disability.

With any living trust-centered estate plan, a Pour-Over Will must also be drafted as a matter of course. The Pour-Over Will is a fail-safe device. We often describe this Pour-Over Will to our clients as sort of a legal safety net. It makes sure that property inadvertently left out of the trust is put into the trust after the death of the maker. Since a Pour-Over Will is very simple, it can be drafted with little effort, and should not add significantly to the cost of a Loving Trust plan.

The same comparisons between will planning and living-trust planning can be made between complex will and trust planning. If a lawyer is spending the time to educate his or her clients on the available options with each approach, and each document has the same tax and people planning provisions, the relative costs of the plans should be theoretically identical.

Despite this analysis, most people would agree that it is common practice for attorneys to charge less for the preparation of wills than for living trust-centered plans. In reality, living trust-centered plans do seem to cost more initially because responsible living trust attorneys who fund their clients' trusts spend considerably more time with their clients, do more work, and accomplish more objectives. They take the time to analyze client assets and to coordinate the title to those assets with the trust plan so that probate and unnecessary taxes will be avoided. They also take the time to listen to the hopes, fears, dreams, values, and aspirations of their clients so that they can properly take care of loved ones both on disability and death. If these steps are not accomplished, no estate planning documents, whether wills or living trusts, will be as effective as they ought to be. This failure to take the time to plan, to think, to analyze is the main result of a great many old-fashioned will-planning/probate plans.

If will-planning/probate lawyers are charging less for wills than for living trusts that have comparable planning, it is most generally because will-planning/probate lawyers are spending less time, doing far less work, and achieving far fewer results. It seems crystal clear that, except for the costs of funding a living-trust plan, there should be no reason why will-planning/probate lawyers and living-trust lawyers should not be charging similar fees for similar services and similar results.

The Cost of a Fully Funded Revocable Living Trust

We are frequently asked how much a Loving Trust estate plan should cost. Given the fact that attorney fees vary dramatically from one geographic locale to another and from one attorney to another, this is a tough question. However, through rubbing shoulders with all kinds of attorneys—general practitioners and estate planning specialists—from all over the country through our advanced seminar programs for practitioners, we have been able to get a rough idea of what lawyers are currently charging for these plans.

Based on the information we have, it appears that living-trust plans that do not contain tax planning or unusually complicated distribution strategies generally cost around $1,500. Living-trust plans with tax planning can cost anywhere from $1,500 to an extreme of $50,000 or more for the truly complicated plan that involves lots of assets and planning. If J. Paul Getty had spent $50,000 or even $500,000 or $5,000,000 on attorney fees to prepare a Loving Trust plan, he would have saved $27,000,000 in probate lawyer fees alone!

If you have a taxable estate, or an estate that will grow into a taxable estate over time—and remember, this includes the face amounts of your life insurance and your retirement benefits—your estate will require tax planning. Tax planning adds time, energy, and sophistication to your estate planning, and will save lots of money. It will also increase the size of your attorney's fee to prepare your plan.

Many people want to get a feel for what prudent estate planning costs and usually ask the question: "How much does *it* cost?" The problem with this seemingly simple and straightforward question is, what is the definition of *it*?

We have experienced the *it* problem all of our professional lives. For example, the telephone rings and an honest and sincere inquiry is made by a prospective client: "I'm thinking of making an appointment with you so that you can plan my estate. What do you charge for a [living trust] [Loving Trust plan] [estate plan]?" How can a lawyer possibly respond to this question?

Perhaps if we step back from the problem a minute, and recast it in a more understandable context, we can see the dilemma that this question poses in the mind of the professional. What if the telephone rang at an automotive dealership: "I want to see you about buying a car, how much does *it* [a car] cost?" The car dealer would have to say, "Do you want a new or used car? Cars come in a great many models. We have Mercedes-Benz and BMWs; we also have compact Fords and Chevys. If I knew what model you wanted I could give you an estimated range depending, of course, on what options you'd like." We could go on with this analogy, but you get the point. Unless an attorney can sit down with his or her client and find out precisely what is wanted and needed, there cannot be an accurate fee quote.

Even if we knew, down to the last feature and option, the hypothetical estate-planning model that was needed, it would still be difficult—unlike the price of a car—to set a firm fee because we would need to know where the lawyer is practicing. It is likely that a Wall Street or Beverly Hills lawyer, regardless of his or her expertise, is going to charge a whole lot more for *comparable work* than a practitioner on Main Street in Liberal, Kansas, or Caseville, Michigan.

In addition, we have to ask ourselves the question, "What is comparable work?" Two painters can paint the same size canvas with paints, and yet the price of their creations will be significantly different. A van Gogh is not going to be the same price as an Ordinary Smith. Like painters, lawyers who practice estate-planning law vary in their credentials and skill levels. Some lawyers listen better than others and write with greater clarity. Some lawyers have the ability to better communicate with their clients and to make them feel comfortable and more secure. Some lawyers are just more adept at what they do. We can go on and on. The point is—just like in every other field—some lawyers practice better than others, and the client is usually going to see the difference reflected in the benefits they and their loved ones ultimately receive and in size of the fee they are quoted.

There is yet another consideration that must be added to the fee equation, and that is the ratio of the benefits received for the dollars spent. This ratio will often determine the real value of the services rendered. In a properly implemented Loving Trust plan, a married couple should expect, at a minimum, probate avoidance on the disability or deaths of both spouses, substantial federal estate tax savings, disability planning for both spouses, and complete implementation of their plans for the surviving spouse, children, and ultimately the grandchildren. The value of the planning will be determined by the specifics of each situation, and the perception of value placed on it by the specific client. Perhaps an example will make this concept more understandable:

> **Unless an attorney can sit down with his or her client and find out precisely what is wanted and needed, there cannot be an accurate fee quote.**

Let's say spouses have combined assets of $1,200,000 and another $1,000,000 of term life insurance. Let's assume their attorney's planning efforts can save them $235,000 of federal estate tax with respect to their assets, and an additional 55 percent ($550,000) federal estate tax on their term life insurance. Let's further assume that their combined probate savings are estimated to be roughly $150,000, and that very thorough and precise instructions are left for the care of each other and their loved ones. What is this planning worth?

Let's compare its *value* to the value of something we have more experience with, say the purchase of a new car. A mid-priced family car costs somewhere between $10,000 and $20,000 these days. What is the value of that car to the family? How much will it be worth in a few years? How about in ten years? How does its value correspond to the value of $785,000 in tax savings, and probate savings of $150,000, and a Loving Trust plan that will span generations?

Proper Loving Trust planning for nontaxable estates should approximate $1000 to $2,500 depending on the attorney, geographic location, and the complexity of its instructions for loved ones. For taxable estates that range from $600,000 to the low millions of dollars, fees ranging from $2,500 to $5000 or more are not unreasonable if irrevocable trust planning is not required. If it is, the fee will generally increase according to the number of additional irrevocable trusts that will be required. For estates into the many millions of dollars, fees that approximate the price of a new car are often the case.

We would like to be more specific. But the factors of geography, complexity of the estate, skill and experience of the lawyer, and the benefit of the value received make generalizations impossible.

These fee estimates are based solely upon the drafting of the Loving Trust plan documentation. They do not necessarily include the lawyer's time in transferring property into your trust, a topic we discuss in chapter 24, "How to Get Property into Your Loving Trust Plan."

We believe that the cost of preparing any responsible estate plan is a terrific bargain when compared with other more mundane outlays and obligations, and that this is especially true when we compare those fees to the ultimate benefits that will be derived by you and your loved ones.

The Deductibility of Funding Fees

The cost of preparing a will or a trust is not tax deductible on your federal income tax return because this is an expense that is considered to be personal rather than for a business or investment purpose. However, a benefit of currently funding a revocable living trust, at least for some people, is that a portion of its cost is income tax deductible. Under the Internal Revenue Code, expenses for the management, conservation, or maintenance of property held for the production of income are tax deductible. The costs of funding a trust fall into these categories.

The costs of funding a living trust are subject to the 2 percent of adjusted gross income floor. That means that a taxpayer must have enough of these types of deductions so that they are in excess of the taxpayer's adjusted gross income. To the extent that they exceed 2 percent of adjusted gross income, these types of expenses are deductible. For those of us who have enough expenses to qualify for the 2 percent floor, the deductibility of the fees reduces funding costs.

The Costs of the After-Death Administration of a Fully Funded Revocable Living Trust

Will-planning/probate advocates sometimes argue that the majority of attorneys' fees in larger estates are related to tax and to other matters that are common to after-death work regardless of whether or not a will or a trust is used. They say that some of the functions that are common to both will and trust planning include:

- Settling disputes among heirs
- Settling claims of creditors
- Federal and state tax returns and audits
- Sales, mortgages, and other transactions dealing with real estate
- Income tax planning

This list may look familiar. It contains the major elements that are considered to be extraordinary services in those states that allow statutory percentage fees for attorneys and executors, which we saw in chapter 1, "The Truth Behind Probate." The fees for these tasks can be charged in addition to the percentage fees allowed by statute! While probate lawyers do not have to charge additionally for these services, the evidence indicates that they often do just that.

Even though some after-death administrative functions are necessary with a trust, they are not as extensive as those required in probate. Disputes among heirs and protracted creditor disputes rarely arise when living trust-centered planning is used. Most after-death trust functions are accounting or tax-related and often can be performed by a competent accountant at significant cost savings. The evidence is strong that accounting fees are likely to be lower than attorneys' fees and that many accountants are qualified to prepare and file federal estate tax and state death-tax returns and to give advice on after-death income-tax planning issues.

The after-death administration of a living trust takes the place of the after-death administration of a probate estate. Both types of administration have a limited time span. The difference between them is that the after-death administration costs of a fully funded living trust are significantly lower than the after-death costs of probate and administration.

The advantage in having a living trust-centered plan is that the *trustee*, rather than the probate court or its rules, determines who the appraiser is, what assets are subject to a formal appraisal, and what assets can be valued without a formal appraisal. Because the trustee instead of the rules of probate and the probate court controls these decisions, there is greater flexibility in the valuation process.

Because of this flexibility, the costs of appraisals are often far less with a living trust-centered plan than they are with will planning/probate. It is clearly better to use a Loving Trust plan to avoid a probate appraisal.

Loving Trust planning eliminates the need for the involvement of an executor. Because the trustee of a living trust takes on the duties of an executor without the burden of probate, it follows then that the executor's fee, or the potential for that fee, is substantially reduced or eliminated when using a revocable living trust. Since, in most jurisdictions, the executor's fee is equal to, or marginally smaller than the attorney's fee, an executor's fee approximating 3 percent of the value of the gross estate can be eliminated by a fully funded revocable living trust.

The Elimination of Court Costs and Filing Fees

Both probate attorneys and trust attorneys generally agree that where a fully funded revocable living trust is used, all traditional court costs, filing fees, and publication and notice costs associated with probate are eliminated. Probate advocates dismiss these court costs and filing fees as not particularly troublesome, especially when applied to larger estates. We think that these fees certainly can prove to be costly in smaller estates and must not only be considered but avoided.

Periodic Accountings

Periodic accountings are necessary with both a trust and a probate estate. In a formal probate proceeding, accounting fees are higher than those generated in an informal administration and with a living trust. Since a living trust does not go through probate and administration, it is not subject to any of the rules associated with probate accounting.

Periodic reports are inherent in trust accounting. If a corporate fiduciary is serving—a bank trust department or trust company—a number of reports will automatically be produced on a monthly or quarterly basis as part of the trustee's fee. If a spouse or other family member is serving, accountings are likely to be informal and, at times, nonexistent. In our experience, the accounting costs associated with a trust are less costly than those of a probate estate simply because they are not subject to probate rules.

What Is the After-Death Cost of a Loving Trust Plan?

We believe that a properly funded revocable living trust with assets of less than $600,000 reduces after-death costs to a negligible amount that in all likelihood will be 0.5 percent or less compared with the 5 to 6 percent associated with probate. In our experience, the percentage is higher on larger estates; their after-death costs when a fully funded living trust is used may approach 0.75 percent.

You should also be aware that a Loving Trust plan is designed to avoid the problem of two probate fees for one generation of property. Rather than creating double probate and double exposure to executors' and attorneys' fees, a Loving Trust plan avoids these fees.

All of the evidence conclusively proves that fully funded revocable living trusts cost significantly less than will planning/probate.

Chapter Nine

LeRoy's Story

Shortly after one of our seminars, LeRoy, a financial planning participant from Abilene, Texas, called us. The first exasperated words out of his mouth were, "Do y'all know of any lawyers in this part of Texas that can do one of these trusts?" We didn't know and felt bad about it. LeRoy had left the seminar extremely excited about Loving Trust planning, but quickly became subdued when he couldn't find a local lawyer to do his planning.

The most common question we are asked, whether by seminar participants or talk-show callers, is how to find a lawyer willing to do a Loving Trust plan. There has definitely been a shortage of legal talent out there willing or able to prepare a Loving Trust plan. We share LeRoy's frustration; not being able to refer other advisers and nonprofessionals to lawyers skilled in Loving Trust techniques has been a great frustration to us.

We want everyone to have a Loving Trust, which can be effectively used in every single state. We are confident that if we just get the word out, they will be broadly taken advantage of by both professionals and the public.

There is no way we personally can do everyone's Loving Trust planning. We tried that and made little headway; the more we did, the greater we found the demand to be. We have done thousands of them over the years. There are select lawyers and firms of lawyers who do them all over the country, and, fortunately, these Loving Trust lawyers are increasing in numbers.

It has long been our goal to educate the public and professionals alike in order to start a Loving Trust momentum. To do this, we have to convince the American public that the Loving Trust planning is the best method for providing for loved ones; we must also build a force of competent lawyers to do the work. We have come a long way in making both of these goals a reality. In 1989, we founded the National Network of Estate Planning Attorneys, an organization of attorneys who are trained in and familiar with Loving Trust planning techniques. In our Authors' Note at the end of this book we have more information concerning this national organization. In 1992, we wrote a new book called *The Living Trust Revolution: Why America Is Abandoning Wills and Probate*. It shows

> **In 1989, we founded the National Network of Estate Planning Attorneys, an organization of attorneys who are trained in and familiar with Loving Trust planning techniques.**

why a living trust-centered plan done the Loving Trust way is always superior to will planning and probate. We suggest that you get this book if you need more information either for you, your attorney, or your other advisers about why living trusts should be used for planning. With the knowledge in this book and the directions we provide, and with the information in *The Living Trust Revolution*, you should be able to get your Loving Trust planning accomplished quickly and confidently.

Keep in mind, however, that you should not be a planning Lone Ranger.

We read a recent best-selling health book about how the food you eat can affect your health, and how, through vitamin supplements, diet, and experimentation, you can strengthen your immune system and feel better. The how-to part of this book was virtually impossible for us to utilize. Changing foods all the time, trying to maintain records, and all of the other methods of self-diagnosis were not practical. Finding the correct vitamins and their proper dosages proved to be expensive and even more difficult for us to do. We finally concluded that the only way we could do what the book suggested was to see the doctor who wrote it. He claimed to have tests that would find our food allergies. He could prescribe and dispense the correct vitamins as well as their dosages.

The book gave us false expectations of what we could do. In the end, we had to go see the "guru" to get the job done. Only the doctor could really apply the principles in the book. Other people may be missing out on the benefits of the doctor's program because, unlike us, they cannot travel to see the doctor. This is a classic Catch-22 where the doctor wins through royalties and the rest of us lose through false expectations.

Parts 2 and 3 of this book are designed to help avoid this syndrome. Part 2 will allow you to design, step-by-step, your own blueprints for your Loving Trust plan. Through our instructions and checklists, you will have a pathway to accomplishing your Loving Trust planning. By examining your every motive, you will be able to build a series of subtrusts, created especially for each of your loved ones, that will make up your Loving Trust. You will be your own Loving Trust architect. Your plans or personal blueprints need only be given to a lawyer to be put into legal language.

Part 3 will show you how to find a lawyer to write your Loving Trust documentation. It will also show you how to use the checklist in part 2 to significantly reduce the time and dollar costs of setting up a Loving Trust plan. We will instruct you on how to work with your lawyer to create a final product that will be tailored to you and your loved ones. We will also show you how to get your property into your trust in order to make it fully operational. This, too, can be done at a low time and dollar cost by using our techniques. In addition, part 3 will show you how you can use advisers to keep your costs to an absolute minimum.

Part Two

HOW TO DESIGN YOUR LOVING TRUST

Chapter Ten

What Do You Want to Do?

All of us have certain feelings and ideas about how we want to be cared for and about how we would like to provide for our loved ones. But, oftentimes, our feelings and ideas are nebulous and hard to express. It sometimes takes the help of others for us to define and articulate our feelings so that they can be understood. The next nine chapters are structured to help you come to grips with your desires and motives for the care and well-being of yourself and your loved ones.

In our law practice we were able to assist thousands of clients in planning for their loved ones. To our amazement, most of our clients expressed remarkably similar feelings and planning motives for their loved ones. In part 2, we offer you a variety of practical and loving planning solutions based on those desires and motives that we have repeatedly identified over our planning careers. We are confident that you can accomplish significant Loving Trust planning by selecting the particular desires and motives that best fit you and your loved ones. Chapter by chapter, we'll give you the opportunity to create your own Loving Trust planning solutions by building on those that we have so often successfully utilized.

The building blocks of your living trust are the subtrusts that are created within it. Every living trust has various subtrusts that lie dormant until some event activates them. Throughout part 2 you will be your own Loving Trust architect. You will select subtrusts that fit your situation and motives that reflect your desires. An architect adds room after room and detail after detail to the blueprints of his or her client's dream home; you will likewise be creating your Loving Trust blueprints for the care and well-being of your loved ones.

You do not have to read all of part 2. You *do* need to read those chapters that pertain to your loving needs and desires. Once you have done that, you only need to select the motive or motives in each chapter that meets your desires. We strongly suggest that you place a check mark next to the motives you select on the checklist that concludes each chapter; doing so will help you to keep track of your choices.

> **Every living trust has various subtrusts that lie dormant until some event activates them.**

Upon completing part 2, you can fill in "My Checklist for Designing My Loving Trust Plan." By simply transferring each of your chapter-by-chapter choices to this master checklist, you will have completed your Loving Trust master blueprint. And you will be able to see a picture of what your Loving Trust plan looks like—how all the various subtrusts work together—by filling in the diagrams we have drawn for you at the end of part 2.

We have found that being able to look at a picture of your Loving Trust plan will allow you to get a better idea of its structure and how it operates. Your diagram should give you a broad overview of its design and should facilitate your understanding of how all its subtrusts interact for the well-being of your loved ones.

In part 2, we refer to "my property" or "my trust" as we take you through the planning alternatives. If you are married, you may be confused or concerned when we say this, particularly if you view your marital property as "ours" because you own it in joint tenancy with your spouse. "How do I convince my spouse that I should take 'our' property and put it in my trust?" is a question that invariably is asked when we share the benefits of Loving Trust planning with our clients. Most married couples own their property jointly. As joint tenants with right of survivorship, they believe that they own this property equally and that they each can dispose of their "mythical" one-half. Once we explain how joint property really works, most couples find it difficult to conceptualize how they should own their property for Loving Trust planning purposes; they have a terrible time coming up with an alternative to their joint tenancy habit.

We almost always receive questions like: "Does all 'our' property have to be put in my husband's name?" "Wouldn't it be better if it was all put in my name?" "Isn't there some way we can still somehow own our property together and still have a Loving Trust plan?"

You can only plan for those assets you own. If you are married and wish to control your marital assets, you could take "your" joint tenancy property and put all of it in your name only. Of course, you would have to get your spouse's permission—a necessary condition that is rarely achieved.

Based on your spouse's feelings, you may opt to put all your marital joint property in your spouse's name as the sole owner, although we doubt if many of our readers would go along with this alternative either.

In our experience, it is far more likely that you and your spouse will select one of two ownership planning approaches:

- Change your jointly held property into tenancy in common property.
- Place property approximating one-half of the total joint property in your name alone, and place the other half in your spouse's name.

If you decide to own your property in tenancy in common, you would own

You can only plan for those assets you own.

half and your spouse would own half of each marital asset held in tenancy in common. You could sell your half, give it away, or transfer it to your own trust; your spouse could do likewise with his or her half. This is a convenient way to own property. For example, the deed to your home would have both your names on it along with the magic legal words " . . . as tenants in common" instead of "as joint tenants." Since most couples that we have done Loving Trust planning for think that their joint tenancy property works just like tenancy in common property, tenancy in common is not a radical departure from their perceived status quo.

If you live in Arizona, California, Idaho, Louisiana, Nevada, New Mexico, Texas, or Washington, your marital property is already owned equally with your spouse—you can plan your half, and your spouse can do likewise—under your state's community property laws. For planning purposes, community property functions precisely like tenancy in common. For those of you who live in Wisconsin, while it is not technically a community property state, the community property rules, for the most part, apply.

Regardless of where you live, if you elect to place half of your marital assets in your name and half in your spouse's name, you each would own, control, and plan those assets titled in your name. Many of our clients have elected to place specific assets in one or the other's name; this was particularly true when one or the other of them brought substantial assets into the marriage.

As an example of this method of eliminating joint tenancy property, you may have your home in your name and your spouse may have a second residence or other property in his or her name.

Some of our clients put some of their property in individual names and other property in tenancy in common, blending the two alternatives together. No matter how you and your spouse choose to title your marital property, the important thing to remember is this: Joint tenancy property *cannot be planned*. This is true regardless of whether you want to use a Loving Trust plan, a bare-bones boilerplate living trust, or a simple will.

"Should my spouse and I each have separate Loving Trust plans?" "Can't we just have one Loving Trust plan for the two of us?" "Which is better, separate Loving Trust plans, or one Loving Trust plan for both of us?" These are other questions that we are almost always asked.

You most certainly can have your own Loving Trust plan, and your spouse can do likewise. Or, if you and your spouse prefer, you can have a single Loving Trust plan that will deal with each of your respective wishes and property; we refer to this approach as a "joint" Loving Trust plan.

It is important that you do not confuse a joint Loving Trust plan with jointly owned property; a joint Loving Trust plan is a Loving Trust plan that uses one revocable living trust document that will manifest both your and your spouse's respective wishes as to your respective property. A joint Loving Trust plan is

Joint tenancy property *cannot be planned*.

nothing more than a plan that has one living trust document with two parts to it: "his" wishes and "her" wishes and "his" property and "her" property.

A joint Loving Trust plan is almost always used in community property states; for specific tax purposes—all beneficial—it should always be used by California couples. In our experience, a joint Loving Trust plan is not used as much in the forty-two non-community-property states as it is in the eight community property states.

One noncommunity-property state in which joint Loving Trust plans are frequently used is Pennsylvania. Pennsylvania imposes, quite illogically, a 6 percent inheritance tax on property passing from one spouse to another through a will or a trust but provides an exemption for such property if it is held as tenants by the entireties. In an attempt to avoid this inheritance tax problem, a joint Loving Trust plan is often used.

In response to the question "Which way is better?" there is generally no right answer. In our experience, the work and costs involved with either approach are about the same. Each spouse has his or her own property and his or her desires with regard to loved ones in either alternative.

Proponents of the joint trust approach say that it takes a shorter trust to accomplish the desires of the planning couple and that it is easier to operate and maintain. Proponents of the "each spouse should have his or her own trust" approach believe that their way is less complicated and cumbersome, because each spouse's wishes and property can be dealt with more efficiently in his or her own trust document. We have no preference; in most cases, both ways work equally well.

For your convenience we have designed "My Checklist for Designing My Loving Trust Plan" in part 2 to reflect *your* desires and *your* planning alternatives. If you are married, your spouse should also check those alternatives that best fit his or her objectives. Once you have both selected your respective planning desires, you both can decide—with the help of your Loving Trust lawyer—whether you would prefer individual trusts or a single joint one.

Part 2 is the loving portion of your Loving Trust plan. It is here that you need to spend your planning time. It is here that you will have the opportunity to examine how you feel about your well-being and the needs and requirements of your spouse, children, grandchildren, parents, and other loved ones. It is this process of self-examination and the thought behind it that is so often neglected in a lawyer's office and in boilerplate how-to-do-it books.

You are the architect of your Loving Trust plan; your lawyer is the contractor who will build it. Your Loving Trust plan will include several legal documents, including a revocable living trust. There will be many technical or legal phrases in your Loving Trust planning. We call these phrases "legalese" or "boilerplate"—standard and repetitive legal language. Just like a construction contractor must follow the appropriate engineering and building-code requirements, so must your lawyer follow the appropriate legal requirements.

A Loving Trust plan's basic principles are based on hundreds of years of law and judicial experience. Every Loving Trust plan needs to be written with the appropriate legal boilerplate. That's where your lawyer comes in. You design it, and he or she builds it to your specifications. Between your knowledge of your loved ones and the planning they require and your lawyer's expertise in legalese, you can readily and inexpensively bring your Loving Trust planning into existence.

Chapter Eleven

How to Provide for Yourself

When we introduced the concept of Loving Trust planning to our clients, many of them became very concerned over what would happen if they signed one. "Will I have to pay fees to a battery of lawyers, accountants, and trustees beginning on the day I sign? Will I lose control of my property? Will I create problems with the IRS? What if I change my mind? Will it change the way I do business?" In essence, they were asking what would happen to their lives if they signed a Loving Trust. Our answer was always the same: "Nothing will happen to change your life if you have a Loving Trust. A Loving Trust is simply your set of instructions that automatically kicks in on your disability or death."

If you are like most of our clients, the odds are pretty good that you have never planned for your disability. We understand when people tell us that it doesn't seem practical to plan for themselves. Most of us have the attitude that no matter how bad things are for others, those things could never happen to us. As a result, we are usually taken by complete surprise when those things do indeed happen to us.

At one time, we too had "it will never happen to us" attitudes. Our attitudes quickly changed when experience taught us that many of our clients became sick, injured, or were otherwise incapacitated prior to their deaths. On numerous occasions we had to go to hospital rooms to have Loving Trust plans signed. On other occasions we were too late; there was nothing we could do.

When emergencies occur, planning mistakes and miscalculations can be made. Not enough thought goes into emergency planning; loved ones are often inadvertently hurt because of hasty planning.

Medicaid Planning

A major concern for most of us is how we are going to be taken care of if we will have to live in a nursing home. Americans are living much longer because of scientific advances. A longer life span means that long-term care is needed more than ever before. Unfortunately, the costs for this care are high. Figures for the cost of skilled nursing care vary, of course, but the average *yearly* cost for 1993 ranged between $25,000 to $48,000.

Most of us would like to qualify for as many governmental benefits as we can so that we can preserve our wealth for our spouses and other loved ones. Since Medicaid is the only significant government program that pays for nursing-home care, it would be helpful if every one of us could qualify for its benefits. However, much to the dismay of many of our clients, only those citizens with low incomes and low net worth are eligible.

Summary of Medicaid Eligibility Requirements

There is a great deal of misunderstanding about who and how one qualifies for Medicaid. Medicaid is a general term for a federally funded and state-funded program that provides, among other benefits, medical assistance to aged individuals "whose income and resources are insufficient to meet the costs of necessary medical services. . . ." Medical services generally include nursing-home care for people who are over sixty-five years of age. Most people don't understand that Medicaid is a federal program that is administered by the states. Because of that, each state has different rules about Medicaid eligibility that qualify under a broad umbrella of federal rules.

For a person to qualify for Medicaid, he or she must be poor. Federal law requires that to receive federal funding each state must have a medical-assistance plan that determines eligibility based on the income and other resources that are available to someone who applies for aid. A married couple's income and property are combined to determine eligibility.

The rules that follow *may* not be accurate when you read this. As of the writing of this chapter, Congress is considering a massive change in the Medicaid rules. Be sure to check with an attorney before you rely on this information.

There are a myriad of rules that apply in determining assets and income for elderly persons seeking Medicaid assistance for nursing-home care. A single person who is trying to qualify for nursing-home benefits is generally allowed to retain only the following assets in order to qualify for Medicaid:

- A home
- $2000 in cash
- Prepaid funeral
- A burial account of up to $2,500
- Term life insurance
- A limited amount of whole life insurance

Let's say you are married and you want Medicaid benefits for nursing-home care, but your spouse does not require nursing-home care. In that case, deciding

Medicaid eligibility is a little more complex. You are called the *institutionalized spouse* because you are the one seeking Medicaid benefits. You can retain the same assets that are allowed to a single person. Your spouse, called the *community spouse*, can retain more assets than you so that your spouse is not totally impoverished.

Each state sets the amount of assets that the community spouse is allowed to retain and still allow the institutionalized spouse to qualify for Medicaid nursing home care. The federal Medicaid law gives limits as to what a state can require as far as the minimum and maximum assets a community spouse can retain. For 1993, the latest year for available figures as of the writing of this chapter, no state could require a community spouse to have assets of less than $14,148 nor can a state set a higher limit than $70,740. You must check your state's law as to what it requires within this range.

If you have more assets in your name than your spouse has in his or hers, there is a period of time within the Medicaid application process where either of you may transfer assets to the other (but not to anyone else) to divide property to meet Medicaid standards. After these assets have been rearranged to give each of you the allowed amount, Medicaid eligibility is determined. If the assets of either of you exceed the allowed amount, then this excess amount must be spent on nursing-home care before you, the institutionalized spouse, will be eligible for Medicaid benefits.

Medicaid law also places limitations on your income. These also vary from state to state. To be eligible for Medicaid, the institutionalized spouse cannot have monthly income in excess of the monthly cost of the nursing home, although states can require lesser amounts. If a state requires a lesser amount, it saves the state money because fewer people qualify for Medicaid benefits.

All income received by an institutionalized spouse is taken by the state to defray the costs of the nursing-home care, after certain allowances are taken into account. Additional income may be allocated to the community spouse if needed to bring the income of the community spouse up to the minimum level. The community spouse can keep all income paid to him or her individually and one-half of joint income.

This summary is not meant to present a definitive survey of Medicaid but to describe just how little net worth and income one can have and still qualify for Medicaid. If a person has more assets or income than Medicaid allows, he or she either has to use personal assets and income to pay for a nursing home, or find a way to qualify for Medicaid without consuming those assets and income.

Lifetime Medicaid Planning

Most people do not want to lose virtually all of their assets and income in paying for a nursing home until they are poor enough to qualify for Medicaid.

HOW TO PROVIDE FOR YOURSELF

They are interested in exploring methods to protect assets and income from the high cost of nursing-home care by qualifying for Medicaid. One solution that people commonly try is to give their assets to close family members. Giving away everything you own means total loss of control over those assets. Once assets are given away, there is no assurance of what will happen to them. If family members spend those assets, get into creditor trouble, or just decide to keep them, there is nothing you can do. And, even if family members use them for your benefit, they can accidentally disqualify you from Medicaid if they give you too much!

There are also federal and state gift-tax ramifications when you give property away or it is given back to you after you have given it away. You must be very careful to understand these ramifications before you give your assets away.

Prior to the Omnibus Budget Reconciliation Act, passed in August 1993, some people attempted to use irrevocable trusts to both qualify for Medicaid and remain in control of their property. These trusts were subject to complex rules, and great care had to be exercised for them to be effective. Even when they were used, it was difficult for the irrevocable trust maker, or his or her spouse, if the maker was married, to have access to the principal or income of these trusts and still maintain Medicaid eligibility. Just as in making outright gifts, there were also potential adverse federal and state gift-tax ramifications of these irrevocable trusts.

Under the new rules passed by Congress in the Omnibus Budget Reconciliation Act, all trust assets, including those held in irrevocable trusts, are considered to be available resources of the trust maker if the trustee has the ability to pay trust assets to the maker. If this is the case, then all of the trust assets are counted in determining Medicaid eligibility. If the terms of the irrevocable trust provide that the trust assets are to be paid to beneficiaries other than the trust maker or the trust maker's spouse, the trust assets are considered to be available resources of the trust maker for sixty months after the first payment of a beneficiary is made. The changes under the new law concerning Medicaid eligibility for individuals who make transfers to irrevocable trusts have eliminated the irrevocable trust as a meaningful Medicaid planning technique.

One potential obstacle to making gifts to family members is a thirty-six-month ineligibility period (sixty months in the case of irrevocable trusts, as discussed above). This rule was invented by the government to discourage people from transferring assets in order to qualify for Medicaid. Originally, this period was thirty months, but under the Omnibus Budget Reconciliation Act, the period was increased to thirty-six months. If assets are transferred by either you or your spouse to someone other than your spouse as a gift within thirty-six months of either applying for Medicaid or entering a nursing-home facility, the government presumes that you made the gift to obtain Medicaid eligibility. If this is the case, immediate benefits are not available to you or your spouse. The thirty-six-month rule applies unless it can be proven the gift was not for purposes of Medicaid eligibility or that the gift was to another person for the benefit of your spouse. But, if the gift is for the benefit of a spouse, the rules limiting the assets he or she can have then come into play, creating yet another Medicaid qualification obstacle. If ever Murphy's Law applies, it is to these very complicated Medicaid rules.

It is clear that there is little lifetime planning that can be accomplished for purposes of Medicaid eligibility. Any planning that can be done involves giving away property with little or no hope of ever getting it back. For most people, the purchase of long-term health care insurance may well be a better solution.

There is more to Medicaid planning than the issue of qualification. A more important question has to be addressed. Does a person want to be subject to state support while living in an institution? Medicaid eligibility means that an individual is essentially at the mercy of state and federal agencies to determine the facilities offered and the minimum standard of care that will be provided. Amounts allotted to an individual for nursing-home care are approved by governmental agencies that may be more concerned with budgetary constraints than with the quality of the care.

If you are interested in Medicaid planning, you should consult a qualified attorney to find out all of the rules that apply in your state.

There are at least two groups of attorneys that you might want to seek out to consult about Medicaid law. One group is the National Network of Estate Planning Attorneys. Members of this network have been trained in the concepts of Loving Trust planning. Many of these attorneys are familiar with Medicaid planning as well as a broad range of other estate planning techniques. There is another group of attorneys called the National Academy of Elder Law Attorneys. These attorneys are vitally concerned with legal issues that affect older people, including Medicaid rules.

> **Almost all our clients have felt that they should be taken care of first; that their own well-being should be the top priority of their "Me" Trust.**

Motives for Planning for "Me"

The motives that we have found most important to our clients over the years in planning for their possible disabilities have related to the priority of care in a "Me" subtrust. Almost all our clients have felt that they should be taken care of first; that their own well-being should be the top priority of their "Me" Trust. They also wanted their dependents—spouses, children, parents, etc.—cared for.

Here are the five motives we commonly see in a "Me" Trust:

11–1 Take care of me and nobody else.

11–2 Take care of my needs first and then my spouse's needs.

11–3 Take care of my needs first, then my spouse's, and then my children's or dependents'.

11–4 Take care of me, my spouse, and my children based solely on our needs, without any priorities among us.

11–5 Take care of me and my children based solely on our needs, without any priorities among us.

11–1 Take care of me and nobody else.

If you are single and have no dependents, this alternative is for you. You have undoubtedly relied upon yourself for your well-being and wish to continue that self-reliance by establishing your "Me" Trust with yourself as its sole beneficiary.

You may want to use this alternative if you are elderly or partially disabled and are being cared for by a relative or close friend. It should be used in lieu of a general power of attorney or putting your property in joint tenancy with a trusted family member or friend. By using this alternative, you can allow the same person or persons you would give your power of attorney to or who would be your joint tenant to care for you by naming them trustees of your "Me" Trust. As your trustees, they would take care of you within the limits imposed by your instructions, without a general power of attorney, joint property, or any other cumbersome device to allow them to help care for you.

11–2 Take care of my needs first and then my spouse's needs.

If your spouse is economically dependent on you, you will undoubtedly want to provide for your spouse's care as well as your own. This alternative provides that both of you are to be taken care of from your trust property, but that your needs are to be taken care of on a priority basis.

Children and other dependents are not relevant in this alternative. Your children may be grown or you may have no children. This alternative assures you that both you and your spouse—and this is true if your spouse is disabled as well—will be taken care of subsequent to your disability.

11–3 Take care of my needs first, then my spouse's, and then my children's or dependents—in that order.

This alternative is the same as alternative 11–2, except that your children or other dependents are added as beneficiaries. This alternative is used when you are married and have minor children or disadvantaged adult children dependent on you. It can be easily modified to include an aged parent or other persons economically dependent on you. The priority in which your trustees are to exercise their care still retains you as your trust's primary beneficiary; your spouse, children, and other dependents follow in that order.

11–4 Take care of me, my spouse, and my children based solely on our needs, without any priorities among us.

We include this alternative to show you that you do not have to make yourself the primary beneficiary of your "Me" Trust. This alternative allows your trustees to look at the economic needs of all your beneficiaries and to care for you and them based solely upon your respective needs.

This mandates that your trustees ask two questions before distributing your trust money. "Is there enough money and property to care for you, your spouse, and your children?" If there is, then your trustees can proceed to care for all of you without determining whose needs are greater. If your trust funds are limited, the second question is, "Who is most in need of those funds?" Your trustees will determine a priority among your beneficiaries based on their respective needs and the funds available at that time.

This alternative gives your trustees the discretion to make the best decision based upon the circumstances at that time. Your trustees are charged with exercising the same judgment and making the ultimate decisions that you would make if you were healthy.

This alternative was almost always used by our clients with good marriages or those with close family ties. It was, by far, the most preferred "Me" alternative.

11–5 Take care of me and my children based solely on our needs, without any priorities among us.

This alternative is specifically designed for the single parent. Like alternative 11–4, it states that your trust funds will be used to take care of you and your children based solely on your respective needs at that time. It was almost always selected by our single-parent clients.

There are six alternatives for a "Me" Trust that follow, including the five discussed here plus an alternative that you can use to create your own motive. Please check the alternatives that most nearly coincide with your desires and motives.

( )   11–1   Take care of me and nobody else.

( )   11–2   Take care of my needs first and then my spouse's needs.

( )   11–3   Take care of my needs first, then my spouse's, and then my children's or dependents', in that order.

( )   11–4   Take care of me, my spouse, and my children based solely on our needs, without any priorities among us.

( )   11–5   Take care of me and my children based solely on our needs, without any priorities among us.

( )   11–6   My own motive: _____

_____

_____

Chapter Twelve

How to Provide for Your Spouse

You may provide for your spouse by designing your Loving Trust so that, at your death, it creates a special subtrust for him or her that we call a "Pocketbook" Trust. A Pocketbook Trust is used to control and protect the property that you want to pass to your spouse on your death; that is its only purpose. It should always be used instead of leaving property outright or directly to a spouse.

The sole beneficiary of your Pocketbook subtrust will be your spouse. The degree of your spouse's control over the property in this trust will be dictated solely by your motives. For example, your Pocketbook Trust can be very liberal. It can give your spouse the right to take and spend any or all of your trust property at any time for any reason. Or it can be very restrictive, severely limiting the benefits your spouse receives.

There are no provisions in a Pocketbook Trust to care for your children, grandchildren, or any beneficiaries other than your spouse. The property in this kind of trust is *solely* for your spouse's benefit. If your trust is liberal and allows your spouse to take funds out when your spouse so chooses, he or she can use them for the benefit of anyone, including children, grandchildren, or others. Your husband or wife can use the funds for others only after those funds are taken out of the trust.

In our seminars, there is usually a woman in the audience who has a purse at her side. We ask her if we can have her purse, and after much prodding, more often than not, she reluctantly obliges. We then tell her that we are planning on opening it in order to share its contents with the rest of the class. As you can imagine, she is appalled at the thought and quickly asks for—or snatches—her purse back. No one can blame her for wanting to keep the contents of her purse private.

Purses and wallets—pocketbooks—were invented to hold personal belongings.

They are convenient and private. Their owner may carry and store personal property without worrying that it will be exposed, helter-skelter, to the prying eyes of sometimes not-so-innocent bystanders.

Now you can understand why we call such a trust a Pocketbook Trust rather than a Marital Trust—its proper technical name.

A Pocketbook Trust springs into existence on your death. The money and property you leave in a Pocketbook Trust are for the benefit of your spouse but are limited by your instructions. These instructions can be liberal or restrictive, depending on your motive.

A Pocketbook Trust is used to keep the affairs of your spouse private. Because it is a subtrust of your Loving Trust, it totally avoids probate at your death. It avoids a living probate if your spouse is disabled or incapacitated. It avoids probate on your spouse's death. It works like your "Me" Trust, but simply has a different beneficiary and a different set of instructions to take care of your spouse after your death. Please remember that you will design it according to your desires and motivations.

The funds in your spouse's Pocketbook Trust may even be protected from your spouse's creditors. We know of a case where a widow was left a substantial amount of money and property in such a trust. Even though the widow's husband named a bank as trustee, the trust had very liberal provisions for her use and enjoyment of her husband's property. She had the right to all of the income—the money her trust made—and access to the principal of her trust at any time and for any reason. She even had the right to leave the money and property in her trust to anyone she wanted to on her death. As you can see, she had full control over the trust and everything in it!

This widow's son was a budding entrepreneur who wanted to be a developer. To get financing for one of his building projects, he asked his mother to sign a promissory note along with him. She did. Soon thereafter her son went bankrupt. The son's creditor sued his mother to collect on the note, won the lawsuit, and then proceeded to try to collect on the note by going after the property in Mom's trust. The creditor's theory was that, since Mom could take money and property out of her trust at any time, the creditor should be able to force her to take the property out and pay him off.

The trustee of Mom's trust refused to allow the creditor to collect from the trust. The creditor sued the bank as trustee and, when the appeals were over and the case decided, the court held that the creditor could not collect from Mom's trust.

Mom's trust had a spendthrift clause—we call it an immunity clause—that prevents creditors from taking trust assets. A spendthrift clause is an instruction to the trustees that the trust property is free from the claims of the beneficiaries' creditors and that the trustees *should never* pay those creditors. Since Mom had

> **The money and property you leave in a Pocketbook Trust are for the benefit of your spouse but are limited by your instructions.**

received her husband's property in trust, the spendthrift clause protected the trust property from the claims of Mom's creditors.

An immunity clause is allowed by almost all states and has long been considered a legitimate safeguard that trust makers can take advantage of for the protection of their loved ones. *It is absolutely mandatory that your lawyer put an immunity or spendthrift clause in your Loving Trust plan for the protection of your loved ones.*

We cannot guarantee that an immunity clause will work in every situation or that other courts will follow this same legal reasoning or result. We do know, however, that immunity clauses have worked for centuries, and we see no reason or likelihood that their effectiveness will be diminished.

If you have already made a leap in logic and concluded that you could set up a trust for yourself that would, of course, include an immunity clause so that you could avoid the claims of your creditors, you will be disappointed to know that your logic has been rejected by the courts. An immunity clause works only for loved ones other than the trust maker!

Perhaps the widow in our story would have liked to have said no to her son but was afraid to confront him. Under our Loving Trust techniques, she could keep her Pocketbook Trust private, even from her son! She could deny his request by saying that it wouldn't be allowed by the terms of the trust or that the other trustees would not approve it. She would, in effect, be using its confidentiality to protect herself from her own children.

Most of our clients immediately understood the beauty of a Pocketbook Trust when it came to controlling their property after their death. They did not, however, so readily understand why they needed one if they loved their spouses and wanted them to have everything on their death. We were perplexed by this until we finally understood that most of our clients incorrectly associated the word "trust" with negative motives, feelings, or results. This is why we always took time with our clients to review the advantages of Pocketbook Trusts over leaving property outright to spouses. We told them that a Pocketbook Trust:

- Avoids a living and a death probate for your spouse.
- Keeps both your affairs and your spouse's affairs totally private.
- Allows your spouse to lean on and get assistance from your trustees.
- Keeps your spouse's creditors—not *your* creditors—from taking what you left.
- Gives your spouse the ability to say no to friends, relatives, and others who are requesting loans or investment opportunities, by blaming the "no" on the terms of the trust or the trustees.
- Can do all of this without restricting your spouse's rights to the use and enjoyment of your property.

Leaving All Your Property to Your Spouse in a Pocketbook Trust

The five most common motives in this area are:

12–1 I want my spouse to have total control over my property.

12–2 I want my spouse totally taken care of, but I want to limit my spouse's right to leave my property on his or her death.

12–3 I want my spouse totally taken care of, but I will decide where my property goes on my spouse's death.

12–4 My spouse can have only the income my Pocketbook Trust earns and nothing more; I will say where my property goes on his or her death.

12–5 My spouse will get only whatever my state's laws require that I must leave him or her.

12–1 I want my spouse to have total control over my property.

If your motive is to give your spouse maximum use and control over your property, this is the alternative for you.

With this alternative, your spouse gets all the income produced by the property in the trust. Your spouse may also use the trust property—the principal—at any time and for any reason. There are absolutely no restrictions on the use of the trust property. In addition, if your spouse is disabled, the trustees will care for your spouse's needs even though your spouse may be unable to ask for assistance. This will avoid the need for court-appointed agents and all of the expense and problems associated with court intervention.

When your spouse dies, the trust property will pass pursuant to your spouse's desires. Here you have purposefully relinquished control to your spouse. However, if your spouse does not specifically create a trust or a will to leave the property, it will automatically pass to those loved ones you have chosen in your Loving Trust plan.

Where both spouses are committed to each other and to leaving property to their mutual children or others, this alternative is very useful. Your spouse does not have to direct where the trust assets will pass on his or her death; they will automatically pass under other terms of your Loving Trust.

This alternative gives your spouse total control by:

- Giving your spouse all the trust income.
- Giving your spouse access to all the trust property whenever and in whatever amounts your spouse desires.

- Instructing your trustees to totally care for your spouse during any period when he or she is disabled or incapacitated.
- Allowing your spouse to leave the trust assets to anyone he or she wants.

This alternative—more than any other—is an "I love you and trust in your judgment" trust. It is used for privacy and to avoid probate, the unscrupulous, and creditors. It does not restrict your spouse in any manner. It is designed to assist rather than hinder your mate.

12–2 I want my spouse totally taken care of, but I want to limit my spouse's right to leave my property on his or her death.

If your motive is to give your spouse maximum benefits from your Pocketbook Trust without giving your spouse maximum control over where your property ultimately goes, this alternative may interest you.

In this alternative, your spouse receives all the income from the trust. Your spouse may also receive principal, *but only when your spouse needs it*. Principal can only be used for your spouse when the trustees determine that it is needed for his or her health, education, maintenance, or support. (These are IRS words that, when used in conjunction with one another, mean that the trust property can be used for almost any conceivable need.)

In this alternative, the trustees are instructed to look to any property or other sources of income your spouse has outside of the trust before parting with trust funds. Trust funds will be used only if no other source of property or income is available to your spouse.

When our secretary reviewed this paragraph, she said, "It sounds like lots of red tape is involved in order for one's spouse to get the money." We replied that she was right, that "need," not "desire," was the requirement here, and that the trustees had to find "need" before parting with the trust funds.

Very often, this alternative is used if a spouse has substantial property of his or her own. It is also commonly used in community-property states (Arizona, California, Idaho, Louisiana, Nevada, New Mexico, Texas, Washington) and Wisconsin because in those states one's spouse already has half of the marriage property in his or her name as a matter of state law.

This alternative allows your spouse to decide who, among a group of beneficiaries, will ultimately receive the trust property. For example, you might leave instructions that upon your spouse's death you want the remaining trust property to pass to your children and grandchildren. Since you cannot predict the future and have considerable confidence in your spouse's judgment, you give him or her the right to decide which children or grandchildren get what. It may be that one of your children has married into a wealthy family and is very comfortable, while one of your grandchildren has a severe health problem and needs money. Your spouse can evaluate the circumstances and allocate the property according to his or her assessment at that later time.

Your spouse can divide all the trust property in any manner, including disinheriting any—but not all—of the members of that group. For example, if your group consisted of your children and grandchildren, your spouse would have to name at least one of them as the beneficiary of the trust funds.

This alternative is often used when spouses are loved, but when their ability to care for themselves is lacking or suspect. We have seen many breadwinner spouses leave such a plan for spouses who have not shown the slightest inclination for understanding investments, basic money management, or business.

12–3 I want my spouse totally taken care of, but I will decide where my property goes on my spouse's death.

If you wish to provide for your spouse without giving your spouse any control over your property, this alternative may interest you.

This alternative is identical to alternative 12–2 with the exception that you determine where the remaining trust property passes on your spouse's death. The decision is entirely yours. Your spouse has no control whatsoever over the ultimate disposition of your property when he or she dies. This alternative is often used by trust makers who have children by a prior marriage and who want to be assured that their property will go to their own children rather than their spouse's family. You would clearly favor using it if your spouse had different ideas than you have about who should ultimately get your property.

12–4 My spouse can have only the income my Pocketbook Trust earns and nothing more; I will say where my property goes on his or her death.

You should select this alternative if you want your spouse to have only the income your property produces and to never have—under any circumstances—the ability to touch your trust property.

In this alternative the trustees are required to pay the trust's annual income to your spouse for the rest of his or her life. Upon your spouse's death, the trust property will pass pursuant to your instructions. Your spouse could never use any of your trust principal under this alternative.

This alternative is most often used in pure federal estate-tax planning situations where a spouse is independently wealthy and would never foreseeably have any need for your principal. By giving your spouse the right to the trust income, all federal estate tax on your property is forestalled until your spouse's subsequent death.

12–5 My spouse will get only whatever my state's laws require that I must leave him or her.

Many states require that upon the death of a spouse, a certain minimum amount of the deceased spouse's property be given to the surviving spouse. In our *Protect Your Estate*, we devote an entire chapter to spousal rights under state law.

It is our belief that even when one attempts to leave his or her spouse the absolute minimum allowed by law, he or she should still leave it in a Pocketbook Trust. This is not as altruistic as it sounds. By leaving property in trust, you can control where it will ultimately go if your spouse either neglects or refuses to take the necessary actions to dispose of it under the terms of his or her own will or trust.

This alternative is designed exactly like alternative 12–1. It gives your spouse complete control over the property in his or her trust. What distinguishes it is that it's funded with the minimum amount necessary to comply with your state's laws.

If this alternative interests you, be sure to ask your lawyer whether under your state's law a Loving Trust plan will allow you to totally bypass your spouse in order to leave your property entirely to other people or charities. In a handful of states, a Loving Trust can be used to get around state will laws requiring that spouses be left certain minimum amounts. In these states, a husband or wife who uses a trust can leave all of his or her property directly to children or others.

If either the amount of property going into the trust or its terms gives your spouse less than he or she would otherwise be entitled to under your state law, your spouse can ignore your trust and take his or her state-mandated legal share.

Some of our clients have responded with, "So what do I have to lose by disinheriting my spouse?" "If he or she doesn't fight it, I've won!" "If he or she doesn't fight it, I'm right back where I would have been if I gave him or her the minimum required under my state's law."

The answer to this argument is that your spouse gets to pick exactly what assets he or she wants when gathering his or her state-given share. In our experience, your spouse will pick the wheat and leave your children or other loved ones with the chaff! Spouses fighting for their rights will always select and take the best property.

There are six alternatives for a Pocketbook Trust in the following checklist. These include the five discussed here, plus an alternative that you can use to create your own motive. Check the alternative that most nearly coincides with your desires and motives.

( ) 12–1 I want my spouse to have total control over my property.

( ) 12–2 I want my spouse totally taken care of, but I want to limit my spouse's right to leave my property on his or her death.

> It is our belief that even when one attempts to leave his or her spouse the absolute minimum allowed by law, he or she should still leave it in a Pocketbook Trust.

( ) 12–3 I want my spouse totally taken care of, but I will decide where my property goes on my spouse's death.

( ) 12–4 My spouse can have only the income my Pocketbook Trust earns and nothing more; I will say where my property goes on his or her death.

( ) 12–5 My spouse will get only whatever my state's laws require that I must leave him or her.

( ) 12–6 My own motive: _____

_____

_____

_____

Chapter Thirteen

How to Provide for Your Family

A Family Trust is a subtrust of your trust that is specifically created on your death for the benefit of loved ones other than just your spouse. Your Family Trust can name just your children as its beneficiaries. It can name your children and your spouse as its beneficiaries. It can name a parent or other loved one as sole beneficiary. It can name any number or combination of beneficiaries you wish.

We often ask our students to think of a Family Trust by picturing a dining-room table packed high with food. Around the table sits a family consisting of a widow, her children, and her deceased husband's elderly parents. The menu has been decided, the food has been prepared according to the deceased husband's instructions, and the meal is being served by a local catering service. The servers are to distribute and apportion the food among each of the family members pursuant to the instructions of the deceased husband.

We further ask our students to pretend that they are planning that dinner. We then ask them to create as many different sets of serving combinations as they can think of. The results of this exercise always amuse us. It doesn't matter whether we are teaching attorneys, accountants, insurance agents, or financial planners. Each profession can get equally bizarre in the serving instructions they contrive in responding to our request. We bring the exercise to a close with: "Replace the food with financial assets and the caterers with trustees, and you've got a classic Family Trust planning situation. The variety of your catering instructions represents the variety of the planning instructions available to you in providing for your loved ones with a Family Trust."

You may ask us, "Why would I want to create a Family Trust?" You would generally do so if you wanted to provide for your children, grandchildren, parents, or other loved ones while your spouse is living.

A Family Trust is not just for loved ones other than your spouse. It can, and

> A Family Trust is a subtrust of your trust that is specifically created on your death for the benefit of loved ones other than just your spouse.

125

most often does, provide for the well-being of one's spouse as well. Your spouse can even be named as the primary beneficiary of your Family Trust.

It is at this point that many of our students express confusion. We tell them to remember the dining-room table analogy and to relax because, as we explain more about a Family Trust, it will become readily apparent how and why they are successfully used by so many different people.

Why Family Trusts Are Used

Family Trusts are generally used for one or more of five reasons. They are used when:

You Wish to Save Your Family Federal Estate Tax

A Family Trust can save a family a great deal of federal estate taxes. Every dollar that is put in a Family Trust is free of federal estate tax up to a maximum of $600,000. Let's assume that you leave $600,000 directly to your spouse, and that your spouse has more than $600,000 of his or her own funds. When your spouse leaves your combined funds to your children, the tax on your $600,000 will be a whopping $235,000! If you leave your $600,000 in a Family Trust for the benefit of your spouse and children, there would be absolutely no federal estate tax.

We discuss the tax ramifications of your Family Trust in Chapter Eighteen, "How to Save Federal Death Tax." If the value of your and your spouse's assets—including life insurance proceeds and retirement benefits—is approaching or is greater than $600,000, you should carefully read Chapter Eighteen, "How to Save Federal Death Tax."

It Is Important to You That Your Family Members Are Provided For

This desire is usually present when a person loves his or her spouse and family but does not believe that the spouse loves or will take care of other family members.

We often see this situation in second marriages. Imagine that you have children by a first marriage and that your spouse also has children by a first marriage. If you leave all your property to your spouse, you can pretty well anticipate that he or she will use it to provide for his or her children's well-being rather than that of your children. This dilemma is easily circumvented with a Family Trust that provides instructions for the care of your children.

This need also frequently comes up with respect to the desire many people have to provide for their extended family members, such as parents or brothers and sisters. Imagine that your spouse dislikes your parents; that their meager savings and social security income is augmented to a large extent by your economic assistance. You are fearful that, should you leave all your property to your spouse, he or she will cut off your parents' much-needed economic assistance. This dilemma is circumvented by leaving appropriate funds in your Family Trust with specific instructions as to how your parents are to be cared for following your death.

You Want Your Family Trust to Pass to Your Children

This desire usually reflects one's concern that his or her spouse just might leave his or her inheritance to a new spouse or to some unworthy person or cause.

This situation almost always surfaces in second marriages. Imagine that your spouse has children of his or her own, or that he or she has no children but is not particularly fond of your family. You would be understandably concerned that your spouse would leave your inheritance to his or her family rather than to your loved ones. Your dilemma could be easily solved with a Family Trust that specifically provides that, after your spouse's death, its funds be distributed, pursuant to your instructions, to the loved ones you specify.

It also frequently occurs when one is concerned about a spouse's emotional stability or his or her ability to make prudent decisions. Imagine that your marriage is a good one—the first for you and your spouse—and that your spouse is an excellent parent to your children. But let's further imagine that your spouse is extraordinarily emotional and easily taken in by the guile of others. You would be understandably concerned that if you left all your property to your spouse, he or she could easily leave it to a new spouse or to someone else who entered his or her life. Your dilemma could be easily solved with a Family Trust that provides instructions to the contrary.

You Wish to Leave Your Property to Other Loved Ones

This desire is usually present when one's spouse is independently wealthy or when—for whatever reason—one chooses to leave property to loved ones other than a spouse.

Imagine that your spouse has received a substantial inheritance from his or her parents and that, though your children are all young adults who are making good on your expectations, they would welcome any available economic assistance to improve their lifestyles. It would certainly be reasonable for you to leave the amount you determine appropriate directly for your children's benefit in your Family Trust.

The need to provide for loved ones other than a spouse frequently occurs when one's love of others is greater than one's marital love. This situation can frequently surface in other than romantic scenarios. Imagine that the child you were always closest to was severely injured in an automobile accident that left him or her a quadriplegic and that your spouse was more concerned about his or her golf game than the well-being of your child. Given this circumstance, it would certainly be understandable for you to want your Family Trust funds to care for your child rather than your spouse.

We often see marriages where convenience has replaced love as a motive for staying together. Imagine that your marriage is such a marriage and that you are particularly close to your children or to your brothers and sisters. It would certainly be understandable if you wished to leave a substantial sum to family members other than your spouse through your Family Trust.

You Wish to Reduce Your Loved Ones' Income Tax Burden

Let's assume that you love your spouse and wish to leave everything to him or her on your death. Let's further assume that you have nothing in common with any of the situations we have illustrated as to why people utilize a Family Trust, but that you are keenly interested in reducing your spouse's income tax burden following your death. A Family Trust could certainly meet your objective.

A Family Trust's ability to reduce income taxes can be easily illustrated. Let's pretend that your spouse is in a high income tax bracket, say 28 percent, and that your children do not pay income tax—a typical planning situation. If you leave all your property outright to your spouse or in a Pocketbook Trust, 28 percent of every dollar your money makes will go to Uncle Sam. Only seventy-two cents of every dollar your money earns can be used to pay for your children's health, support, maintenance, and education.

If you create a Family Trust that allows your trustees to provide for your children, income tax can be saved. Children fourteen years of age or older will be taxed on their trust income at their own bracket, less their own allowable exemptions. This means that they could be paying income tax in the 15 percent bracket on a great deal of their trust income rather than at the 28 percent bracket, a saving of 13 percent. Children under fourteen receiving income from a trust are subject to the so-called Kiddie Tax, which generally means that any unearned trust income received by a child in excess of $1000 is taxed in the top tax bracket of the child's parents.

A Family Trust can be created as your only Loving subtrust, or it can be created at the same time and in addition to the Pocketbook Trust for your spouse. For our purposes, your Family Trust, like your spouse's Pocketbook Trust, lasts only until your spouse dies. On your spouse's death a new subtrust is created called a Common Trust for your children and grandchildren.

How You Should Allocate Your Property Between Your Pocketbook and Family Trusts

When you establish your Pocketbook and Family Trusts, you must make the decision as to how much of your property will be allocated between the two trusts. If saving federal estate tax is one of your motives for designing and creating your Loving Trust plan, chapter 18, "How to Save Federal Death Tax," will help you determine how you should allocate your property in conjunction with federal estate-tax planning.

If your estate is valued at less than $600,000—as are the majority of all Americans' estates—the only restraint on how you divide your property between the two trusts will be your spouse's right under your state law to a certain percentage or dollar amount of your property. Put another way, the minimum amount that you can allocate to your Pocketbook Trust is the amount that your state's law requires you to leave your spouse. Most states' laws require that surviving spouses get a portion of their deceased spouse's property. To find out what the law is in your state, you will have to ask your lawyer or refer to the appendix in *Protect Your Estate*, which briefly explains each state's law concerning spousal rights. Once you know the "magic" minimum, you can thereafter allocate as much as you like to your Family Trust.

As you think about how you would like to allocate your property between your Pocketbook and Family Trusts, keep in mind one very helpful concept. In our judgment it is not wise to allocate your property between the two, using actual dollar amounts. For example, let's assume that you have $100,000 and your intention is to leave one-fourth of it to your spouse. Do not say "$25,000 to my spouse in my Pocketbook Trust and the balance in the Family Trust." The value of your property may be less than $25,000 when you die, which would mean that your children will not receive any of your property. Or the value could increase greatly, leaving your spouse with relatively little to provide for his or her needs. With inflation, deflation, and all the other changes that occur, using a dollar figure can be very dangerous.

Always choose a percentage of your property that you wish allocated between your Pocketbook and Family Trusts. Use half-and-half, or one-third/two-thirds, or sixty/forty; use any percentage you think appropriate. This will always give you a result that will allocate your property the way you want without all the problems associated with naming a fixed dollar amount.

As you review and decide upon which Family Trust alternative best fits your motives, keep in mind the precise allocation that you want to make. Also keep in mind that your allocation decision may change based upon your desires and the loving alternative you ultimately select. Following are those *non-tax* allocation alternatives we have seen commonly used:

> With inflation, deflation, and all the other changes that occur, using a dollar figure can be very dangerous.

13–1   I want all my property to pass to my spouse in my Pocketbook Trust.

13–2   I want my spouse to receive whatever he or she is entitled to under state law with the balance passing to my Family Trust.

13–3   I want my property equally divided between my Pocketbook and Family Trusts.

13–4   I want _____ percent to pass to my Pocketbook Trust and _____ percent to my Family Trust.

13–5   I want all my property to pass to my spouse in my Family Trust.

Using a Sole Family Trust

In some situations, a Family Trust is used without a Pocketbook Trust. If you live in a community property state (Arizona, California, Idaho, Louisiana, Nevada, New Mexico, Texas, or Washington), or in Wisconsin, one-half of your marital property is yours to do with as you want at your death. The other half belongs to your spouse. You may also have what is referred to as "sole and separate property," property that is solely yours. It is not legally considered to be part of the marriage property.

Since your community property spouse will also have half of the marital property, you may want all your property to pass to your Family Trust based upon any one or more of the desires that we have already discussed. Under this circumstance a Pocketbook Trust may not be needed.

However, you should not necessarily elect to use a sole Family Trust if the combined value of your half of the marital property and the value of your sole and separate property is more than $600,000. If it is, and one of your motives is to reduce federal estate tax, read Chapter Eighteen, "How to Save Federal Death Tax." After you do, it is likely that you will be adding a Pocketbook Trust to your Loving Trust plan.

Motives

You can design your Family Trust in order to provide liberally for your spouse, or you can design it so that your spouse is not even a beneficiary. Between these two extremes you can design your Family Trust in any manner you like. Some of the more common Family Trust alternatives that we have seen repeatedly used over the years are:

13–7   I want primarily to care for my spouse by providing him or her with as many benefits and as much control as possible.

13–8   I want to provide for my spouse and my children based upon their respective needs, while giving priority to the needs of my spouse. I

> **You can design your Family Trust in order to provide liberally for your spouse, or you can design it so that your spouse is not even a beneficiary.**

want my children and grandchildren to get what is left after my spouse's death.

13–9 I want to provide for the respective needs of my spouse and my children, but if my spouse remarries, I want to provide only for my children.

13–10 The same as alternative 13–9, except that I want my spouse taken care of during any period of time that he or she is single.

13–11 I want to provide for the respective needs of my spouse, my children, and other loved ones and will set forth my priorities.

13–12 I want to provide for loved ones other than my spouse.

13–7 I want primarily to care for my spouse by providing him or her with as many benefits and as much control as possible.

This alternative is often selected by happily married couples whose only motives are to reduce federal estate taxes and provide complete control and benefit to the surviving spouse, while providing secondary care for other family members. Use of this alternative assumes complete confidence in one's spouse.

If this alternative fits your desires, you would name your spouse as a co-trustee of your trust. You would also give him or her the power to fire co-trustees at any time and for any reason, so long as a replacement is named pursuant to your instructions. The provisions of your Family Trust would give your spouse:

- all the income the trust earns,
- the greater of $5000 or 5 percent of the funds each year as a matter of right without having to show any need,
- the opportunity to have his or her every need for health, support, maintenance, or education paid for by the trustees on a first priority basis, and
- the right to leave whatever is left in the trust at his or her death to family members in whatever amounts or percentages the spouse chooses.

The secondary provisions of your Family Trust will provide for the health, support, maintenance, and education of your children.

It is readily apparent that should you select this alternative, you would be giving your spouse awesome power and control over your Family Trust. As a co-trustee your spouse would have the power to make every decision with respect to the investment of and the withdrawal from the trust funds. Should your spouse and his or her co-trustees disagree about any decision, your spouse could simply fire that trustee, and a replacement that you have previously named in your Loving Trust plan will take over.

The income from the trust will all be paid to your spouse, and will therefore be taxed in your spouse's personal income-tax bracket. This might be considered poor income-tax planning. However, that criticism would be of no consequence to you since income tax planning is not one of the motives associated with this alternative.

The bizarre configuration of $5000 or 5 percent was not selected on an arbitrary basis. It represents a right expressly authorized by the Internal Revenue Code; that is the only reason it exists. You would obviously take advantage of this right, since your motive in using this alternative is to provide your spouse with the absolute maximum bundle of rights possible, while still avoiding federal estate tax on the Family Trust funds.

Your spouse's right to be cared for with respect to his or her every need for health, support, maintenance, and education is of critical importance in meeting your liberal requirements. These words come right out of the Internal Revenue Code; they mean literally everything. Since your spouse is both a trustee and the primary beneficiary of the trust, he or she should have absolutely no difficulty removing funds for legitimate needs.

Your spouse's power to control the Family Trust funds continues even subsequent to his or her death as a result of the fourth benefit this alternative bestows. You can give your spouse the right to leave the balance of the trust to any person or persons in any amounts or percentages that he or she selects—the only qualification being that you set the parameters as to the group your spouse can select from. In this alternative, the group is your children and grandchildren. It could just as easily be your spouse's family or any other group.

13–8 I want to provide for my spouse and my children based upon their respective needs, while giving priority to the needs of my spouse. I want my children and grandchildren to get what is left after my spouse's death.

This alternative is generally used by happily married couples who are interested in maintaining the pre-death status quo and who are also interested in reducing their family's income taxes. It is commonly selected by those people who love their spouses and who have children or grandchildren who are dependent upon them or their spouses. This alternative was the one most frequently selected by our clientele over the years.

If it fits your desires, you would most likely wish to name your spouse as a co-trustee of the trust. You would also give him or her the power to fire a co-trustee at any time and for any reason, so long as a replacement is named. The provisions of your trust would be:

- I want my trustees to take care of my spouse and children in their every need for health, support, maintenance, and education from the income and principal of my trust.

- In caring for my loved ones, I want my trustees, at all times, to give primary consideration to the needs of my spouse.
- Whatever is left in my Family Trust on my spouse's death shall immediately be used for the care of my children and grandchildren, pursuant to further subtrusts that I will create in my Loving Trust plan.

The key to this alternative is its flexibility. It allows your spouse to use all the Family Trust funds—both income and principal—to care on a "needs basis" for your beneficiaries. It also makes manifestly clear that your number-one priority is your spouse's welfare.

This type of Family Trust is often called a "spray" or "sprinkle" trust. It gets its name from the fact that it operates just like a nozzle on your garden hose. Income and principal can be directed at one beneficiary, in the same way you can adjust the garden hose nozzle to a hard, accurate jet of water. Income and principal can also be diffused among many beneficiaries, just as the nozzle can be adjusted to give a broad, soft spray of water for a garden full of tender flowers.

A sprinkle or spray trust can offer significant income-tax advantages. Spraying income over a lot of income-tax brackets creates less income tax in most cases than directing incomes into one bracket.

There is also a gift tax problem that can be circumvented with this alternative. The gift tax problem can be easily illustrated:

Assume that Mr. Jones left a Family Trust that gave his spouse all its income each year and provided that the principal could be made available only to Mrs. Jones. Further assume that Mrs. Jones wanted to make gifts to her children of her surplus funds after she paid her income taxes.

Her lawyer would tell her that any gift she made in excess of $10,000 would be subject to federal gift tax laws. If Mrs. Jones took principal from the Family Trust and then attempted to give it to her children, her lawyer would tell her the same thing.

Contrast Mrs. Jones's plight with your spouse's under this alternative. Your spouse as a co-trustee would have the right to care directly for the needs of your Family Trust's beneficiaries without having first to pay the money to himself or herself. Since your trustee-spouse could pay the money directly from the Family Trust to your beneficiaries there would be no gift and, therefore, no federal gift tax.

A major difference between this alternative and our first alternative is that your spouse will not have the right to leave any of the Family Trust property to whom he or she wants on death. This alternative locks in trust funds for the benefit of your children and grandchildren.

A vast majority of our clients took particular delight in this provision. It appeared that they thought it both fair and appropriate. Their thinking went something like this: my spouse has his or her own funds (independent monies, community property share, or a Pocketbook Trust) and can leave them to anyone he or she desires. My Family Trust represents my share of our marriage, and I want its funds ultimately to go to my loved ones.

13–9 I want to provide for the respective needs of my spouse and my children, but if my spouse remarries, I want to provide only for my children.

This alternative is identical to our previous alternative with one exception. It gives a spouse benefits from the Family Trust only so long as that spouse remains single. If he or she should remarry, this alternative automatically and permanently removes that spouse as a Family Trust beneficiary. A spouse cannot return as a beneficiary even if he or she is later widowed or divorced.

This alternative is often selected by the same people who selected alternative 13–8, but who are sensitive to the potential conflict-of-interest dilemma their spouses may find themselves in following remarriage.

We can best illustrate this dilemma by sharing a conversation that occurred many years ago in our offices:

> Martha came to us for advice with respect to a trust dilemma. Her first husband left property to her and their children in a Family Trust. As primary beneficiary she could have whatever she needed whenever she needed it. She loved her second husband very much, and wanted to be loyal to him. Unfortunately, he was an extremely poor provider. They quickly went through her independent money, and he was constantly harassing her to invade the funds of the Family Trust for their mutual benefit.
>
> Our client was beside herself. She wanted to be loyal to her second husband and acquiesce to his demands. On the other hand, she did not want to disinherit her children by bleeding the Family Trust. If she refused to invade the Family Trust, she was fearful that her second husband would perceive that she was disloyal and divorce her. If she invaded it, she was fearful that there would be nothing left for her children.
>
> Martha was in tears during most of the interview. Unfortunately, we could not offer her any advice or direction that would alleviate her burden. She had to make a decision, and she couldn't win regardless of how she made it.

This alternative is specifically designed to circumvent Martha's dilemma. It allows your spouse to continue to care for your children as a co-trustee of the trust. It also gives your spouse the ammunition to tell that subsequent spouse that he or she cannot touch a penny of the Family Trust as a result of remarrying. It takes the heat off your spouse while allowing your spouse to continue caring for your children.

13–10 The same as alternative 13–9, except that I want my spouse taken care of during any period of time that he or she is single.

This alternative is exactly like alternative 13–9, except that if your spouse is no longer married, then your spouse again becomes a beneficiary of the Family Trust.

This alternative is used by people who are concerned about their spouse's well-being following a divorce from or death of a subsequent spouse. It manifests much love and concern for one's spouse.

If you use this alternative for your spouse, he or she would always be a beneficiary of your Family Trust during any period of time that he or she is single. Your spouse could marry and divorce several times or lose subsequent mates to death and still be a beneficiary of your Family Trust during interim unmarried periods.

13–11 I want to provide for the respective needs of my spouse, my children, and other loved ones and will set forth my priorities.

This alternative is used in those situations where a person is very much concerned about the well-being of loved ones in addition to members of his or her immediate family.

It is commonly used by people who view that they are responsible for aged parents, disadvantaged brothers or sisters, or needy nieces and nephews. It is used to include close family friends as additional Family Trust beneficiaries.

If this alternative fits your desires, you would name loved ones in addition to your spouse, children, and grandchildren as beneficiaries of your Family Trust. You will create a nightmare for your trustees unless you provide them with a list of which beneficiaries are to be given first nod with respect to the income and principal of your Family Trust.

Let's assume that you have named your spouse, children, grandchildren, parents, and your spouse's parents as your Family Trust beneficiaries. Let's further assume that each has substantial needs for the same trust-fund dollar. You must provide your trustees with what we refer to as a priority list, in effect saying: "Here's the way I would spend my money caring for my loved ones." In our example, you might say: "I want primary consideration given to the needs of my spouse and thereafter to my children, grandchildren, parents, and finally my spouse's parents, in that order."

We point this out to you because in our experience it is a frequent problem and concern in the trust world. There are often times when there are simply not enough funds available to adequately provide for the needs of all of a trust's beneficiaries. This situation always causes significant consternation among the trustees and can frequently result in threat of litigation and actual courtroom

You will create a nightmare for your trustees unless you provide them with a list of which beneficiaries are to be given first nod with respect to the income and principal of your Family Trust.

battles. Your loved ones will avoid all of this and your desires will be effected if you will take the time to set forth your priorities.

13–12 I want to provide for loved ones other than my spouse.

You may want to create a Family Trust where your spouse is not a beneficiary. This alternative is designed exactly like the spray or sprinkle trust found in alternative 13–8 with the exception that your spouse is not a beneficiary.

This alternative is frequently used when your spouse is independently wealthy or in second-marriage situations where it is critical that your children are exclusively provided for by a Family Trust.

A key decision that has to be made is whether you would be comfortable having your spouse as a co-trustee of your Family Trust. If you choose not to name your spouse as a co-trustee, your spouse would not have any control over the trust funds. If it is your desire to place your spouse in a trustee's role, then your spouse will be able to exercise control over the Family Trust by exercising his or her judgment in implementing your instructions.

We have never seen a consensus among our clients as to when one should and should not name a spouse as a trustee under this motive. It is our experience that every situation is unique. However, it is our strong belief that you should not name your spouse as a trustee when using this alternative unless you have extraordinarily strong and good reasons to the contrary. People who are disinherited are often full of bitterness and rancor.

The Family Trust alternatives that we have discussed are listed below. Please take a moment to check the alternatives that most closely meet your desires and motives.

How to Allocate Between My Pocketbook and Family Trusts

( )   13–1   I want all my property to pass to my spouse in my Pocketbook Trust.

( )   13–2   I want my spouse to receive whatever he or she is entitled to under state law with the balance passing to my Family Trust.

( )   13–3   I want my property equally divided between my Pocketbook and Family Trusts.

( )   13–4   I want _____ percent to pass to my Pocketbook Trust and _____ percent to my Family Trust.

( )   13–5   I want all my property to pass to my spouse in my Family Trust.

( )   13–6   My own motive: _____

_____

_____

_____

How I Want My Beneficiaries Provided For
from My Family Trust

( )   13–7 I want primarily to care for my spouse by providing him or her with as many benefits and as much control as possible.

( )   13–8 I want to provide for my spouse and my children based upon their respective needs, while giving priority to the needs of my spouse. I want my children and grandchildren to get what is left after my spouse's death.

( )   13–9 I want to provide for the respective needs of my spouse and my children, but if my spouse remarries, I want to provide only for my children.

( )   13–10 The same as alternative 13–9, except that I want my spouse taken care of during any period of time that he or she is single.

( )   13–11 I want to provide for the respective needs of my spouse, my children, and other loved ones, and will set forth my priorities.

( )   13–12 I want to provide for loved ones other than my spouse.

( )   13–13 My own motive: _____

_____

_____

_____

Chapter Fourteen

How to Provide for Your Minor Children

A major planning problem that we have frequently encountered relates to what we called "ledger mentality" in chapter 4. You'll recall our story about John and Wayne and how they had a penchant for keeping a ledger on every penny spent on behalf of each of their children, periodically making the appropriate adjustments so that the sums spent on each were exactly the same. In our experience, most people do not subscribe to this approach to parenting, yet that is precisely how they care for their children and grandchildren on death.

Life insurance and employee benefit designations that leave property "share and share alike," "equally," or "per stirpes" mandate exact ledger equality regardless of the needs and relative economic circumstances of the children. Simple-will or bare-bones living-trust planning that leaves property in this fashion also creates ironlike inflexibility and oftentimes has disastrous results.

Your trust has a special subtrust—called a Common Trust—that comes into existence for your children after both your and your spouse's death. It is specifically designed to make sure that your children are cared for based on their needs rather than through some arbitrary division or amount arithmetically created by an insensitive adviser. It fully complies with the concept that you love your children equally but wish to care for them based on their needs, that there is nothing so unequal as the equal treatment of unequals. It only terminates when your youngest child has attained some age or requirement that meets with your desires.

In our seminars, we refer to the Common Trust as a "Chicken or Vegetable Soup Pot Trust." Can you recall your mom's soup specialty? If it was like our moms', it had just about everything in the pantry and refrigerator in it. When it was ladled out, the hungrier children at the table got more than those who were not as hungry. Some got more meat, because that was their favorite; some got more vegetables or rice or noodles. If a particular brother or sister had a penchant for a particular ingredient, that ingredient was always found in abundance in his or her bowl. Mom controlled and monitored the whole process to make sure that everyone was nourished and as happy as possible, and she ultimately decided who got what.

A Common Trust is designed to act like Mom's soup pot. Its trustees replace Mom's function and decide who gets what based upon the relative needs and desires of the children. Just as Mom ladled out the soup, your trustees distribute your property to your children based upon each child's needs as they compare to the needs of the other children with respect to the available trust resources.

We may love our children the same, but we do not treat them the same. The cornerstone of your Common Trust is this: When it comes to minor children, need is more important than equality. Your Common Trust's purpose is to provide for all your children's needs from a common source just as if mother or father were living and doing just that.

Allow us to contrive an extreme example that illustrates the need for a Common Trust:

> Assume that you have two children, a twenty-four-year-old electrical engineer and a five-year-old aspiring ballerina. Further assume that your entire estate—including life insurance—is $100,000. We doubt that you would leave $50,000 to each child knowing that your son is making a fine living and that your ballerina has sixteen years to go to reach adulthood or to complete college.

Since truth can be stranger than fiction, let's take a look at a more typical situation that frequently occurs in the probate courts across the country when a Common Trust is not used:

> Parents of three children, aged seven, thirteen, and eighteen, died in an accident. The parents left a will that created a separate death trust for each child. The parents' property was divided equally among the three separate trusts. The seven-year-old was injured in the same accident that killed her mother and father. Medical bills mounted quickly and by the time she reached eleven years of age, her trust property was completely gone. Her two sisters' trusts had substantial amounts of money and property in them. Unfortunately, none of the property in these trusts could be used for the seven-year-old. She became a ward of the state, even though her two sisters had a great deal of property.

Because the parents chose to immediately establish separate trusts for their children, they created an iron curtain between the children. Had these parents been given the opportunity to create a Common Trust, they would have undoubtedly jumped at the chance. They would have been able to keep all of their property in a Common Trust until the youngest child reached a certain age or achieved a certain level of education. Then, and only then, would whatever property that was left be divided among their children, either outright or to their respective separate trusts. If these parents had utilized a Common Trust, all of their children

Your Common Trust's purpose is to provide for all your children's needs from a common source just as if mother or father were living and doing just that.

would have been able to share in their property based on actual need, rather than on an arbitrary percentage or arithmetical division.

Had our storybook parents not been killed, we are sure they would have spent their money caring for their truly needy child. They would not have said, "No more for you, you've used your one-third. You're on your own." The question again surfaces, "Why should we do on death something we would never consider doing in life?"

To be effective, we believe a Common Trust needs to have certain critical provisions that are often overlooked.

Need Is More Important Than Equality

The first and foremost provision of an effective Common Trust is an instruction to the trustees that each child is to be cared for based upon his or her needs as measured against the other children's current and anticipated needs and the amount of trust resources available. It is important that you instruct your trustees that it is permissible to spend more on one child if that is what needs to be done. Make sure that your Common Trust is a soup pot trust. That's what it is all about.

Assist Your Guardians

Instruct your trustees to use the trust funds to assist the guardians of your children in caring for and raising them. Let's face it, if you and your spouse die and leave your children in your sister and brother-in-law's care, they are going to have their hands full, not to mention their house, their car, and their lives. Allow your trustees to use your trust money and property to help your guardians.

It is entirely foreseeable that the guardians of your loved ones may need to put an addition on their home to properly house your children. They may need a station wagon or van to replace their two-door sedan or sports car. They may need to change or add a great many things in order to make their lives, and the lives of your children, comfortable as a result of adding your family to theirs. Most of our clients have expressed their sensitivity to this requirement and have instructed us to "Be sure to provide that our children's guardians are provided with whatever they reasonably need to care for our little ones."

Allow for Advances

Clients who have children with a significant age disparity are caught on the horns of a major planning dilemma. If they immediately distribute their property equally to their children, they are ledger planning. If they leave it all in a Common Trust until their youngest child attains a certain age, they may be punishing their older children with respect to their economic needs for such things as

> It is important that you instruct your trustees that it is permissible to spend more on one child if that is what needs to be done.

establishing a business or profession, purchasing a home, paying for their weddings, etc.

This dilemma is solved with instructions that we refer to as "extraordinary advancement" language. In our Loving Trust plans, our trustees are allowed to advance money or property to an older child for extraordinary needs or opportunities. However, there are conditions that must be met before such an advance is made. Our trustees have to determine if the particular child's need is a good one. Does he need funds to purchase a home? Does he need such a home? Is it appropriate for his and his family's needs? Is it fairly priced? If your trustees' investigations support the need for such an extraordinary request, they must make an additional determination before providing the requisite funds.

They must further ask, "Is there enough money in the soup pot to satisfy this need or request, while still leaving enough for the anticipated care of his younger brother?" Put another way, "If the money is given to my older son to purchase a new home, could that advancement in any way adversely affect my younger son's rights to funds for the basics: health, support, maintenance, and education?" This is a tough question to answer, but it needs to be answered before the trustees can make an advancement. If there is any doubt in our trustees' minds, they should not make the advancement.

You should provide your trustees with instructions that they are always to be mindful that the Common Trust is for all your children; that one child's special business or nonessential social needs are not to be satisfied when there are younger children with basic needs (such as food, clothing, education, etc.).

An advancement is not a gift that would deprive your other children of their ultimate share of your property. Many of our business-oriented clients referred to this advancement procedure as an interest-free loan to an older child that will automatically be paid back when the Common Trust splits into Separate Trusts or outright shares for all the children.

A few real examples should bring this concept to life for you:

> In the mid-sixties we worked on a trust that did not provide for advancements from its Common Trust. Its beneficiaries were a young man named Tom, who was twenty-six years of age, and a daughter named Sue, who was nineteen years of age. Tom was a successful young executive and Sue was a high-achieving college sophomore.
>
> Tom went to his deceased parents' trustees with the request that they advance him funds to purchase a fast-food franchise. There were considerable funds in the trust, and its terms stated that it would terminate in two years when his sister reached age twenty-one. Unfortunately, however, its terms did not provide advancement language. The trustees felt bad because their investigation concluded that his proposed venture was both sound and very exciting. But their

. . . one child's special business or nonessential social needs are not to be satisfied when there are younger children with basic needs . . .

hands were tied; he would have to wait two years for such funds. Two years later he had the funds, but the business opportunity had passed him by.

If our young entrepreneur's parents had provided advancement instructions, he could have made a good career and business investment without hurting his sister's financial rights in any way.

Let's assume that there was $500,000 in the Common Trust and Tom's request for $100,000 was honored by the trustees; when his sister, Sue, turned twenty-one there was $400,000 in the Common Trust. Given our advancement language, Sue would have received $250,000 and Tom would have received $150,000.

Let's assume the same situation, only let's change the facts a little. Assume that the trust contained advancement language, and that it had only $200,000 in it; that Sue was only fourteen, a freshman in high school, and she had a learning disability. Would the trustees make the advancement? Put yourself in the trustees' shoes. Tom would be asking for half of the Common Trust funds. Sue would need expensive tutors and it would be seven years until she reached age twenty-one. Would the remaining $100,000 be enough to provide for her health, support, maintenance, and education? If we were the trustees, we would not advance the funds. Would you?

Advancement language is designed to enable your trustees to do what you would do under the same set of circumstances. That is its only purpose.

Providing for the Death of a Beneficiary

Your Common Trust must also provide a method for distributing its property in the event one of your children dies before the Common Trust terminates. Our Loving Trust instructions make it clear that if one of our children dies while the Common Trust is in existence and that child has children (our grandchildren), then our son's inheritance will be preserved—in trust—for our grandchildren. For example, if you have three children and the oldest dies leaving two children of his or her own, then when the Common Trust is divided, that dead child's share will be split equally among your grandchildren. During the time the Common Trust is still in existence, however, the grandchildren will be cared for with the chicken-soup pot just as if they were your children.

If one of our sons dies and leaves no children, then his share will pass equally to our other children when the Common Trust is divided up. We feel, and so have the vast majority of our clients, that this is the fairest way to handle a deceased child's inheritance with respect to the Common Trust. You may choose to handle it differently. If you do, simply state to whom and how you want the funds to pass.

Define When the Common Trust Will End

The final provision needed in an effective Common Trust is at what time, or upon what event it will end and the property in it be divided.

We have found that almost all our clients have liked the instructions that we include in our Loving Trust plans for needs versus equality, assistance for guardians, advancements, and the death of beneficiaries. They have had different opinions, however, as to when their Common Trust should end and its funds split into Separate Trusts for each of their children.

Some of the alternatives that we have seen repeatedly used over the years are:

14–1 All my children are adults. I do not want a Common Trust.

14–2 I want my Common Trust to end when my youngest child is twenty-one years of age.

14–3 I want my Common Trust to end when my youngest child is twenty-three or completes college, whichever happens first.

14–4 I want my Common Trust to end when my youngest child is _____ years of age.

14–1 All my children are adults. I do not want a Common Trust.

A Common Trust is almost always used when one leaves minor children. If you have only adult children, you would generally skip this trust and move on to Separate Trusts for your children as described in chapter 15, "How to Distribute Your Children's Property."

14–2 I want my Common Trust to end when my youngest child is twenty-one years of age.

Twenty-one has historically been the popular age for children to be considered adults and on their own. This alternative calls for the Common Trust to terminate when your youngest child attains that magic age of majority.

The variations that can be used in this alternative are endless. Any age can be substituted for twenty-one.

A few of our clients have opted to utilize the Common Trust far past the time when their youngest child has attained the age of twenty-one. In such cases, we have reminded them that the age chosen is only used to terminate the Common Trust and divide it equally among their children's Separate Trusts. However, a very small percentage of our clientele became so intrigued with this concept that they designed their Loving Trust plan to keep their Common Trust in existence for the entire lifetimes of all of their children. When asked for our thoughts on the subject, we always shared our Loving Trust planning for our children, but quickly continued, "It's your Loving Trust plan, and you can do whatever you want. It is entirely up to you. We encourage you to do what you feel is best for you and your children."

14–3 I want my Common Trust to end when my youngest child is twenty-three or completes college, whichever happens first.

We would like to give our children the opportunity to receive a college education. That is why our Common Trust stays in force until our youngest children reach age twenty-three or complete college, whichever occurs first. Our reasoning is simple. If we live as long as we think we will, we are going to make sure that each of our children haves every chance to go to college. If we die before each of our children have this opportunity, we want to make sure that each has the opportunity of finishing his/her undergraduate college education before our Common Trust terminates and is divided into Separate Trusts for each of our children.

In discussing this alternative with our clients, we have stressed that if a child does not finish his or her undergraduate college education by a certain age it would be wise to terminate the Common Trust before the "professional student" drains away his or her siblings' inheritance. The age you use depends upon your particular perceptions and desires. You may like the concept but think that twenty-three is too old or too young. You can certainly substitute any age that you think appropriate. Some of our clients have even instructed us to substitute graduate or professional school graduation requirements as their Common Trust termination provision.

We do not particularly care what colleges our children attend, but we do care that they attend an accredited university. This is why we set forth certain minimum standards in our Common Trust before authorizing our trustees to expend funds for educational purposes. We have carefully written our Loving Trust plan to reflect what we would do if we were to make the decisions on how our money was being spent on our children's education.

14–4 I want my Common Trust to end when my youngest child is _____ years of age.

This is identical to alternative 14–2, except that it allows you to pick the age that your youngest child must attain for your Common Trust to terminate.

The Common Trust alternatives that we have discussed are listed on the following page, including an alternative that you can use to create your own motive. Take a moment to check the alternatives that most clearly meet your desires and motives.

HOW TO PROVIDE FOR YOUR MINOR CHILDREN

( )   14–1 All my children are adults. I do not want a Common Trust.

( )   14–2 I want my Common Trust to end when my youngest child is twenty-one years of age.

( )   14–3 I want my Common Trust to end when my youngest child is twenty-three or completes college, whichever happens first.

( )   14–4 I want my Common Trust to end when my youngest child is _____ years of age.

( )   14–5 My own motive: _____

_____

_____

_____

Chapter Fifteen

How to Distribute Your Children's Property

You can immediately divide your property among your children upon your death or you can leave it in a Common Trust that will divide it among your children at a later time. Either way, you will eventually be dividing your property among your children. The question that remains to be answered is, how do your children receive their shares? You could certainly leave them their inheritance outright. We discussed this bare-bones planning approach in chapter 4. A better alternative is to leave each of your children with a Separate Trust that will provide instructions for his or her individual care and for the orderly distribution of your funds pursuant to your desires and motives.

A Separate Trust, as its name implies, is a subtrust of your trust that is funded and designed to take care of a specific beneficiary. Separate Trusts for your children can be created immediately upon your death or upon the deaths of you and your spouse. They can also be created upon the termination of your Common Trust.

This chapter will outline and discuss several methods of distributing property to a child from his or her Separate Trust. The methods we share with you are those that have been most commonly selected by our clients over the years.

Just as a properly designed Common Trust should have certain instructions in it, a Separate Trust should contain instructions as to how your trustees should administer it prior to distributing its funds. We will discuss the basic operating instructions that each of your children's Separate Trusts should contain before providing you with your distribution alternatives.

Advance Distributions

While each of your children's inheritance is in his or her Separate Trust, your trustees will almost always be instructed to make distributions to your son or daughter for his or her every need. You will recall that the legal words that convey this instruction come right out of the Internal Revenue Code regulations. They are "education," "health," "maintenance," and "support." By instructing your trustees to so care for your children, you can be assured that they will be well taken care of.

You can amplify your instructions to your trustees by instructing them to meet your children's extraordinary needs. For example, we instruct our trustees to assist each of our children in starting a business or profession, purchasing a home, meeting the expenses of a wedding, or any other extraordinary need that may surface.

Your child's Separate Trust need not be like a bank vault or safe-deposit box that is meant to be kept perpetually locked with its contents rendered unavailable. It can be designed to be a living and compassionate vehicle that fully implements your instructions for the care and financial well-being of each of your children. It can be structured as a buffer between your children and the cruel reality of an aggressively competitive marketplace.

Your Separate Trust instructions are meant to help, teach, and encourage your children in the ways of money and spending. Like us, most of our clients have instructed their trustees to be liberal in caring for the needs of their children, emphasizing that the preservation of the trust funds is not as important as taking care of the children's needs. We have always viewed revocable living trusts that are part of our Loving Trust plans as people-oriented trusts that conjure up visions of Thanksgiving dinner, roaring fireplaces, and joyful family reunions rather than stingy, cold, and heartless devices that only say no to the children.

We have encountered a minority of clients who, for whatever reasons, did not subscribe to our liberal Separate Trust philosophy. These clients had desires that were the opposite of ours. They wanted to be assured that their trust instructions were restrictively conservative. Their desires were more like J. Paul Getty's than ours. They wanted to preserve their children's trust funds and only wanted to provide for advancements on a most rigorous and exacting basis.

In your Loving Trust planning you can select one of the approaches that is most conducive to your thoughts about and feelings for your children.

15–1   I want my trustees to liberally provide for each of my children.
15–2   I want my trustees to provide only for the health, education, support, and maintenance of each of my children.

The Premature Death of One of Your Children

A standard instruction found in our Separate Trusts deals with the premature death of a child. If one of our sons dies before taking all the property from his

> **Your child's Separate Trust need not be like a bank vault or safe-deposit box that is meant to be kept perpetually locked with its contents rendered unavailable. It can be designed to be a living and compassionate vehicle that fully implements your instructions for the care and financial well-being of each of your children.**

Separate Trust, we provide that the funds should go to whomever he wants—that is, if he took the time and attention to leave a will or a trust of his own.

It is our desire that our sons leave whatever was left for them to anyone they want, including family, friends, or charity. It is our feeling that if our sons care enough for someone to take the time to plan for him or her, their wishes should be respected. On the other hand, if he doesn't take the time to make a will or trust of his own, we provide that the balance of his Separate Trust share will pass equally to his children, our grandchildren, or, if he doesn't have children, then it will pass to his brother's trust.

Over the years, we have found that roughly 50 percent of our clients have liked this Separate Trust feature. The remaining half did not want to give a child the power to direct where unused trust funds would be distributed. It was the feeling of these clients that it was their money and they would determine where it went on a child's premature death. The bulk of these clients directed that it went to their deceased child's children. If there were no grandchildren, they wanted the funds to pass equally to their other children. A small percentage of our clients chose to leave the funds to their deceased child's spouse or to some other person or charity.

You can select the approach that most clearly meets your desires and motives from the two that follow:

> 15–4 I want my child's trust property to pass pursuant to my child's directions.
>
> 15–5 I want my child's trust property to pass to my child's children or, if none, to my other children.

Distribution Alternatives

Like a Common Trust, a Separate Trust can have a limitless variety of distribution alternatives. Your Loving Trust planning can provide for a single distribution from each of your children's Separate Trusts or for multiple distributions. It can provide for distributions at different ages or on special occasions. It can provide unique distribution provisions that differ from one child to another; each of your children do not have to be planned for in exactly the same way—unless they are exactly the same and you wish to treat them just that way.

Some children have the ability to handle financial affairs better than others. There is no rule stating that children, grandchildren, or other loved ones need to have exactly the same Separate Trust instructions and provisions. Children often have different needs that require different planning approaches. Your Loving Trust plan allows you to comfortably meet those needs and to be secure in the knowledge that your love and caring will survive you.

Like a Common Trust, a Separate Trust can have a limitless variety of distribution alternatives.

HOW TO DISTRIBUTE YOUR CHILDREN'S PROPERTY

Following are eight alternatives that were commonly selected by our clientele. We hope that one or more of them will match your desires and motives. At the very least, their broad spectrum will enable you to create your own Separate Trust distribution instructions.

Most of the Separate Trust alternatives refer to mandatory distributions by the trustees. However, living trusts that are included in Loving Trust plans usually have a paragraph that instructs the trustees to keep a child's funds in trust if he or she is disabled or chooses to leave them there to be taken at a later date.

15–7 I want my property distributed to my children immediately.

15–8 I want my children to have immediately whatever they want from their Separate Trusts.

15–9 Make two distributions to my children, one-half at a minimum age, the remainder at another stated age.

15–10 Make two distributions to my children, the first at a minimum age, or immediately if that age has been met, the second to occur five years from the date of the first distribution.

15–11 Make four distributions to my children, the first to occur at a minimum age, or immediately if that age has been met, the second through fourth to occur every five years.

15–12 Make multiple unequal distributions, the first to occur at a minimum age, or immediately if that age has been met, the others at stated ages.

15–13 Make no mandatory lifetime distributions to my children, but take care of my children in whatever way they need, whenever they need it from the trust funds.

15–14 Make entirely different distribution patterns for each of my children.

15–7 I want my property distributed to my children immediately.

Despite our admonitions to the contrary, we have had clients who have insisted that their property be immediately distributed outright to their children. This alternative is almost always chosen when there are adult children who have proven themselves responsible.

If your children are adults and you have absolutely no concern about their financial ability, this alternative may be for you. However, we must ask you to carefully reflect on your position. Do you remember the problems we addressed with regard to disability? Assume that your daughter has a heart attack and is unable to care for herself. If you left her inheritance directly to her, she would be unable to utilize your funds without court intervention. She would be in the same predicament as Groucho.

A well-designed trust would have a provision for just this situation. It would tell your trustees to take special care of your disabled daughter and to hold off making any outright distributions to her until such time as she is able to care for herself. In effect, it would give your trustees the option to continue her Separate Trust for her benefit.

Another concern we would like to share before you select this alternative centers on our earlier discussion of immunity or spendthrift clauses. You will recall that life insurance proceeds are generally immune from the claims of creditors because of this clause. So, too, are funds left in properly designed Loving Trust plans. If you leave your property to your children in a Separate Trust, it is probable, under your state laws, that your children's creditors will not be able to take your trust funds to satisfy any indebtedness owed to them by your children.

We are generally opposed to outright distributions. However, if that is your desire, this is the alternative for you.

15–8 I want my children to have immediately whatever they want from their separate trusts.

This alternative is what we have offered our clients in lieu of an outright distribution or division. It is designed to accommodate those parents who have adult children who have proven themselves to be mature when it comes to financial matters.

If you leave your property outright to such children, you will expose their funds to both their creditors and the probate court in the event of a disability. These are risks that do not have to be taken.

If instead you leave your child's inherited property in a Separate Trust with instructions that provide that he or she is to receive whatever trust funds he or she requests at any time, you will have circumvented these problems.

Your child's Separate Trust will function just like the liberal Pocketbook Trust we discussed in chapter 12. It will keep his or her inheritance confidential, avoid a living probate, and, most likely, avoid the claims of creditors.

We heartily recommend this alternative to anyone who is seriously considering the first alternative. It provides significant benefits.

15–9 Make two distributions to my children, one-half at a minimum age, the remainder at another stated age.

This alternative delays any mandatory distribution to your children until each child reaches a certain minimum age. When the required age is reached, one-half of your child's Separate Trust is his or hers to use without having to show or prove need. When your child reaches the next stated age, the remainder of his or her Separate Trust will likewise be distributed.

> **If you leave your property to your children in a Separate Trust, it is probable, under your state laws, that your children's creditors will not be able to take your trust funds to satisfy any indebtedness owed to them by your children.**

If your child has already reached the second stated age by the time of your death, he or she would receive all of his or her inheritance in one distribution. For example:

> After my Common Trust ends, each of my children shall receive an equal share of my property to be held in a Separate Trust.
>
> When each of my children reaches age twenty-five or, upon the creation of this Separate Trust, if any child of mine is already twenty-five, then pay out one-half of my child's trust property to him or her. When my child is thirty or, on the creation of this Separate Trust, if my child is already thirty or older, then pay out the balance of the trust property.

Under this example, if at the time that the Separate Trusts are created, one of your children is twenty-three, then all of that child's property will remain in his or her Separate Trust. The trustees will care for the child out of his or her Separate Trust for health, education, maintenance, and support. The trustees will be liberal, if you choose, and will allow advancements for the extraordinary purposes you have set forth in your instructions. When your child is twenty-five, he or she will be entitled to receive one-half of your trust property; the other half will be distributed to your son or daughter at thirty.

What if your child is twenty-six at your death? If that is the case, one-half of your child's Separate Trust property will immediately be distributed; the other half will stay in trust until he or she is thirty.

What if your child is thirty-one on your death? If your child is thirty or older when the Separate Trust is formed, then he or she will receive an immediate distribution of the entire trust property.

The assumption implicit in the selection of this alternative is that if children are under twenty-five they are not experienced enough to be trusted with their inheritance. If they are over twenty-five, but under thirty, they should be given a chance to flex their financial muscles with half of their inheritance. If they are thirty years of age or older, they should be trusted with their entire inheritance.

There is nothing special about these ages. They are an example of what can be done under this alternative. If you like how this alternative is designed, but are not happy with the ages, you can replace them with others that better fit your desires.

15–10 Make two distributions to my children, the first at a minimum age, or immediately if that age has been met, the second to occur five years from the date of the first distribution.

For some reason, a substantial percentage of our clients felt that two distributions five years apart seemed to be the ideal method for distributing property to their children. Here, emphasis is placed on the minimum age that triggers the first distribution.

A Separate Trust designed under this alternative would have instructions something like this:

> After the Common Trust ends, each of my children shall receive an equal share of my property to be held in a Separate Trust.
>
> Pay one-half of each child's Separate Trust to him or her at age twenty-five. If my son or daughter is over twenty-five when this Separate Trust is formed, distribute one-half of its funds immediately. Distribute the other half five years from that date.

A child who is under the age of twenty-five when his or her Separate Trust is created will not receive an immediate distribution. The trustees will care for the child based upon need until the child reaches twenty-five, when one-half will be distributed. The other half will remain in trust and will always be available to the child, based on the trustees' judgments and your instructions, until it is distributed five years later.

What if a child is over twenty-five when the Separate Trust is formed? There will still be two distributions five years apart. A child who is thirty-one when the Separate Trust is formed will receive one-half of the trust property immediately. The other half will remain in the Separate Trust until the child reaches thirty-six.

The unique quality of this alternative is that regardless of your children's ages at your and your spouse's deaths, they will always receive their shares in two distributions five years apart. It specifically addresses the adage that "Age does not a wise person make. Experience does."

15–11 Make four distributions to my children, the first to occur at a minimum age, or immediately if that age has been met, the second through the fourth to occur every five years.

This alternative is similar to alternative 15–10. However, here four distributions are called for rather than just two.

An example of how this alternative is typically designed is:

> After my Common Trust ends, each of my children shall receive an equal share of my property to be held in a Separate Trust.
>
> Pay one-fourth of the Separate Trust funds to my child when he or she is thirty. If my child is over thirty when this Separate Trust is formed, pay out one-fourth immediately. Pay out the balance in three additional equal distributions, each distribution being five years apart.

If your child is twenty-two when the Separate Trust is created, there would be no immediate distribution. The trustees would provide for your child from the trust funds pursuant to your instructions. Your son or daughter would receive one-fourth of the trust property at thirty. At thirty-five, forty, and forty-five, three additional equal distributions would be made. If your child is over twenty-five at the time the Separate Trust is created, say thirty-two, then one-fourth would be paid immediately and the other three installments would be paid at thirty-seven, forty-two, and forty-seven.

In our experience, four distributions would be the upper distribution extreme. There is a drawback in using too many installments. They can become cumbersome and make some children unnecessarily and overly dependent on your trustees' judgments. This does not mean that you can't select a hundred distributions in designing your Separate Trusts, but you should have good reasons for doing so.

15–12 Make multiple unequal distributions, the first to occur at a minimum age, or immediately if that age has been met, the others at stated ages.

Distributions from the Separate Trust do not have to be equal in amounts, nor do they have to be five years apart. If you wish to give a child multiple distributions in different amounts, you can certainly do so. Any distribution can be delayed for as long as you choose.

Following are instructions that illustrate this approach:

After the Common Trust ends, each of my children shall receive an equal share of my property to be held in a Separate Trust.
Pay one-fourth of the Separate Trust to my child when he or she is thirty-five. If my child is over thirty-five when the Separate Trust is created, pay out one-fourth immediately. When my child is fifty, pay out another fourth. When my child is sixty, pay out the balance of the Separate Trust.

This alternative can be adapted to meet a variety of motives. Sometimes it is used to make uneven distributions at set intervals. For example, the clause may be written to state that if your child is over thirty-five when the Separate Trust is created, then one-third of the trust property is paid immediately. The remainder is paid fifteen years later.

This alternative is also used to make as many distributions as you desire; it is not limited to two. It is also used to make other types of uneven distributions, such as three distributions of 20 percent, 30 percent, and 50 percent. This alternative can accommodate almost any motive or desire you may have with respect to designing uneven distributions from your children's Separate Trusts.

15–13 Make no mandatory lifetime distributions to my children, but take care of my children in whatever way they need, whenever they need it from the trust funds.

For some children, especially the disadvantaged, it is better to keep your property in trust for them all their lives. They will never be able to adequately manage money or property. Your trustees will always have to supervise their financial affairs pursuant to your instructions. Other children simply cannot handle finances or wealth. Many parents have shared with us that they have a child who has a proven inability to manage his or her financial affairs.

We have most frequently seen this alternative used to protect a child from himself or herself or from others where there is:

- A learning disability
- A drinking, drug, or gambling problem
- A spouse who is irresponsible or who is perceived to have married for money
- No motivation for the child to achieve and succeed on his or her own
- An irresponsible, spendthrift child who has no regard for responsible financial behavior
- Fear that the child will give his or her inheritance to a cult or sect with little regard for his or her own well-being

The list is endless. If you have a parental situation where you are fearful of putting significant sums of income or property in the hands of a child, this might be the alternative for you.

You would select this alternative if you wish to protect and provide for a particular child for his or her lifetime. You would instruct your trustees to provide for whatever your child needs for his or her education, health, maintenance, and support. You would further instruct your trustees to examine your child's other sources of income and to determine whether or not that income needed to be supplemented from the child's Separate Trust funds.

You can certainly include instructions directing your trustees to give assistance to your child in order to start a business or profession, purchase a home, or any other extraordinary opportunity. Or, if you choose, you could instruct your trustees to provide only the bare necessities for your child's well-being.

Most of our clients who have utilized this alternative have designed it to help and protect their children. They did not design it as a parsimonious vehicle to deprive a child of his or her inheritance.

This Separate Trust alternative generally passes the trust funds directly to grandchildren, other children, or wherever else you wish the funds to go upon

For some children, especially the disadvantaged, it is better to keep your property in trust for them all their lives.

your child's death. Its very structure dictates that you do not give your child the right to dispose of the trust funds on his or her death.

15–14 *Make entirely different distribution patterns for each of my children.*

It is not necessary, or in some cases even desirable, to treat all your children the same when distributing property from their respective Separate Trusts. One of your children may be totally self-sufficient and need no guidance. Another may be just the opposite. You may have different hopes and fears with respect to each of your children. If so, you might wish to address and manifest those hopes and fears by designing different provisions in each of your children's Separate Trusts.

We had a client who immigrated to this country shortly after the Second World War. He was a very successful self-made man who held strong views. "You know," he said to us, "I believe with all my heart that men and women should be treated for what they are, not for what gender they happen to be. I am a real believer in equal rights for all. It's just too bad that it's not that way. Women are not equal with men. They get taken advantage of, and I want to make sure my girls are protected. My boys need protection, but not as much as my girls. My boys are not subject to as much discrimination."

He had us draft his Separate Trusts differently for his sons and his daughters. His design went something like this:

> My sons shall receive two distributions from their Separate Trusts. One-half of the trust property will be distributed when a son is twenty-five or when his Separate Trust is created, whichever is later. The balance will be distributed five years after the first distribution.
>
> Each of my daughters shall receive one-fourth of their property when they reach twenty-five or at the creation of the Separate Trusts, whichever is later. Five years after that distribution, a second distribution will be made of one-third of the remaining trust balance. All of the other trust property will remain in trust for the life of each of my daughters to care for their every need. When a daughter of mine dies, her trust property shall pass to her children.

You may not agree with what this client did, but you have to agree that he was able to set forth his views and make them work in his trust. It was his feeling that women needed more protection than men. Right or not, it was his trust and his property. His Separate Trusts manifested his concerns and fears and addressed them in a constructive and loving manner.

We used this example to demonstrate what you can do with your property if you have particularly strong desires or motives that differ from child to child. If you do, you can fully express all your desires in your Loving Trust planning.

The Separate Trust alternatives that we have discussed are listed below. Please check the alternatives that most closely meet your desires and motives.

Advancement Distributions

( )   15–1   I want my trustees to liberally provide for each of my children.

( )   15–2   I want my trustees to provide only for the health, education, support, and maintenance of each of my children.

( )   15–3   My own motive: _____

_____

_____

_____

Premature Death of a Child

( )   15–4   I want my child's trust property to pass pursuant to my child's directions.

( )   15–5   I want my child's trust property to pass to my child's children or, if none, to my other children.

( )   15–6   My own motive: _____

_____

_____

_____

Distribution Alternatives

( )   15–7   I want my property distributed to my children immediately.

( )   15–8   I want my children to have immediately whatever they want from their Separate Trusts.

( )   15–9   Make two distributions to my children, one-half at a minimum age, the remainder at another stated age.

( )   15–10 Make two distributions to my children, the first at a minimum age, or immediately if that age has been met, the second to occur five years from the date of the first distribution.

( )   15–11 Make four distributions to my children, the first to occur at a minimum age, or immediately if that age has been met, the second through the fourth to occur every five years.

( )   15–12 Make multiple unequal distributions, the first to occur at a

> minimum age, or immediately if that age has been met, the others at stated ages.

( ) 15–13 Make no mandatory lifetime distributions to my children, but take care of my children in whatever they need, whenever they need it from the trust funds.

( ) 15–14 Make entirely different distribution patterns for each of my children.

( ) 15–15 My own motive: _____

_____

_____

_____

Chapter Sixteen

How to Give to Charity

Are you charitable? Do you make regular gifts to your favorite charities? Do you tithe and make love offerings to the Lord's work?

Most of us are charitable. We make meaningful gifts to our church, Christian organizations, and to our communities. We take great joy in participating in God's work. We care about others and involve ourselves in charitable activities by giving of our resources and time.

Giving of our resources and time is a Christian trait. Many of us go about our lives secure in the knowledge that, as Christians, ours is a lifetime of abundance lived under a promise that we cannot out-give God.

Unfortunately, many of us give little or no thought to continuing our charity after we are gone.

A meaningful estate plan using Loving Trust techniques is designed to allow you to give what you have to whom you want, the way you want, and when you want, and to save every last tax dollar and cost possible. It gives you the opportunity to share your hopes, fears, dreams, values, and aspirations with those who survive you. It allows you to plan as if you were there, leaving a little of you in the daily lives of your loved ones.

If your charitable walk with Christ is a regular part of your life, why should it stop on your death? Many of us would be quick to answer that "We will be better off with Him, and our worldly worries and concerns should be left behind us." But what about our worldly love? What about our ability to further His work on earth after we depart?

Our main concern should be to provide for the needs of our loved ones in our absence; to leave instructions for continued good stewardship over the worldly wealth we had entrusted to us. We would ask you to consider that your generosity and the insights that accompany it can survive you; that your Christian stewardship can be just as important after you are gone as it is while you are alive.

Think of the joy you feel when you are able to make a difference through a gift of your resources or time. Is it possible for you to continue to make a differ-

If your charitable walk with Christ is a regular part of your life, why should it stop on your death?

ence through charitable giving after you are gone? Are there ways that will allow your charitable gifts to be monitored after your death to insure the integrity of your stewardship and prudence? The answer to each of these questions is an unqualified "Yes."

Christian giving does not have to stop with death; through His gifts and proper estate-planning techniques, it can survive death and bring help and comfort to those who most need our generosity.

As you read this chapter, ask yourself these questions: "Am I responsible for practicing good stewardship with respect to the resources God has given me both during my lifetime *and* after my death?" "When I'm no longer here, is it important that I see to it that what I've accumulated continues to advance His work?" "When time ceases for me, can I still make investments in eternity, or, as Jesus called it, 'lay up treasures in heaven'?"

Giving to the Lord's work through your planning can be an enormously gratifying experience. By leaving a written testimony of your faith, you can have the satisfaction of knowing that you'll make a positive, perpetual statement about your devotion to Him.

Giving to charity through a properly designed plan can generate significant tax benefits. Christians who do not understand this generally render unto Caesar what is not his due. They leave too little to the Lord's work, and more than their fair share to the IRS. By doing proper planning, you will be able to decrease income, estate and gift taxes, and distribute those savings among family members and His work.

If properly accomplished, your charitable gifts will be fully deductible to your estate. This means that if your estate is in the 55 percent bracket, the Internal Revenue Service will pay 55 percent of every dollar you leave to charity rather than to government largesse. There are also considerable income-tax benefits that you can receive as a result of your after-death charitable planning.

Many of us have assets that have grown substantially in value since we acquired them; assets that, whether by prudent investment, inflation, or a combination of the two, have increased many times over. If we sell these assets during our lifetimes, we'll pay income tax on their appreciation. If we give them to charity without proper planning advice, it is likely that we will not receive the benefit of their full market value under increasingly restrictive income-tax laws. By giving to charity with artful advice, we will benefit both ourselves, family members, and the charities of our choice; we can add His work to our affordable list of planning possibilities.

You do not have to choose between benefiting your family's needs and God's work; you can do both. If you believe in providing for your loved ones and for your Christian ministry, you will want to consider a number of charitable alternatives. To honor God by returning to Him some of what He has given you, and

> You do not have to choose between benefiting your family's needs and God's work; you can do both.

to ensure meeting your loved ones' needs, carefully consider which of these alternatives most closely fits your desires.

16–1   I want to give specific assets to my favorite charities on my death.

16–2   I want to give cash gifts in specific amounts to my favorite charities on my death.

16–3   I want to make cash gifts that represent specific percentages of my estate's value to my favorite charities on my death.

16–4   I want to make cash gifts of specific amounts that cannot exceed a certain percentage of my estate's value to my favorite charities on my death.

16–5   I want to create a subtrust in my Loving trust plan that will make gifts in perpetuity to my favorite charities after my death.

16–6   I want to create a charitable foundation in my Loving trust that will make gifts according to my charitable philosophy to public charities that meet that philosophy.

16–7   I want to give my home or farm to charity, but live in it during my life.

16–8   I want to create a special separate trust for charity to which I can transfer some or all of my assets that will give me a lifetime income, and benefit charities on my death or upon my spouse's death following mine.

16–9   I want to create a special separate trust that will give its income to charity during my life, but which will give its assets to my loved ones on my death.

16–10 I want to purchase life insurance in order to meet my charitable desires.

16–1 I want to give specific assets to my favorite charities on my death.

This motive can be easily accomplished in your Loving Trust if you accurately describe the assets and the charities you wish to receive those assets. Your estate will get a deduction for the fair market value of the assets on your death.

16–2 I want to give cash gifts in specific amounts to my favorite charities on my death.

This is a commonly used technique that can be dangerous. Property values go up and down. Most of us arrive at the value of our specific cash gifts by estimating the value of those gifts as a percentage of the total value of our estate. If the value of our estate changes dramatically, the impact of our gifts will also change dramatically. For example:

> I instruct my Trustee to give my church the sum of $20,000 at my death. At the time I sign my trust, my estate is worth $200,000. I am giving 10 percent of my estate to my church. But, when I pass away ten years later, the value of my estate has doubled to $400,000 so that I have given only 5 percent of my estate to my church.

This can work the other way too. Assume that the country goes through a massive depression subsequent to your planning instructions and that the value of your estate is only $40,000 on your death. In this case, your specific gift of $20,000 would equal 50 percent of your estate!

When making cash gifts of specific amounts, it is important to constantly monitor your estate size in order to make sure that your intentions are precisely carried out.

16–3 I want to make cash gifts that represent specific percentages of my estate's value to my favorite charities on my death.

This technique puts a premium on flexibility. It allows you to increase or decrease the amount of your gifts in direct proportion to the value of your estate. This simple technique can protect your loved ones if the value of your estate goes down and can protect your charities if the value of your estate goes up.

This technique can be used to create escalating or de-escalating amounts based upon the size of your estate. For example:

> I leave my church 10 percent of my estate if its value is between $100,000 and $200,000. If my estate is less than $100,000, I leave my church 5 percent, and if my estate is more than $200,000, I leave it 20 percent of my estate.

16–4 I want to make cash gifts of specific amounts that cannot exceed a certain percentage of my estate's value to my favorite charities on my death.

This technique attempts to combine the first two alternatives into one that will retain the certainty of the first and the flexibility of the second. For example:

> I leave my church the sum of $5000, as long as that amount is equal to or less than 10 percent of my estate. If it is greater than 10 percent of my estate, I leave my church the sum of $2,500.

This technique can also be used to qualify a percentage gift as well. For example:

> I leave my church 10 percent of my estate as long as the amount of my gift is not less than $1000 or more than $20,000.

16–5 I want to create a subtrust in my trust that will make gifts in perpetuity to my favorite charities after my death.

This alternative is used to benefit specific charities by giving them a share of the income that specific property earns each year after your death. For example:

> I leave the sum of $100,000 in trust for the benefit of my church and Christian organizations A and B. Each year after my death my trustees shall distribute all of the income or 5 percent of the trust principal, whichever is greater, equally among these charities.

If you choose to leave your assets in trust, it is important that you make your charitable intentions very clear to your attorney, so that he or she can make sure that your gifts will qualify for all of the available tax benefits.

16–6 I want to create a charitable foundation in my trust that will make gifts consistent with my charitable philosophy to public charities that agree with my philosophy.

This is a powerful alternative that provides great flexibility in continuing your ministry and the Lord's work. It works like this:

> A charitable subtrust is created in your Loving trust that will spring into existence on either your death, your spouse's death following yours, or upon your children's deaths, if you leave them property in trust.

The trust names specific trustees that can be the same as, or different from, the trustees of the other subtrusts in your Loving trust.

Care should be taken to name those trustees who share your charitable interests, and who have the wherewithal and judgment to follow your instructions within the Christian spirit in which they were given.

Oftentimes a combination of individual and professional trustees are selected. Individuals are named for their understanding and commitment to your charitable causes. Professional trustees are selected for their investment and administrative know-how.

It is important that you provide for a succession of trustees in the event of a trustee's resignation, disability, death, or removal.

Your charitable subtrust should contain detailed instructions with descriptions of your charitable purpose and philosophy. Your instructions will give your trustees specific direction as to how they should go about distributing the trust's annual income within your overall charitable philosophy.

If you select this alternative, you may wish to provide a list of charities that would qualify for the trust income if the trust were to come into existence the day you signed it. For example:

If you choose to leave your assets in trust, it is important that you make your charitable intentions very clear to your attorney, so that he or she can make sure that your gifts will qualify for all of the available tax benefits.

I want to leave the sum of $200,000 in trust for the benefit of Christian youth. My trustees shall not be constrained in the organizations they determine shall qualify as long as they are public charities in good standing under the nonprofit organization laws of the United States.

A listing of those charities that would qualify as worthy recipients as of the date of my trust is as follows: *Here you would list those charities that you have been regularly supporting during your lifetime.*

Your instructions should allow your charitable trustees reasonable discretion in what organization they select to receive the trust's income each year. They should also be very clear on what your likes and dislikes are. This is your stewardship, and the clearer you are, the easier your trustees' task will be in carrying them out.

Your attorney will make sure that your trust qualifies under the charitable laws as a qualified charitable foundation, and that all the appropriate safeguards are followed to assure its continued charitable status. He or she will also be sure to put in procedural safeguards so that your trustees cannot do anything that is not totally consistent with your charitable intent and instructions. Your attorney will also add language making it clear that only charities that are qualified under IRS guidelines will be the recipient of gifts from your foundation. This will insure that the gifts will be tax deductible.

With this alternative, that portion of your wealth that you elect to leave to the Lord's work can stay in trust for worldly perpetuity. For each year after your death, the income or a selected percent of the trust principal will be distributed among the public charities that meet your criteria. With this charitable planning technique, you can create a vehicle that will replace you and carry your stewardship forward until Judgment Day.

If your charitable foundation makes more income than the laws require it to pay out, that income can be added to the principal of your trust so that it will continue to grow and make even more income for your charitable beneficiaries.

If you elect this alternative, you will want to make sure that your gift is meaningful enough to justify the time and expense of operating the foundation. If you would like to create a charitable foundation but do not have the necessary resources, consider coupling this alternative with alternative 16–10, "I want to purchase life insurance in order to meet my charitable desires."

16–7 I want to give my home or farm to charity but also live in it during my life.

You can make a gift of your residence and still live in it rent-free during your lifetime. You can also receive any income it generates. On your death it will automatically pass to the charity free of federal gift, estate, or income tax. This is called a gift of a remainder interest.

You will also gain an income-tax advantage by using this alternative. The value of the remainder interest is calculated under IRS tables. That value is deductible on your current income-tax return. If the value of the deduction is greater than your ability to use it, it may be carried forward for five consecutive years as well.

16–8 I want to create a special separate trust for charity to which I can transfer some or all of my assets that will give me a lifetime income.

To accomplish this technique, you will have to create a separate special trust called a Charitable Remainder Trust in addition to your basic Loving trust plan. A Charitable Remainder Trust is a trust to which you make a gift of property. You retain the income from the trust property and designated charities to receive the property after your death. You can name one or more charities, and even reserve the right to change those charities right up to the time of your death.

If you wish, you may even designate that, after your death, the income will continue for your spouse or your children and that your designated charities will only receive the property upon their deaths. The trust can be structured so that your loved ones receive a percentage of the income the trust earns each year or a predetermined percentage of the value of the assets in the trust.

Do not get confused by Charitable Remainder Trusts. In essence they are very simple. The income belongs to you or other family members and the principal belongs to a charity or charities that you name in the trust. Since you are giving away property and retaining only its income, you get a current income-tax deduction based on the value of what you have given up. This value is computed under tables provided by the IRS; it can often generate a very sizeable current income-tax deduction.

16–9 I want to create a special separate trust that will give its income to charity during my life, but which will give its assets to my loved ones upon my death.

This technique is often used by good stewards who are high-income earners; people who do not need any more income in their daily lives and who want to benefit the Lord's work without giving away their children's inheritance. It is called a Charitable Lead Trust.

A Charitable Lead Trust is the opposite of a Charitable Remainder Trust because the income from the trust assets goes to charity while the principal goes to your loved ones after your death. Since the principal of the trust ultimately goes to loved ones, the Charitable Lead Trust's terms for your loved ones will usually be identical to those of your Loving trust. The income earned by the assets in the Charitable Lead Trust is deductible according to a set of fairly complicated rules and restrictions and requires the assistance of your professional advisors.

16–10 I want to purchase life insurance to meet my desires for charitable giveng.

Many charitable Christians lament the fact that they cannot afford to leave more to the Lord's work. They have limited resources and families who will need those resources. These Christians wish they had surplus resources so that they could continue their contributions to the Lord's work.

Life insurance can provide an answer to the "resource dilemma" faced by many Christians. Most of us have purchased life insurance at one time or another to create an estate for the benefit of our loved ones. We have sacrificed to pay premiums in order to create a larger pool of money for our loved ones upon our death.

Life insurance is purchased with a loving motive: We care enough about the future of our loved ones to pay today so our loved ones will benefit tomorrow. Can this same motive and technique be used for the Lord's work? The answer is a resounding "Yes!" We can purchase life insurance that will go directly to charity under most of the techniques we have already discussed.

If this alternative is properly structured by your advisors, the premium payments are fully deductible on your income-tax return. In addition, the death proceeds are not subject to federal estate tax.

For many of us, life insurance may be the only way to continue our gifts of love to His work after we are gone. For others of us, this technique will augment our estates and provide a way for us to say "thank-you" in Christ's name for the countless material blessings we have been given in our business and financial lives.

16–11 My Own Alternative Plan

The essence of estate planning with Loving Trust techniques is giving what you have to whom you want the way you want and when you want. This mandate should carry over to your Christian giving to charity and should free your spirit for even more creative ways of giving.

If you would like to know about charity, you should seek out the advice and counsel of the leaders of your favorite charities. You can be sure that they will do everything possible to assist you and to answer your questions. They will usually be able to provide you with good written materials on the subject and will gladly work with your advisors to assist them in meeting your wishes. There are many excellent texts available on the specifics of charitable giving that your charitable leaders can make available to you. For a general, yet more complete overview than is possible in this chapter, we recommend our chapter on "Giving It to Charity" in *Protect Your Estate*.

The charitable alternatives that we have discussed are listed below, including an alternative that you can use to create your own charitable plan. Take a moment to check the alternatives that most clearly meet your desires.

( )   16–1   I want to give specific assets to my favorite charities on my death.

( )   16–2   I want to give cash gifts in specific amounts to my favorite charities on my death.

( )   16–3   I want to make cash gifts that represent specific percentages of my estate's value to my favorite charities on my death.

( )   16–4   I want to make cash gifts of specific amounts that cannot exceed a certain percentage of my estate's value to my favorite charities on my death.

( )   16–5   I want to create a subtrust in my Loving Trust that will make gifts in perpetuity to my favorite charities after my death.

( )   16–6   I want to create a charitable foundation in my Loving Trust that will make gifts according to my charitable philosophy to public charities that meet that philosophy.

( )   16–7   I want to give my home or farm to charity, but live in it during my life.

( )   16–8   I want to create a special separate trust for charity to which I can transfer some or all of my assets that will give me a lifetime income.

( )   16–9   I want to create a special separate trust that will give its income to charity during my life, but which will give its assets to my loved ones on my death.

( )   16–10 I want to purchase life insurance to meet my desires for charitable giving.

( )   16–11 My own alternative plan: _____

_____

_____

_____

Chapter Seventeen

How to Ultimately Distribute Your Property

Lawyers refer to planning for the ultimate distribution of your property as the "ultimate remainder," a term that sounds somewhat depressing. To many it conjures a picture of Armageddon. That picture is accurate, because that is exactly what ultimate remainder means—Armageddon. We knew a family (a husband, wife, and two children), who left on a trip in their new camper and never came back. They were killed instantly in a tragic and senseless car accident. One moment they were alive and happy, the next, dead.

Losing a family in a single accident is horrifying to think about. But when providing for loved ones, it has to be addressed. What would happen to your property if the worst happened and your entire family was killed in a single catastrophic accident? Your Loving Trust planning should be designed to answer this question. The ultimate remainder is used to pass your property to distant family, friends, or charity if your immediate family doesn't survive you.

When you die without a will or a bona fide will substitute, your state's law determines who will receive your property. This law, called the law of descent and distribution, also applies if your whole family is killed, unless you provide for an ultimate remainder in your trust.

Most states' laws mandate that the next set of living relatives on your family tree will get your property. For example, if your parents are living and you, your spouse, and children all die in a single accident, your parents would receive your property. If your parents are deceased, but you have brothers or sisters, then they will receive your property. Each state has a complex system of determining who is the next relative, or generation of relatives, on the family tree to receive your property.

As you can imagine, the laws of determining heirship can get quite complicated. In law school, we learned about the "Doctrine of the Laughing Heir." It comes from the mental picture that is formed when a poor, working person is

> When you die without a will or a bona fide will substitute, your state's law determines who will receive your property.

informed that a distant relative has died. This heir has never heard of or met the now-deceased relative. At first, the reaction is one of sadness. When that poor heir finds out that there is a sizable inheritance and he is the only legal heir, out comes a whoop of joy as he laughs all the way to the bank.

When we mentioned ultimate remainders to our clients, we elicited some fairly strange reactions. Most people began to fantasize, and even agonize, over what should be done. We have had clients delay signing their Loving Trust plans for months while they contemplated an ultimate remainder.

Ultimate remainders are important. They are a facet of your Loving Trust planning that allows you to control your property even in the worst scenario imaginable. However, the odds of ultimate remainders ever having to be used, at least for most families, are incredibly small. Nevertheless, in good planning everything is possible, and it is necessary that you squarely face this possibility and attempt to resolve it in your own mind.

Determining an ultimate remainder is not so important that it should cause you to delay completion of your entire Loving Trust plan. A Loving Trust plan can be changed at any time with little trouble or expense. If you cannot decide what to do with respect to your ultimate heirs, select one of the following ultimate remainder alternatives and sign it. It is better for you to have your plan in force for you and your immediate loved ones while you are deciding on the specifics of your ultimate remainder than it is to do nothing while you are thinking about a contingency that will most likely never occur.

Over the years we have found that ultimate remainders fall into one of four categories. We have turned these categories into four different alternatives:

17–1   I want one-half of my property to pass to my heirs and one-half of my property to pass to my spouse's heirs under my state's laws.

17–2   I want all my property to pass to my heirs under my state's laws.

17–3   I want my property to pass to certain individuals.

17–4   I want all my property to go to charity.

17–1 I want one-half of my property to pass to my heirs and one-half of my property to pass to my wife's heirs under my state's laws.

This alternative is used when one spouse owns most of a family's property in his or her name. If the whole family were to die in one accident and no ultimate remainder was in effect, then by law all the property would pass only to the owner's relatives. Many people do not like this result. They would rather have their property pass equally to their family and their spouse's family.

Use of this alternative reflects the attitude that even though one spouse is the owner of the marriage's property, the property is treated as if it were owned equally

> **It is better for you to have your plan in force for you and your immediate loved ones while you are deciding on the specifics of your ultimate remainder than it is to do nothing while you are thinking about a contingency that will most likely never occur.**

by each spouse. It is by far the most common ultimate remainder alternative that we see used. Most of our clients have had little or no concern about using state law to determine who will ultimately receive their property.

17–2 I want all my property to pass to my heirs under my state's laws.

This ultimate remainder follows the laws of your state. It simply reaffirms that you wish your property to pass to your heirs as they are determined under state law. This alternative is commonly used if you are single. If none of your Loving Trust beneficiaries is alive at your death, then state law will determine who on your family tree will receive your property.

You may want to use this alternative if you are married and you and your spouse each have property in your own names. Your spouse will leave his or her property to his or her heirs and you will do likewise with yours.

17–3 I want my property to pass to certain individuals.

Rather than rely on your state to determine who your ultimate remainder heirs will be, you may wish to specifically designate them.

Of all the ultimate remainder alternatives, this one presents the most potential for problems. What if the ultimate remainder beneficiaries you name are not alive when you and your immediate family die?

There are two methods of solving this problem. The first is to state that if an ultimate beneficiary dies, the property that would otherwise go to him or her would pass to his or her heirs under state law. This approach assumes that you want your property to follow that beneficiary's family lines.

The second approach is to name several contingent beneficiaries. If a beneficiary is not living when the ultimate remainder is needed, then the other named beneficiaries would share your property equally. Of course, if you ran out of these beneficiaries, your property would pass by your state's laws anyway.

You can see why some people get carried away with ultimate remainder clauses. The "what if" game can be played forever, and a solution never reached. On this one, we urge you to play the odds. Name whom you want to name as your ultimate remainder beneficiaries, decide on backup beneficiaries, and use your state's laws.

17–4 I want all my property to go to charity.

You may decide that if your immediate family cannot have your property, it should go to a charity or charities. You can use any of the alternatives in chapter 16, "How to Give to Charity," if you would like to include a charity as part of your ultimate remainder.

There are five alternatives for an ultimate remainder in the following check-list. These include the four we have discussed, plus an alternative that you can use to create your own motive. Please check the alternatives that most nearly coincide with your desires and motives.

( )   17–1   I want one-half of my property to pass to my heirs and one-half of my property to pass to my spouse's heirs under my state's laws.

( )   17–2   I want all my property to pass to my heirs under my state's laws.

( )   17–3   I want my property to pass to certain individuals.

( )   17–4   I want all my property to go to charity.

( )   17–5   My own motive:

_____

_____

_____

Chapter Eighteen

How to Select Your Trustees

What do my trustees do?" and "How do I select my trustees?" are two questions that we are frequently asked when we lecture on Loving Trust planning. This doesn't surprise us because choosing trustees has traditionally been viewed as one of the most difficult tasks a person must undertake when establishing any type of trust. While choosing your trustees is certainly important and will involve serious deliberation, we suspect that many professionals have so muddied the trustee waters that choosing a trustee is often viewed as a much harder process than it really needs to be. With the answers to these two questions, we believe that you should be capable of selecting your Loving Trust trustees with a minimum of anxiety and deliberation.

What Do My Trustees Do?

Very simply, your trustees will follow your instructions in administering your Loving Trust property for the benefit of your loved ones.

Follow Your Instructions

Your trustees must be able to understand your instructions. Your Loving Trust planning will be only as effective as the breadth and clarity of the instructions you leave and the wisdom that you have employed in selecting your trustees. If your instructions are sparse and ambiguous, your trustees will have to care and provide for your loved ones by relying on their mores and judgments in lieu of yours. Sparse, incomplete, or ambiguous trust instructions will place significant pressure on your trustees. They will either have to substitute their philosophy for yours, or be so careful in not violating what they guess your loving intent to be that they become unresponsive and, as a result, do little to care for your loved ones.

A "bare-bones" trust puts both your trustees and your beneficiaries in an extremely bad position. Your trustees will not be comfortable because they will not have a well-defined path to follow, and they will be justifiably concerned

> Your Loving Trust planning will be only as effective as the breadth and clarity of the instructions you leave and the wisdom that you have employed in selecting your trustees.

about their liability for making incorrect judgments. Your beneficiaries will suffer as a result of the incorrect or unmade decisions of their underdirected "bare-bones" trustees.

We do not believe that you would entrust your loved ones to a baby-sitter without giving that sitter thorough instructions. Regardless of the competence of the baby-sitter, you will not want his or her notions of how to care and provide for others to override yours when it comes to your children. The same is true for your trustees. No matter how good your trustees are, leaving them with incomplete instructions will force them to make decisions that you might not make.

Those people who preach that the only good trust is a short or bare-bones trust are generally misinformed or uncaring.

Most of us spend our entire lives providing for loved ones and accumulating property to promote their comfort and well-being. We sacrifice daily pleasures in order to purchase disability and life insurance. We have a great deal to say when asked about how we discharge our spousal and parental duties. Given a choice, we would not want our loving care and guidance to end abruptly with our death or disability.

You should design your Loving Trust plan with the same thoroughness with which you run your household. If concise instructions accomplish your goals, then by all means use them. But if you opt for brevity only to reduce the length of your Loving Trust documentation, you will shortchange your loved ones. Do not let anyone intimidate you with respect to the length of your trust instructions. As long as they are clear and complete, you will not have to apologize to anyone. Bare-bones planning will make Murphys out of your trustees and a shambles of your loving intentions.

Many people have a great concern, bordering on outright fear, that their trustees will not do what they are supposed to do. We are often asked, "How do I know that my trustees will do any of the things I've instructed them to do?"

A trustee's actions are very highly regulated by the laws of all states and the decisions of their courts. There is an important rule of law that states, "There is no duty known to the law greater than that duty which a trustee owes to the beneficiary of a trust." This is an extraordinarily powerful and far-reaching statement of the law with respect to your trustees' duty to follow your instructions in caring for your loved ones.

Your trustees have an absolute legal obligation to care for your Loving Trust beneficiaries with the highest standards of prudence and care mandated by our entire legal system. They can be brought to task and sued for not following your instructions. The law makes it clear that they are on the hottest of all legal hot seats if they do not act prudently within the instructions you have provided.

Administer Your Loving Trust Plan

While you are alive and well, your Loving Trust property will be under your direct control. There will be absolutely no constraints on you or your Loving Trust property. You will continue—just as you always have—paying your bills, collecting your income, buying and selling things, filing your tax returns, and performing all of the innumerable functions that are part of living in our society.

Upon your death or disability, someone has to take over all these tasks. If you do not have a Loving Trust plan, the probate court will assume them. If you have a Loving Trust plan, your trustees will do so according to your instructions. They will perform all the tasks that are required to care for you, your loved ones, and your property.

How much administration your Loving Trust planning needs will depend on the extent and mix of your trust property and the completeness of your instructions. Your trustees will have to keep records of all their transactions, as well as file all necessary income tax returns. They will be accountable to your beneficiaries for all their actions.

The longest chapter in our trust is devoted to giving our trustees the power to accomplish and implement our instructions. Most bare-bones trust planning skimps or totally ignores these critically important trustees' powers. If your trust does not give your trustees the power or legal authority to accomplish your instructions, then your trustees will have to go to the probate court and get the judge's approval before doing so.

When we were children, our parents would frequently send us to the store to purchase cigarettes for them. The storekeeper would not sell them to us unless we produced a note from our parents saying that it was all right. Think of the storekeeper as the law and the child's notes as the trustee's power portion of your Loving Trust plan. The trustee's power gives your trustee the power to do whatever is necessary to administer your trust pursuant to your instructions.

Every state has laws that automatically grant authority to trustees. These laws attempt to be complete, but in our experience, they are often silent with respect to specific situations. When that happens, your trustees will have to seek the judge's direction. A well-designed Loving Trust plan gives its trustees the power to do everything necessary in order to accomplish its maker's instructions.

We wholeheartedly believe that your Loving Trust plan would be bare-bones without this important language. Please insist on it when working with your lawyer.

> A well-designed Loving Trust plan gives its trustees the power to do everything necessary in order to accomplish its maker's instructions.

How Do I Select My Trustees?

Your trust must always have at least one trustee to operate it. No trust has an autopilot that keeps it on course when there is no one to run it. No matter how many years your Loving Trust planning lasts, it will always have to have at least one trustee who is following and implementing your instructions.

Trustees are named in one of two ways. You can name them or a local judge can name them. If you choose the former, you would name your initial trustees in your trust; you would also provide for their replacement in the event of death, disability, or resignation by prenaming who you would like their replacements or successors to be. Your replacement trustees are referred to as successor trustees.

If you fail to name a trustee, or if for some reason the trustees you do name are unable or unwilling to serve, a local judge will name a trustee for you. When confronted with this situation, the judge almost always names a bank trust department. Our law will not allow a trust to fail because it doesn't have a trustee.

Your trustee selection process should take into consideration different circumstances as you name your trustees. Who should be your trustees when you are alive and well? Do you want different trustees on your disability? What individuals, banks, or trust companies should be your trustees after your death? In the case of individuals, how do you wish to replace them if they die, become disabled, or choose not to serve?

You May Be Your Own Trustee

All our clients wanted to be an initial trustee of their own trust. We recommend that you choose to do so in designing your Loving Trust planning. Many people hold the incorrect view that when they establish a trust they must name an independent trustee to operate it. Many hold the equally incorrect opinion that their trustee must be a bank that will immediately charge a fee for being a trustee in name only.

You may choose to retain a bank or other professional trustee while you are alive. However, if you do, they will charge you a fee if there is property in your trust. You do not have to name an institutional trustee as one of your initial trustees! Professional trustees are usually named as initial trustees only when there is significant property that the maker wants to have professionally managed.

As an initial trustee of your trust, your duties will be minimal. We will explain how you accomplish the few tasks you will have to perform with regard to your trust in chapter 24, "How to Get Property into Your Loving Trust Plan."

You do not have to be anxious about the trusteeship of your trust while you are alive and able to act as your own trustee. It is when you cannot act as a trustee or take care of yourself that your choice of trustees becomes critical.

No trustee will ever be as good at the job as you are. As long as you are healthy and lucid, you should be your own trustee.

> **No trustee will ever be as good at the job as you are. As long as you are healthy and lucid, you should be your own trustee.**

You Need a Co-trustee

We recommend that you name an additional co-trustee of your trust. If you become disabled or die and do not have a co-trustee, there may be no one to take over the trust reins. If that is the case, a local judge will need to get involved in order to pass the reins. Imagine the following:

> You are a spectator at a track meet. A major relay event is about to take place. The gun goes off and the race is on. Your team does well, as each of your first two runners leads his opponent and makes a smooth hand-off of the baton to his teammate. Your third runner expands the lead, but as he attempts to hand the baton to the anchorman he clumsily drops it. Your team's hopes of victory end with the falling baton.

Now, imagine that you are your trust team's lead relay runner. As the initial trustee and lead runner you do well and hold your own, taking care of yourself and your trust property. Suddenly you become disabled or die. It's time to hand the baton to the next runner or trustee. But there's no one there. The baton drops to the earth and will stay there until a local judge picks it up and hands it to a successor trustee named by the court.

Let's assume that you named your spouse as one of your initial co-trustees. While you are alive and healthy, he or she is a trustee in name only. Now let's assume that you become disabled. Your spouse, as your co-trustee, becomes an active trustee. The baton does not drop to the earth.

Your co-trustee spouse will continue to administer your trust following your disability. He or she will hand the baton to your successor trustee if that is what your instructions provide. If your instructions provide for a successor co-trustee, your spouse will offer the baton to and share it with your replacement co-trustee.

If you are single, the same continuity problem presents itself, except that you will not have the convenience of naming a spouse as your co-trustee. You will have to name another family member, good friend, or perhaps one of your professional advisers as your initial co-trustee.

If your trust has at least one other co-trustee, you will not have to be concerned that the probate court will get involved in order for your "trustee baton" to be passed on. If your trust has two or more trustees, you can be assured that it will be continuously administered without any outside or public intervention.

If you decide that you wish to act as your sole trustee, you can certainly do so. The only danger is that if you become disabled or die, there may be a period during which your trust has no trustee. Until someone notifies your new trustee that you are disabled or dead, your trust is not going to be administered for anyone's benefit.

You may have some concern or fear that if you initially name a co-trustee, you may lose some control over your property. If you properly design your Loving

Trust plan, this will not be the case. Your trustees work for you at all times. While you are alive and healthy they must do what you tell them—not more, not less! After your disability or death, the only thing that changes is that they will receive your orders through your Loving Trust instructions rather than directly from you.

You may terminate a co-trustee at any time and for any reason. While you are alive and well, you can maintain complete control of your Loving Trust planning. Naming another trustee does not deprive you of any control. As the maker of your trust, you may hire and fire trustees at will. You can delegate as little or as much authority as you want to another trustee. You can structure your Loving Trust plan so that your co-trustee can only pass the baton to successor trustees on your death or disability.

If you are happily married, it is common practice for you and your spouse to act as co-trustees of your trust. We would certainly recommend that you do so. You should not be concerned that by doing so you will create problems for yourself later on if you have domestic difficulties or go through a divorce. You may terminate your spouse as a trustee at any time, for any reason. During the time your spouse is a co-trustee, he or she does not control your property. Your mate follows your lead and instructions and, as a trustee, awaits your disability or death to pick up the baton and follow your trust instructions.

Both you and your spouse will remain as trustees until subsequent events trigger a change. You will remain a trustee until you become disabled, die, or simply resign. Your spouse will remain a trustee until he or she becomes disabled, dies, resigns, or is terminated.

You need to select your initial co-trustee. You will also need to name who you want to be your successor trustees upon your disability or death and the termination, resignation, disability, or death of one or more of your trustees.

The Characteristics of a Good Trustee

You want to make sure that your successor trustees have the capability of administering your Loving Trust instructions with skill and empathy for your loved ones. Finding a trustee with these characteristics is very difficult and, in most cases, impossible. This is why we almost always recommend that our clients name multiple co-trustees. You can select your trustees so as to blend their talents and virtues in order to create a collective "super-trustee."

"Many hands make light work" and "Two heads are better than one" are adages that apply to trustee selection. When it comes to trustee selection, too many cooks don't spoil the broth, they make for a more efficient kitchen.

In selecting your trustee team you should be looking for individuals or institutions that will:

- Be knowledgeable with respect to beneficiaries.

> **Your trustees work for you at all times. While you are alive and healthy they must do what you tell them—not more, not less!**

- Have a liking or empathy for your loved ones.
- Know how to manage and invest your funds.
- Understand your thinking.
- Be collectible for any mistakes that are made.

If you understand the relative advantages and disadvantages of institutional and individual trustees, the difficulty of your selection task should be greatly reduced.

Using a Bank or Other Trust Department as a Trustee

There is a lot to be said for naming an institutional or professional trustee. Bank trust departments and local trust companies are organized to provide trust services to you and your loved ones for a fee. They have staffs of highly trained and qualified trust specialists who work with trust documents and beneficiaries daily. Professional trustees are thorough and will make objective decisions based on the facts as they see and interpret them. They are usually not influenced by emotional issues that could taint their objectivity.

Institutional trustees are geared to administer trusts. With banks of computers and sophisticated equipment, they keep fabulous records and create and maintain all the accounting information that anyone could reasonably want.

Because institutional trustees are corporations, they cannot die or become disabled. The fact that they will outlive the trusts they administer has been reassuring to many of our clients.

Many of our clients and seminar students have been concerned about the viability of their local banks. While bank failures occur, banks are legally structured and regulated in such a way that their trust customers do not have to fear that their assets will be taken to satisfy claims of the bank's creditors or stockholders. The trust assets of a financial institution are segregated from the assets and liabilities of the institution itself. That means that creditors of the financial institution cannot seize trust assets to satisfy debts.

The main advantage we see in naming a financial institution as one of your trustees is based on a concept that we call "collectibility." Because all trustees are liable to their trust beneficiaries for their mistakes, it is important that they can back up their liability with cash or other assets. If your trustees make a mistake, they are liable for the damages sustained by your trust and its beneficiaries.

If your trustees make a major blunder and lose your trust funds, they would be absolutely responsible for making good their mistake and making your trust whole. But, if they have no money or assets of their own, they obviously cannot make good on their mistake. You won't be able to take "blood from a turnip" just because that turnip is a trustee.

Financial institutions usually have lots of money and other assets. They have the ability to make good on their errors. That is why we frequently recommend that our clients use them as co-trustees in building their trustee team.

There are also disadvantages associated with naming a professional trustee. They may be so objective that they take all the love out of your Loving Trust planning. While their employees most likely will know you, in all likelihood, they will not know your loved ones. And it's unlikely that they will know you and your thought processes well enough to "read between the lines" in your Loving Trust instructions to further infuse your planning with empathy. We are not suggesting that their employees are not caring or capable of emotion. They are simply paid professionals who will predictably "follow the book" in discharging their institutional trustee duties.

There are a few other disadvantages of using a professional trustee. For one thing, there is employee turnover in a trust department. Go-getters on the rise use trust departments as springboards to bigger and better things. This turnover can be disconcerting and disruptive to your loved ones. Furthermore, because of their liability, institutional trustees tend to be conservative at times. They analyze, consider, and have meetings. Their conservatism is also reflected in their investment results. The bad news is that they may not significantly outperform the market. The good news is that they seldom lose or squander their funds. They rightly believe that it is more important to preserve the principal of their trust accounts with modest rates of return than to invest in high-yield, high-risk investments. Many of our clients look at this conservative mandate as a definite and reassuring advantage.

Using Individuals as Trustees

Family members, friends, colleagues, and advisers are often named as Loving Trust trustees. Since they are not professional trustees, they are free from much of the cumbersome apparatus that goes with an institutional trustee. Like institutional trustees, they have their advantages and disadvantages. By their very nature, individual trustees are less likely to be objective than are institutional trustees. Any individual you would select will most likely know you and your family. He or she may even know a great deal about your business and investment affairs. The odds are good that your individual trustees will be subject to beneficiary pressures and that they will be more likely to make decisions based on a touched heart than on an objective and dispassionate intellect.

You have the opportunity, while you are alive and healthy, to share your Loving Trust planning with your individual trustees in order to communicate the essence of your beliefs and desires with respect to your loving instructions. Your trustees can be schooled in becoming knowledgeable about your Loving Trust planning. They should read this book and our book *Protect Your Estate*. They should have an opportunity to read your Loving Trust plan and to ask you and your other advisers any questions they may have.

You can certainly name your lawyer, your accountant, your financial planner, and your life insurance agent as trustees. Any one or more of them may have the knowledge and expertise to act as your trustee. Each of them may also have invaluable knowledge with respect to your business and financial affairs. They may also be close to and have a particular empathy for your family members. It is likely that they will also have a professional objectivity that will temper their emotions. In our opinion, many advisers make excellent co-trustees. They are often an overlooked trustee source.

Almost all individual trustees have some drawbacks. Their lack of objectivity can cause squabbles among your loved ones. They may do too much reading between the lines in your Loving Trust instructions and fail to follow them. They may try too hard and get so close to the trees that they can't see the forest.

Individual trustees—and this is a major drawback—may not be collectible for their mistakes. When a trustee makes a mistake such as failing to follow trust instructions or acting in a negligent manner, that trustee must pay any damages incurred by the beneficiaries. For individual trustees, this means that their personal property can be used to pay for these damages if they have no liability insurance. Does your sister or brother have the resources to make good on his or her mistakes if they lose or squander your trust fund? What about Joe, your best friend and colleague? Does your lawyer, CPA, investment adviser, or trusted life insurance agent have the requisite resources? If they don't, you should think twice about naming one of them as a sole trustee.

If you are thinking that you or your individual trustees can purchase trustee liability insurance, think again. Obtaining liability insurance is a growing problem, and it is next to impossible to purchase liability insurance to cover a trustee. Even if you could purchase it, say from Lloyd's of London, it would be prohibitively expensive. The cheapest coverage that we have found, therefore, is for you to name a large bank or trust company as one of your co-trustees.

By law, institutional trustees must post all their assets as their performance bonds. These professionals usually charge less than 2 percent annually on the value of your property to provide their services. We think of their fee as the cost of an insurance policy, and in today's market it is a bargain.

Individual trustees are mortal. They can go bankrupt or become disabled. They can die prematurely. They can become embezzlers, drug addicts, or alcoholics. They can move to distant lands. They can decline to be your trustee when their time comes to serve.

We recommend that you name more than one individual as your successor trustee. We also recommend that you give serious consideration to naming a professional trustee to serve with them because of the insurance factor professional trustees bring to the table. Name your trustees in teams that will work best for you and your loved ones in the event of your death or disability.

Selecting Your Trustees

While you are alive and well, you should be a co-trustee of your trust. If you are happily married, your spouse, barring exceptional circumstances to the contrary, should be your co-trustee.

If you are single, or you do not choose to name your spouse as your initial co-trustee, you may act as sole trustee, but you would be better advised to name a close family member, friend, colleague, or one of your closest advisers as a co-trustee.

Upon your disability, you should provide for successor trustees as your replacement. You can name any number of successor trustees to act in your stead. They can join your spouse or other individual co-trustee, or they can replace him or her as well as yourself.

It is important that your Loving Trust instructions list who you wish your disability trustees to be. It is equally important that you provide for their replacements in the event they cannot serve.

You must stipulate who your Loving Trust trustees will be following your death. They can be the same as your disability trustees, or they can be entirely different. Do not forget to provide for their replacements. It is critical that your Loving Trust planning always have a succession of trustees to assure continuity in its administration.

In the event a trust fails to provide for replacement trustees or if the replacement trustees named in a trust cannot serve, the trust is still valid. The same is true if replacement trustees refuse to serve, which is their prerogative. (There is no law that forces any trustee named in a trust to actually serve.) "No trust shall fail for want of a trustee" is one of the cornerstones of trust law. Beneficiaries of a trust that does not have a trustee, no matter the reason why, can always go to a court and have the court appoint a trustee. The trust is still valid. Happily, the court only names a trustee; it does not have the right, in most cases, to exercise any control over either the terms of the trust or its beneficiaries.

If you are fortunate, you will have the opportunity to select among several well-qualified individuals in whom you have much faith. But if you are like most of our clients, you will not have this luxury. You may have only one or two individuals you would feel comfortable naming. You may feel uncomfortable naming any individual trustees, in which case you may choose to name an institutional trustee to act when you die or become disabled.

In designing your trustee team, please remember that institutional trustees offer distinct advantages and that they often blend well with individual trustees as co-trustees. By combining an individual trustee with an institutional trustee, you can maximize the advantages and minimize the disadvantages of each. By working together, they can provide expertise, collectibility, and administration tempered with love, empathy, and caring. We highly recommend that you consider such an option.

Before we offer you those alternatives most commonly selected by our clientele over the years, there are still two issues that you need to address when selecting your trustees: control and cost.

Control

Your trustee is controlled by the terms of your Loving Trust instructions and by the law governing trustees in your state. However, when you name a trustee in a Loving Trust plan, you are not going to be around to see that trustee in action. It may be that even with much thought and the best of intentions, you have made a bad choice.

Most of the "bare-bones trusts" that we have reviewed over the years fail to take into consideration that a trustee may do a bad job. These trusts do not have any method for the beneficiaries to terminate a trustee who just isn't doing a very good job.

While you are alive and well, you can terminate any trustee at any time, for any reason. If you are happily married, we suggest that you give this same termination right to your spouse upon your disability or death. If you have adult children, we suggest that you next give these termination powers to a majority of your children. If your children are minors, you should consider giving termination powers to your children's guardians. The same would hold true for a majority of your beneficiaries, regardless of who they are.

By always giving your loved ones the power to terminate a trustee, you continue to control through their control. A trustee doing a poor job ought to be replaced. In fact, if your trustees know they can be terminated they will probably do a better job and be more responsive to the needs and sensitivities of your beneficiaries. If you *do not* wish your beneficiaries to have this right—this is clearly your prerogative—don't give it to them.

You should give your loved ones the power to terminate your trustees only if you place substantial restrictions on its use. We strongly suggest you provide instructions that if a trustee is terminated, that trustee must be replaced with another trustee whom you have named in your Loving Trust instructions.

We are often asked, "What happens if my beneficiaries fire all of the trustees I have named?" Our last line of defense provides that, in that event, an institutional trustee must be named. We know that your beneficiaries will not dupe or unduly take advantage of one of these professionals. We even give our beneficiaries the power to terminate professional trustees, but if they do that, they have to name another institutional trustee as a replacement.

Giving your beneficiaries termination powers, so long as they are coupled with the power to appoint your replacements, is good planning. It provides a system of checks and balances and adds significant flexibility to your Loving Trust planning.

Cost

Your Loving Trust instructions should provide that your individual trustees get paid for acting as your trustees. Trustees work hard and have significant responsibilities and significant personal liabilities.

When it comes to a close friend or family member, many of us will take on responsibility, work hard, and even endure some personal liability, regardless of whether we are paid or not. Somehow, though, this kind of work all too often gets shuffled to the bottom of our stacks, left undone until all of our profitable work is finished. We believe that you will get better performance from your individual trustees if you provide Loving Trust instructions that your trustees are to be paid. If they are family members or friends, they may decline their compensation. The key to such instructions is that they can receive a trustee's compensation if they earn it and elect to receive it.

Every state has laws regulating trustee fees. Some states' laws specify that trustee fees will be a certain percentage of the trust property. Others provide that trustee fees will be governed by whatever fees are customarily charged in a given area or that they will be governed by whatever is reasonable in a particular community.

Institutional trustees always charge a fee for their services. All of them have written fee schedules that they will be happy to provide to you. We believe that their fees are very reasonable for the liability they assume and the work that they do. Most fee schedules provide for higher percentage charges for smaller trusts; many do not take trusts below a certain dollar value. You can readily find out what your bank or trust company charges by asking for their fee schedule.

We have listed those alternatives that are commonly selected by our clients, plus an alternative that you can use to create your own motive. Please take a moment to check the alternatives that most nearly coincide with your desires and motives. For your convenience, we have broken these alternatives into four categories:

1. Naming my trustees while I am alive and well
2. Naming my successor trustees on my disability
3. Naming my successor trustees on my death
4. How my beneficiaries may terminate my trustees

Naming My Trustees While I Am Alive and Well

( )   18–1   I will act as my sole trustee.

( )   18–2   My spouse and I will act as my co-trustees.

( )   18–3   I will act as a co-trustee along with:

( )   18–4   My own alternative:

_____

_____

_____

_____

Naming My Successor Trustees on My Disability

( )   18–5   The following individuals or institutions will act as my successor trustees in the order I have set out (if I do not name an institution, at least two individual trustees must always serve):

( )   18–6   The following individuals or institutions will *replace all my initial trustees* and will act in the order I have set out (if I do not name an institution, at least two individual trustees must serve):

( )   18–7   My initial co-trustee must choose a major institutional trustee to serve as successor co-trustee. When my initial co-trustee can no longer serve, this institutional trustee shall continue to serve alone.

Naming My Successor Trustees on My Death

( )   18–8   My disability trustees will continue to serve. They will be replaced by the following individuals or institutions in the order I have set out (if I do not name an institution, at least two individual trustees must serve):

( )   18–9   My disability trustees will be replaced by the following individuals or institutions in the order I have set out (if I do not name an institution, at least two individual trustees must serve):

( )   18–10 My initial co-trustee must select a major institutional trustee to serve as co-trustee. When my initial co-trustee can no longer serve, this institutional trustee can serve alone.

How My Beneficiaries May Terminate My Trustees

( )   18–11 My spouse can terminate any of my successor trustees. After my spouse is no longer a trustee, a majority of my beneficiaries can terminate any of my successor trustees. When all my successor trustees have either been terminated or they are no longer available, my beneficiaries must choose a major institutional trustee.

( )   18–12 A majority of my beneficiaries can terminate any of my successor trustees. When all my successor trustees have either been terminated, or they are no longer available, my beneficiaries must choose a major institutional trustee.

( )   18–13 My own alternative:

_____

_____

_____

_____

0001-19688-1

Chapter Nineteen

How to Save
Federal Death Tax

Just as most of us have come to accept the old adage that "nothing is certain but death and taxes," many of us have come to believe that death *means* taxes. Fortunately, for most Americans, death taxes, or at least the federal death tax, are not inevitable.

In 1981, the Economic Recovery Tax Act significantly reduced the federal government's taxation of estates. Today the value of an estate, less all its liabilities, must exceed $600,000 to be subject to the federal death or estate tax. Recent statistics show that a mere 3.5 percent of estates pay federal estate tax.

If You Have Not Changed Your Federal
Estate-Tax Planning Since 1981

The Economic Recovery Tax Act so changed the precepts of federal estate- tax planning that any planning you accomplished prior to its enactment is probably totally obsolete. If you did federal estate-tax planning before the Economic Recovery Tax Act was passed, you must change your planning now. Your current planning very likely creates unnecessary federal estate taxes upon your death. This is especially true if you live in Arizona, California, Idaho, Louisiana, Nevada, New Mexico, Texas, Washington, or Wisconsin. The new law has had its greatest impact on these community property states.

We can't emphasize enough the urgency and importance of our request. We have observed that only a small percentage of people with pre-1981 plans have bothered to change their planning. We suspect most people believe that the Economic Recovery Tax Act's benefits automatically apply to them. Unfortunately, the truth is just the opposite. If you want to take advantage of its ample benefits, you need to redo your planning.

> . . . for most Americans, death taxes, or at least the federal death tax, are not inevitable.

How Big Does Your Estate Have to Be?

For tax to be one of your planning motives, the value of all your property, including your life insurance proceeds—reduced by the value of all your debts—must approach or exceed $600,000. If you are married, the combined net value of your and your spouse's property must approximate $600,000 to warrant federal estate-tax planning.

Federal Estate-Tax Planning for Single People

If you are single and you wish to do federal estate-tax planning, you are faced with a very difficult task. The federal government does not give any special federal estate-tax breaks to single people. Most federal estate-tax planning done for singles deals with sophisticated lifetime gifts, special life insurance trusts, and other complex measures beyond the scope of this book.

We strongly recommend that you concentrate on designing your Loving Trust planning, as explained in chapter 21, "How to Plan If You Are Single," and that you work closely with a good tax lawyer. We would also recommend that you read *Protect Your Estate*. We wrote this text primarily with larger estates in mind. It will provide you with estate-tax planning strategies by acquainting you with many of the finer tax-planning points.

Given the difficulty of planning for a single person's federal death taxes, most of our single clients ultimately opted to purchase considerable amounts of additional life insurance to cover their tax liability. In effect, they viewed federal estate tax as a liability that could only be covered or offset by adding more money to their estate.

If you are single and wish to cover your federal estate-tax liability with additional life insurance, you should be absolutely sure that you work closely with your lawyer and your insurance agent in dovetailing your insurance into your Loving Trust planning; absent good planning, your life insurance will be subject to federal estate tax. A little later in this chapter, we will share an effective way to purchase life insurance by using an irrevocable life insurance trust so that it is free from federal estate tax.

The Unlimited Marital Deduction

If you are married when you die, the federal government gives your spouse a significant tax break called the unlimited marital deduction. If you leave your property to your spouse—it does not matter whether you do so outright or in trust—it will *not be subject to federal estate-tax.*

In its simplest form, this is how the unlimited marital deduction works:

Esther Feld is wealthy. She decides to leave all her property outright to her husband, Fred, at her death. When she dies, none of her property—regardless of its value—will be subject to the federal estate tax, as long as she and Fred are still married at the time of her death.

The marital deduction allows you to pass unlimited amounts of property to your husband or wife free of federal estate tax. This remains true even if you wish to leave your property to your spouse with severe restrictions placed on its use. The only requirement you must meet in order to qualify for this wonderful tax benefit is that you must give your spouse the right to all the income your property produces each year.

Esther left all her property to her husband, Fred, in trust. Her trust instructions could have stated that Fred was to receive only the interest, dividends, and other income that Esther's trust property produced each year.

Even with Fred's receiving this meager benefit from his wife's inheritance, it would qualify for the unlimited marital deduction. Esther's property would not be liable for federal estate tax.

The only right you must give your husband or wife with the property you leave him or her in order to qualify for the unlimited marital deduction is the right to the income from that property, paid at least annually, for the rest of his or her life.

You may certainly choose to be more liberal in providing for your spouse and still have your inheritance qualify for this tax bonanza. The law only requires that your spouse annually receive the income.

The property that you leave your spouse will, however, be subject to federal estate tax when your spouse dies. The reason that the federal government is so kind to married couples is that they know that if the value of a husband and wife's property is large enough, there will eventually be an estate tax. Like circling vultures, the federal tax collectors know it is only a matter of time before they can feed.

Your $600,000 Tax-Free Amount

Every person gets a $600,000 tax-free amount that they can pass to loved ones. If this amount is not wisely used, it can be "lost" and tax paid where it doesn't have to be paid. For example:

Let's assume that Esther leaves her entire estate of $1,000,000 directly to Fred and that Fred has no property of his own. He would receive the money tax-free because of the unlimited marital deduction. But keep in mind that Esther did not use her $600,000 tax-free amount.

However, on Fred's subsequent death, his federal estate tax on the $1,000,000—

even after his $600,000 tax-free amount is used to offset it—would be $153,000!

Had Esther properly planned her tax strategy and used her $600,000 tax-free amount, there would absolutely be no federal estate tax on either her death or Fred's. Esther could have designed her Loving Trust plan something like this:

My Loving Trust plan will take care of me first. When I die, it will create two subtrusts. One will be a Family Trust for our children. I will leave my tax-free amount of $600,000 to this Family Trust.

I want the remainder of my property to go to Fred in a Pocketbook Trust. He can have all the income and all the trust property for whatever he wants. My trustees shall take care of him if he is ill or disabled. He can leave what is left in this Trust to whomever he wants on his death. If he doesn't, its remaining funds will go to my Common Trust for our children.

A diagram of this Loving Trust plan would look like this:

"Me" Trust
$1,000,000

Pocketbook Trust   Family Trust
$400,000 $600,000

Esther's Loving Trust plan totally avoids federal estate tax because it fully uses the unlimited marital deduction and her $600,000 tax-free amount. It accomplishes this because:

All the property in Fred's Pocketbook Trust qualifies for the unlimited marital deduction.

The $600,000 in the Family Trust is subject to federal estate tax, but is offset by Esther's $600,000 tax-free amount.

When Fred dies, the property in the Pocketbook Trust will be more than offset by Fred's $600,000 tax-free amount. The $600,000 in the Family Trust will not be subject to tax because it was subject to federal estate tax on Esther's death.

Esther's federal estate-tax planning utilized both her and Fred's tax-free amounts in addition to Esther's unlimited marital deduction. Her situation clearly demonstrates that despite the lure of the unlimited marital deduction, it is better to use Pocketbook and Family Trusts than it is to leave everything directly to your spouse.

Your Pocketbook and Family Trusts

If you are married and one of your desires is to achieve federal estate-tax planning, your Loving Trust plan will always have a Family Trust and one or two Pocketbook Trusts.

Whether your Loving Trust has one or two Pocketbook Trusts will be determined by your non-tax motives, and will, to a large degree, depend upon the value of your property. If the value of your property exceeds $1,200,000, you should consider using two Pocketbook Trusts. If the value of your property lies somewhere between $600,000 and $1,200,000, you will usually utilize a single Pocketbook Trust for your spouse's benefit.

Whether you have one or two Pocketbook Trusts in your Loving Trust plan is irrelevant for federal estate-tax savings purposes. One Pocketbook Trust and one Family Trust will always maximize federal estate-tax savings for married couples. The number of Pocketbook Trusts that you create will be based solely on your non-tax motivations.

Non-Tax Motives

Even though reducing federal estate tax is one of your primary motives, your non-tax motives will totally influence the Pocketbook and Family Trust alternatives you ultimately select.

> Let's assume that Esther has $2,000,000 and that Fred is still penniless. Let's further assume that the couple's state law mandates that a spouse has an absolute right to half of a deceased spouse's property. In our situation, Fred would have legal right to $1,000,000 of Esther's property at her death.
>
> Esther has confided to us that she loves Fred and her children, and she wishes to leave everything she owns to them. She also desires to avoid every last dollar of federal death tax possible. Esther also shares her concern that she doesn't want Fred to disinherit the children because he is taken in by another woman or because of some other equally aberrant behavior. Given Esther's desires, we would recommend two Pocketbook Trusts and a Family Trust within Esther's Loving Trust:
>
>> Esther's Family Trust would have her tax-free amount of $600,000 in it. It would provide for Fred and their children, but would remove Fred as a beneficiary if he remarried. Its funds would automatically pass to the children's Common Trust—free of federal estate tax—on Fred's subsequent death.
>>
>> Esther's first Pocketbook Trust would be funded with the amount Fred would be entitled to under state law, in this case, $1,000,000. Its instructions would provide that he could have whatever he wanted, whenever he wanted it. It would be tax-free because of Esther's unlimited marital deduction.
>>
>> Esther's second Pocketbook Trust would be funded with $400,000. It would give Fred all its income at least annually. It would also instruct the trustees to provide for Fred's needs out of the principal of the trust so long as he didn't remarry. It would further provide that its funds automatically

One Pocketbook Trust and one Family Trust will always maximize federal estate-tax savings for married couples.

pass to Esther's Common Trust for the children on Fred's subsequent death. It would also be tax-free because of the unlimited marital deduction (all it has to give Fred is its annual income).

Esther used two Pocketbook Trusts because they served her desires better than just one. She used the first to liberally provide for Fred with what he was otherwise entitled to under state law. She created the second to provide for him on a more regulated basis in order to protect their children's inheritance.

Given Esther's desires, you can see how your non-tax motivations will greatly affect the design of your Loving Trust tax strategies.

The instructions you choose to place in these various trusts will be determined by the alternatives you selected in chapter 12, "How to Provide for Your Spouse," and chapter 13, "How to Provide for Your Family."

Allocation of Your Property Between Your Subtrusts

Federal estate-tax planning is primarily concerned with how much of your property you place in your Family Trust and how much you place in your respective Pocketbook Trusts. It is purely a numbers game. The amounts that you will allocate between these various subtrusts will be based on the size of your estate and your non-tax desires.

As we set out the various allocation alternatives for estates between $600,000 and $1,200,000, you will see you have only a few choices.

Please keep the following concepts in mind as you review these allocation alternatives:

- If you are married and you die before your spouse dies, all the alternatives will totally eliminate federal estate tax on your death.
- State and local death taxes may not be eliminated. Your lawyer may have to make modifications to your Loving Trust plan to reduce or eliminate them.
- There will be a federal estate tax due on your spouse's subsequent death if the combined value of your estates exceeds $1,200,000.
- For easy calculation purposes, we are assuming that the value of your Loving Trust property does not increase after your death.

Federal estate-tax planning, although at times complex, can usually be easily accomplished by most lawyers with the help of an accountant, a sharp insurance agent, or a financial planner who is familiar with federal estate-tax planning. Our goal is to give you an overview of the process, to acquaint you with the concepts, and to provide you with the basic planning alternatives.

Our clients have often been concerned about the specifics of how their property will be allocated among their various subtrusts. "Will our home go in the

Family Trust or in one or the other of the Pocketbook Trusts? What about my bank accounts, retirement benefits, and other property? In which trust will my life insurance proceeds be placed?"

The answer to all these questions is that your trustees, after your death, will make all those decisions by taking into consideration your family members' respective needs and the federal estate-tax laws at that time. In chapter 6, "Our Loving Trust Plan," we provided that our residences should be placed in Pocketbook Trust One. Other than that, we left the process of allocating specific property to our trustees, and so should you.

The Value of My Estate Is Between $600,000 and $1,200,000

If the value of all your property is between $600,000 and $1,200,000, you should most likely create a single Pocketbook Trust to accompany your Family Trust, although you can create two under certain circumstances. We have already discussed the instructions that you should place in these respective trusts in chapter 12, "How to Provide for Your Spouse," and chapter 13, "How to Provide for Your Family."

If saving federal estate tax is one of your primary desires and the value of your estate is between $600,000 and $1,200,000, there are four alternatives for allocating your property between your Pocketbook and Family Trusts. Because of the complexity of federal estate-tax planning, we do not suggest that you invent your own alternative in this area.

Following are the motives that our clients have commonly selected over the years. Each is designed to put different amounts in your different subtrusts in order to avoid federal estate tax. Which alternative you select will depend upon your own desires and motives.

19–1　I want my first $600,000 to pass to my spouse in my Pocketbook Trust and the remainder to go to my Family Trust.

19–2　I want up to my first $600,000 to pass to my Family Trust and the remainder to go to my spouse in my Pocketbook Trust.

19–3　I want my property equally divided between my Pocketbook and Family Trusts.

19–4　I want my spouse to receive whatever he or she is entitled to under our state law, with the next $600,000 of my property passing to my Family Trust, and whatever is left—if any—passing to my Pocketbook Trust Two.

19–1 I want my first $600,000 to pass to my spouse in my Pocketbook Trust and the remainder to go to my Family Trust.

This alternative uses your unlimited marital deduction and both your and your spouse's tax-free amounts to save federal estate tax. There is no federal estate tax on the $600,000 going to your Pocketbook Trust because of your unlimited marital deduction. On your spouse's subsequent death, this $600,000 would also be offset by his or her tax-free amount. There is no tax on the Family Trust because of your tax-free amount. On your spouse's subsequent death, whatever is left in the Family Trust will pass to your children free of federal estate tax.

A few allocation examples should help you to see how this alternative works:

If you have $600,000 of property, it would all go to your Pocketbook Trust. If you have less than $600,000 it would do likewise.

If your property is valued at $700,000, the first $600,000 would pass to your Pocketbook Trust and $100,000 would go to your Family Trust.

If your property is valued at $900,000, $300,000 would go to your Family Trust; at $1,100,000, $500,000 would go to your Family Trust; at $1,200,000, $600,000 would pass to your Family Trust.

This alternative is commonly selected by people who love their spouses and want them to have and control as much of their property as possible, while still achieving federal estate-tax planning. By selecting this alternative you would be emphasizing your desire to provide liberally for your spouse.

19–2 I want up to my first $600,000 to pass to my Family Trust and the remainder to go to my spouse in my Pocketbook Trust.

This alternative also uses your unlimited marital deduction and both your and your spouse's tax-free amounts to save federal estate tax. In fact, it is exactly the same as alternative 19–1 except that it funds your Family Trust before your Pocketbook Trust.

It is commonly selected by people who love their spouses but who are concerned that their spouses' subsequent behavior or mistakes may squander their children's inheritance. It assures you that your children will be cared and provided for with your $600,000 tax-free amount.

This alternative is often used in community property states. In a community property state, one-half of the property acquired in a marriage is owned by each spouse. By state law, each spouse has full control over his or her half and may dispose of this property in any manner.

If you live in a community property state, your share of the community property, plus all your sole and separate property, is yours to dispose of as you see fit. Since your spouse already owns one-half of your marital property, you would allocate the first $600,000 of your community share to your Family Trust. This will maximize your federal estate-tax savings and assure that your children are provided for with your tax-free amount.

19–3 I want my property equally divided between my Pocketbook and Family Trusts.

This alternative also uses your unlimited marital deduction and both your and your spouse's tax-free amounts to save federal estate tax. It divides your property equally between your Pocketbook and Family Trusts. As a result, your Pocketbook fund will be free of tax because of your unlimited marital deduction. Your Family Trust fund will avoid federal estate tax up to your $600,000 tax-free amount. On your spouse's subsequent death, the first $600,000 in the Pocketbook Trust would be tax-free because of his or her tax-free amount; the Family Trust funds will automatically pass tax-free to your children's Common Trust. ·

In "Our Loving Trust Plan" in chapter 7, we wanted at least half of our property to pass to our children. This is not an uncommon motive. Many of our clients have expressed the desire that their children receive at least half of their property. People who express this desire usually view the marriage as a partnership, a fifty-fifty proposition. They express their love for their spouse and children equally, and wish to leave their property to them equally. If that is your desire, this alternative may be for you.

19–4 I want my spouse to receive whatever he or she is entitled to under our state law, with the next $600,000 of my property passing to my Family Trust, and whatever is left—if any—passing to my Pocketbook Trust Two.

If you use this alternative you may have to create two Pocketbook Trusts if the value of your property—after your spouse's state-mandated share is placed in Pocketbook Trust One—exceeds your $600,000 tax-free amount. Here is how this happens:

You have $1,000,000 of property. Under your state law, your spouse is entitled to one-third of your property, or $333,333. You place that amount in your Pocketbook Trust One.
You would like your remaining $666,667 to go into your Family Trust. Unfortunately, this is $66,667 more than your tax-free amount. If you put it all in your Family Trust, $66,667 will be subject to federal estate tax.
To avoid this tax, you create a second Pocketbook Trust for the remaining $66,667. Your instructions in Pocketbook Trust Two are very restrictive. They give your spouse only the Trust's annual income for his or her lifetime (you'll recall that this is the minimum requirement for the unlimited marital deduction).

Upon your spouse's death there will be no federal estate tax, just as there wasn't any at your death. The $333,333 in Pocketbook Trust One plus the $66,667 in Pocketbook Trust Two are offset by your spouse's tax-free amount. The property in your Family Trust automatically passes to your children tax-free.

This alternative will automatically adjust for your state's law. You should consider selecting it if you desire to give your spouse the absolute minimum amount of your property possible under your state's law.

The Value of My Estate Is Over $1,200,000

If you wish to reduce your federal estate tax, and the value of your property is over $1,200,000, you will always allocate $600,000 worth of your property to your Family Trust on your death. This will assure that your $600,000 tax-free amount will be used. It also keeps that sum, plus any increase in its value, out of your spouse's estate on his or her subsequent death.

If the value of your property is over $1,200,000, your family will pay some federal estate tax on your spouse's subsequent death. If your desire is to ultimately pass your property to your children or other loved ones, there is no way to avoid second-death federal estate tax. This certain tax reality can be illustrated as follows:

John Miller has $1,500,000. He is bound and determined to totally avoid federal estate tax while still totally providing for his wife, Mary Kay, and his three children.

He was exasperated when we told him that the best tax planning we could do, while still meeting his other desires, was to have his children pay $153,000 of tax after his and Mary Kay's deaths. He challenged us to prove it.

We explained that there were only so many ways he could allocate his property within his trust:

He could leave all $1,500,000 to Mary Kay. There would be no tax on his death because of the unlimited marital deduction. On Mary Kay's death, tax would have to be paid on the $900,000 left after setting off Mary Kay's tax-free amount.

He could leave half of his property, or $750,000, to his respective Pocketbook and Family Trusts. On his death that would generate an immediate tax on the $150,000 left to the Family Trust over his tax-free amount.

He could leave his $600,000 tax-free amount to his Family Trust and $900,000 to his Pocketbook Trusts. That would only generate tax on Mary Kay's subsequent death on the $300,000 over her tax-free amount or $153,000, by far the best tax alternative.

We told John what we have told countless clients. "We can keep all your property free of federal estate tax on your death if your spouse survives you. We can keep your Family Trust and $600,000 of your spouse's tax-free amount free of federal estate tax on his or her subsequent death. Any funds in addition to that $600,000 tax-free amount will be liable for federal estate tax."

Popular federal estate-tax planning strategies involve deferring your taxes to your spouse's subsequent death and making sure that your $600,000 tax-free amount immediately funds your Family Trust.

People with property valued at over $1,200,000 should consider using two Pocketbook Trusts. The larger your estate, the more likely it is that you would do so. You would elect to use two Pocketbook Trusts in order to better control what happens to your property subsequent to your death. The case of Earl and Debbie illustrates such a need:

> Earl Johnson has worked hard in a real estate development career and has amassed property worth $2,000,000. He loves his wife, Debbie, and his three children. He wants Debbie to be fully cared for after his death. He also wants to make sure that his children will receive half of his property on her death.
>
> In achieving his objectives, Earl would first allocate his $600,000 tax-free amount to his Family Trust. As you know by now, it will be tax-free on both his and Debbie's deaths. Because he loves Debbie and views that half of his property is attributable to her efforts, he leaves $1,000,000 to her in his Pocketbook Trust One, with liberal instructions for her care.
>
> Earl leaves the balance of his property, $400,000, to his Pocketbook Trust Two. Debbie will receive all its income and whatever amounts of the property itself as will be needed to care for Debbie.
>
> On Debbie's subsequent death, all the funds in both Earl's Pocketbook Trust Two and his Family Trust will automatically pass to his children in his Common Trust. Please note that the sum of the two is $1,000,000; half of Earl's property will pass to his children just as he desired.

A second Pocketbook Trust is used both to qualify for the unlimited marital deduction and to control where and how that property is distributed. In most cases it is used to make sure that your children receive its funds on your spouse's subsequent death.

The following alternatives for allocating your property to your respective Pocketbook and Family Trusts are designed to avoid federal estate tax on your death and to minimize it on your spouse's subsequent death. Whether you use one or two Pocketbook Trusts will depend upon your "people motives" rather than technical tax motives.

19–5   I want to save federal estate tax and thereafter care for my spouse as much as possible with a single Pocketbook Trust.

19–6   I want to save federal estate tax; I also want to take care of my spouse

Popular federal estate-tax planning strategies involve deferring your taxes to your spouse's subsequent death and making sure that your $600,000 tax-free amount immediately funds your Family Trust.

and to be assured that my children will have one-half of what's left of my property on my spouse's subsequent death.

19–7 I want to save federal estate tax, while giving as much of my property to my children as possible.

19–5 I want to save federal estate tax and thereafter care for my spouse as much as possible with a single Pocketbook Trust.

Since your motives indicate that you will not be particularly concerned with what your spouse does with your property subsequent to your death, you will need only one Pocketbook Trust under this alternative.

This alternative first allocates $600,000 to your Family Trust and then places the balance of your property in your spouse's Pocketbook Trust.

If the value of your property is $2,000,000, this alternative would be diagrammed as follows:

Pocketbook Trust	Family Trust
$1,400,000	$600,000

This alternative is commonly used by people without children and by those who have extraordinarily good marriages and faith in their spouses.

19–6 I want to save federal estate tax; I also want to take care of my spouse and to be assured that my children will have one-half of what's left of my property on my spouse's subsequent death.

This is the alternative that we chose in our Loving Trust plan in chapter 7. It first allocates your $600,000 tax-free amount to your Family Trust. It then allocates one-half of your total property to your Pocketbook Trust One. The balance of your property will go to your Pocketbook Trust Two. This is the alternative that Earl and Debbie Johnson chose in our earlier example.

If your property is valued at $2,000,000, this alternative can be diagrammed as follows:

Pocketbook Trust One	Pocketbook Trust Two	Family Trust
$1,000,000	$400,000	$600,000

Upon your spouse's subsequent death, the funds in Pocketbook Trust One will pass to whomever your spouse leaves them to. If he or she neglects to do so, they will automatically pass to your children's Common Trust. All your funds in Pocketbook Trust Two and all your Family Trust property will automatically pass to your children's Common Trust on your spouse's subsequent death. And there you have it, at least one-half of your remaining property—$1,000,000—will be locked-in for the benefit of your children.

19–7 I want to save federal estate tax, while giving as much of my property to my children as possible.

Two Pocketbook Trusts and a Family Trust are created by this alternative. It first allocates the amount required by your state's law to your Pocketbook Trust One. It then places your $600,000 tax-free amount in your Family Trust. The balance of your property is placed in your Pocketbook Trust Two.

This alternative is exactly the same as its counterpart for estates between $600,000 and $1,200,000. If your state's law mandates that your spouse receive one-half of your property, and you have $2,000,000, it would be diagrammed as follows:

Pocketbook Trust One	Pocketbook Trust Two	Family Trust
$1,000,000	$400,000	$600,000

If your state's law mandates that your spouse receive one-third of your property, it would be diagrammed like this:

Pocketbook Trust One	Pocketbook Trust Two	Family Trust
$666,667	$733,333	$600,000

Your spouse would receive only the amount required by your state's law in Pocketbook Trust One and only the income from Pocketbook Trust Two. He or she would not receive any benefits from your Family Trust. At your spouse's death, all the funds in Pocketbook Trust Two and your Family Trust will automatically pass to your children's Common Trust. Should your spouse neglect to dispose of Pocketbook Trust One's funds, they, too, would automatically pass to your children's Common Trust.

Because the complexities of providing for loved ones increases as your estate grows larger, it is imperative that you seek the services of a lawyer who understands federal estate-tax planning. Chapters 23, "How to Find a Loving Trust Lawyer," and 24, "How to Work with and Pay Your Lawyer," will be of great help to you in this endeavor. You should also utilize the services of your other advisers; chapter 26, "How to Get Your Advisers Involved to Save Your Time and Money," will tell you how to do just that.

Protect Your Estate explains sophisticated federal estate-tax planning techniques in nontechnical terms. We suggest that you read it if you wish to get a better grasp of how you can reduce your federal estate taxes.

The Irrevocable Life Insurance Trust

A very common estate-tax planning technique is for a single person with an estate worth over $600,000 or for a husband and a wife whose combined estates are worth over $1,200,000 to purchase life insurance to pay off their federal estate-tax liability. This very logical approach, however, doesn't work very well.

Most people are shocked to learn that life insurance is subject to the federal estate tax. They believe that life insurance escapes federal estate tax and passes to loved ones intact. This confusion likely begins with a discussion of income tax because it is true that life insurance is *income-tax-free*, but it is not generally federal estate-tax–free. For married couples, this confusion is then reinforced with the belief that the unlimited marital deduction somehow magically insulates their children and grandchildren from the devastating effects of the federal estate tax. Whatever the reason for this confusion, a great many Americans leave far less life insurance proceeds than they pay for as a result of not taking into account the ravages of the federal estate tax.

If you have a taxable estate, anywhere from 37 percent to 55 percent of your life insurance proceeds will be paid out to the federal government in the form of federal estate tax. *You actually have far less insurance than you think you have. Because of that, you may well be paying 37 percent to 55 percent more for your life insurance coverage than you should be paying.*

> Jay and Laura planned using Loving Trust planning techniques. When Jay died, no federal estate tax was due. However, on Laura's death, her taxable estate, without life insurance proceeds, was $1,000,000. The federal estate tax on $1,000,000 is $153,000.
>
> Laura owned a life insurance policy on her life with a face value of $250,000. This was added to her estate, so that her taxable estate, for federal estate tax purposes, was $1,250,000. The federal estate tax due was **not** $153,000—it was $255,000. The life insurance that Jay and Laura thought was worth $250,000 was really worth only $147,500. A whopping 41 percent of the life insurance was lost to federal estate tax.

There is a special type of trust available that can keep life insurance death proceeds free from federal estate tax, and it is an integral part of Loving Trust planning for those people who have taxable estates. This trust is called an *irrevocable life insurance trust*.

An irrevocable life insurance trust is specifically designed to be the owner and the beneficiary of life insurance policies. When the life insurance proceeds are paid into the trust upon the death of its maker, the proceeds are *not included* in the maker's estate for federal estate-tax purposes. As a result, 100 percent of the life insurance proceeds can be used for the benefit of loved ones pursuant to the maker's instructions.

Jay and Laura used Loving Trust planning techniques, including an irrevocable life insurance trust. When Jay died, no federal estate tax was due. However, on Laura's death, her taxable estate, without life insurance proceeds, was $1,000,000. The federal estate tax due was $153,000.

Laura's life insurance was owned in an irrevocable life insurance trust. It had a face value of $250,000. All of the proceeds were free from federal estate tax. A total of $102,500 of federal estate tax was saved.

An irrevocable life insurance trust is a sophisticated planning device. It has been approved by the Internal Revenue Service and the courts, so it is not a wild gimmick. It is a legitimate planning vehicle and ought to be a part of the Loving Trust planning of anyone who has a taxable estate and who either has life insurance or has the ability to purchase life insurance.

If you think that you are a candidate for this type of planning, you should seek out an attorney and a life insurance agent who are intimately familiar with irrevocable life insurance planning. An irrevocable life insurance trust has many technicalities that must be strictly followed so that the trust will meet your planning objectives, be flexible, and be drafted and maintained in such a way that it will keep your life insurance proceeds federal estate-tax free. Done correctly, an irrevocable life insurance trust is one of the best estate-tax planning techniques there is.

If you or your estate planning advisers would like to know more about the irrevocable life insurance trust, we have written a comprehensive book on the subject entitled *The Irrevocable Life Insurance Trust*. It is published by Loving Trust Inc. and can be ordered through your local bookstore.

The tax allocation alternatives that we have discussed for estates between $600,000 and $1,200,000 and those over $1,200,000 are listed below so that you may check that alternative that most clearly meets your desires and motives.

> **Done correctly, an irrevocable life insurance trust is one of the best estate-tax planning techniques**

The Value of My Estate Is Between $600,000 and $1,200,000

()   19–1   I want my first $600,000 to pass to my spouse in my Pocketbook Trust and the remainder to go to my Family Trust.

()   19–2   I want my first $600,000 to pass to my Family Trust and the remainder to go to my spouse in my Pocketbook Trust.

()   19–3   I want my property equally divided between my Pocketbook and Family Trusts.

()   19–4   I want my spouse to receive whatever he or she is entitled to under our state law, with the next $600,000 of my property passing to my Family Trust, and whatever is left—if any—passing to my Pocketbook Trust Two.

The Value of My Estate Is Over $1,200,000

( )   19–5   I want to save federal estate tax and thereafter care for my spouse as much as possible with a single Pocketbook Trust.

( )   19–6   I want to save federal estate tax; I also want to take care of my spouse and to be assured that my children will have one-half of what's left of my property on my spouse's subsequent death.

( )   19–7   I want to save federal estate tax, while giving as much of my property to my children as possible.

Chapter Twenty

How to Leave Your Personal Property

You might have some very special personal possessions that you wish to provide for in your Loving Trust planning. Jewelry, collections, keepsakes that have been in the family for generations, or even personal papers or diaries are just some of the items our clients have been particularly concerned about when planning for their loved ones. Or you may want to leave your personal property in a special manner, even though it may not be of special value or significance. In either case, your Loving Trust planning can be designed to pass your personal property to whom and in what way you want.

Maintaining control of personal property is exceedingly difficult for people who choose to do will planning. The legal complexities and requirements of wills make them inconvenient and expensive methods for passing personal property. Here's why.

Before we began practicing law, we knew a woman named Marian who had several pieces of jewelry and some antique furniture that had been in her family for generations. It was very important to Marian that certain members of the family inherit these heirlooms so they could be passed from generation to generation. Marian had a will that spelled out exactly which family member would get which item of jewelry or furniture. Unfortunately, Marian constantly kept changing her mind as to who should get what. Each time Marian wanted to make a change, she would go to her lawyer's office and have him make a codicil to her will. On each occasion, she would have to go through all the formalities of changing her will, a process that is complex and time-consuming. It is also expensive. The lawyer had to charge Marian for the time it took to make the changes. Marian was not happy with the expense, and her lawyer wasn't happy with what he viewed to be unimportant nuisance work.

Making Changes to Your Trust

A revocable living trust is a very simple document to change. It does not require complex legal formalities, nor does it require a trip to the lawyer's office each time a change is necessary.

A change to a living trust is called an amendment. You only need to make your changes in writing. That is all there is to it. This simple process effectively amends your living trust.

There are dangers in being able to make changes so easily. Changes in the technical provisions of your trust may invalidate other provisions or so confuse your trustees as to make your trust virtually impossible to interpret. Even baby-sitters get confused if you leave them conflicting or cryptic directions. That is why you should be very careful about what you change and why. You should send any changes you want to make to your lawyer to make sure that the change is not going to inadvertently affect some other portion of your Loving Trust plan.

Luckily, however, changes in how you want to leave your personal property will almost never affect the other provisions of your Loving Trust plan. They can frequently be made with little cost or no involvement by your lawyer. Your lawyer should simply be notified each time you make changes on who is to receive personal property. It will take only a few minutes for your lawyer to review and file such changes. This protection will cost you little or nothing and will help both you and your lawyer make sure your Loving Trust plan is still in good operating order.

What Is Personal Property?

Personal property is property such as furniture, jewelry, clothes, antiques, books, and collections of all kinds. It is not business property, cash, investments, land, or any other income-producing property. The kind of personal property we are talking about is technically called "tangible personal property." If you have a question as to specific property, ask your lawyer. You will quickly find out the answer. Most states have very specific definitions of what constitutes tangible personal property.

Because this type of property is so "personal" in nature, well-drafted trusts contain an entire section dealing specifically with it. In our Loving Trust plan, this section is in three parts:

Leaving your special personal property to special loved ones
Leaving the remainder of your personal property to loved ones
Instructions for resolving disputes over who is to get what personal property

> . . . changes in how you want to leave your personal property will almost never affect the other provisions of your Loving Trust plan.

Leaving Your Special Personal Property to Special Loved Ones

Leaving special personal property to special loved ones is accomplished by a Memorandum of Personal Property that itemizes your special property and names whom you would like to leave it to. A Memorandum of Personal Property is not allowed in all states; check with your attorney to make sure that it is available in yours. A copy of the Memorandum of Personal Property that we used in our practice can be found on page 205.

As you can see, all you have to do is write down a description of the property you wish to leave and the name of the person who is to receive it. Not only does it look simple, it is simple to use. You only need to make sure that you sign and *date* several copies, one of which is to be sent to your lawyer.

The date is critical, because if you change your mind, the Memorandum of Personal Property that is the most recent will prevail. Failure to date the Memorandum of Personal Property may well invalidate it.

We have a suggestion that many of our clients have used very successfully. Sometimes, even though you write down a short description of property, it is hard for some people to determine exactly what you mean. On larger pieces of personal property—furniture, paintings, and the like—take some white adhesive tape and write the name of the person who is to receive it on the tape. Attach the tape to the back or underside of the property so it can be identified.

Some of our clients have used photographs for the same purpose. The point is, be as clear as you can about what's what and who gets it. Confusion is not what trustees and loved ones need.

Leaving the Remainder of Your Personal Property

Property you do not specifically leave by Memorandum can be passed by more general instructions contained in your trust.

Most married people prefer to leave most of their personal property to their spouses. The revocable living trust in our Loving Trust plan instructs the trustees to give all personal property not specifically left to loved ones by Memorandum of Personal Property to the surviving spouse.

What if you are single or your spouse dies before you do? Then personal property can be divided among your children equally, or in any manner you choose. You can even have it pass exactly like the other property that is in your trust. How you leave the remainder of your personal property, just like how you leave specific items of personal property, is entirely at your discretion. You only need to make your lawyer aware of your desires.

Resolving Disputes Over Who Gets What Personal Property

In our experience, some of the most intense and angry battles that heirs get into involve personal property. Because it is so personal in nature, and because it can be very valuable, disputes inevitably arise. Prevention is the best medicine when it comes to avoiding these kinds of disputes.

For example, let's say that you have three children and your spouse is no longer living. You instruct your trustees to divide your personal property equally among your children. Your two daughters both want your jewelry. Your son and one daughter both want your collection of feather hats. Then there is the furniture, the photographs . . . well, you get the idea. Everybody is mad and makes a mountain out of a molehill.

We solve this problem by instructing the trustees to do the following:

> If my children cannot agree as to how they would like to divide my personal property within a reasonable period of time, then you, trustees, divide it the way you think is fairest. If there is no fair way, and no agreement can be reached, sell it and divide the proceeds equally among my children.

When faced with the "Okay, we'll sell it!" choice, children usually find it prudent to reach an agreement. We highly recommend that you insist that this language, or language similar to it, is contained in your trust.

Minor Children

Minor children, as we stated in chapter 15, "How to Distribute Your Children's Property," cannot effectively own property, even personal property. You should have Loving Trust instructions that state that if you have minor children, your trustees can select which personal property they will immediately receive and which will be held for them until a later date. For instance, you may instruct your trustees to divide your personal property among your three children as they work it out among themselves, but if one of them is only ten years old, he or she will be outnegotiated by his or her older brothers and sisters. To protect the ten-year-old, the trustees will act for him or her.

In our trust, we instruct the trustees to be mindful of the desires of the minor children. Even minors can be attached to certain items of their parents' personal property.

Property that is not directly passed to minor children will be added to their trusts or given to their guardian for safekeeping.

You should have Loving Trust instructions that state that if you have minor children, your trustees can select which personal property they will immediately receive and which will be held for them until a later date.

Bare-bones Boilerplate Trusts and Personal Property

Most bare-bones living trusts ignore personal property. More often than not, these trusts leave it to be taken care of by the provisions of a Pour-Over Will (a Pour-Over Will is a special will that leaves property to a living trust, but like any other will, it is controlled by the probate process). Not only is the personal property subject to probate, but the bare-bones boilerplate trust usually has terse or nonexistent terms as to how to give that property to loved ones. Whether this is an oversight or a product of preoccupation with short documents, we do not know. We do know that how you wish your personal property to pass to your loved ones is something that should be addressed in your Loving Trust.

Neither wills nor bare-bones boilerplate trusts can effectively and simply leave your personal property to your loved ones. In a will, leaving your special personal property generally creates problems when you want to make changes and assures that all your personal property will go through the probate process. Bare-bones boilerplate trusts dismiss personal property as part of the domain of wills, making the bare-bones boilerplate worthless to those who have special personal property for special people. Your Loving Trust plan can make leaving this property convenient for you, your loved ones, and your trustees.

MEMORANDUM OF DISPOSITION OF TANGIBLE
PERSONAL PROPERTY OF [YOUR FULL NAME]

Pursuant to the terms of my Loving Trust dated _____, I hereby request my Trustee(s) to distribute the following items of nonbusiness tangible personal property as follows:

Description of Tangible   *Recipient of Tangible*
Personal Property   *Personal Property*

If a recipient of a particular item of nonbusiness personal property does not survive me by thirty days, such item shall be disposed of as though it had not been listed in this memorandum.

Dated:

Witness [Your Full Name]

Chapter Twenty-One

How to Plan If You Are Single

Without a surviving spouse to temper the greed and bitterness that often occur in death's aftermath, disgruntled heirs can be more aggressive, belligerent, and avaricious than they might otherwise be.

Most of the literature that deals with wills, trusts, and planning for loved ones ignores the needs of the single person. It's almost as if the single person were purposefully shunted to the side. Commentators seem to forget that single people also have loved ones who need to be provided for. With the divorce rate continually hovering at the 50 percent level, and with increased numbers of widows, widowers, and individuals who simply prefer to remain unmarried, it seems a shame that more is not written about how the single person can plan for loved ones.

If you are single, you should have a Loving Trust plan. Whether you are elderly with adult children and grandchildren, divorced with children of your own, or unmarried for any other reason, it is imperative that your concern and instructions for your loved ones survive your disability or death. Even if you are completely career-oriented, and have no thoughts of family or marriage, a Loving Trust plan is something you should seriously consider; it can provide for your disability and for your parents or other loved ones on your death.

Every Loving Trust need and benefit that we discussed in part 1 applies as much to you as it does to married people. In fact, its benefits may well be more important to you, since you have only yourself to depend upon.

Without a surviving spouse to temper the greed and bitterness that often occur in death's aftermath, disgruntled heirs can be more aggressive, belligerent, and avaricious than they might otherwise be. It is very possible that your heirs may be more hostile than those of a married person.

Because your Loving Trust planning is governed by significantly less-complicated legal rules than a will, and because it avoids both living and death probates, it is not likely that there will be expensive and bitter court battles over you or your property "à la Groucho." Your Loving Trust planning allows you to continue to provide for yourself and your loved ones following your disability or death.

Unfortunately, single people are often mistakenly characterized as loners

206

whose thoughts and feelings center only on themselves. In our experience, nothing could be further from the truth. Your Loving Trust planning can quickly dispel any such stereotype by conveying your hopes, fears, dreams, and ambitions for your loved ones with a dimension that simple wills or bare-bones living trusts rarely accomplish.

It is critical that you plan for your potential disability. Without a spouse to watch over you and provide for your welfare, you should rely upon your Loving Trust instructions for your care.

Your trust begins with a "Me" Trust, as do all Loving Trust plans. At your death, it will either immediately create a Common Trust or Separate Trusts for your children or grandchildren, or Separate Trusts for your other loved ones.

Your "Me" Trust

Your "Me" Trust may well be more necessary for you than its counterpart for a married person. You will not have a mate to rely on during the period of your disability. You will not be able to depend upon a spouse's judgment with respect to decisions about nursing-home care, institutionalization, and other equally grave matters. Because spouses often share their feelings about what they want to occur if they become disabled, many decisions can be made in the absence of written instructions.

If you become disabled, it is likely that you will not have a "partner" to look after you and handle the myriad problems that will arise as a result of your disability. You may or may not have close relationships with mature and responsible loved ones. Either way, you will be at the mercy of the probate court and may be at the mercy of self-serving supposed friends and acquaintances.

Your "Me" Trust can empower true friends and close loved ones to act as your trustees or "surrogate mates," following your desires and protecting you and your interests.

A business or marital partner is supposed to look after the partnership's pocketbook to make sure that expenses are kept to a minimum. We have seen too many cases where no one was around to monitor the expenses of a disabled single person. As a disabled single person, you would be more liable to be fleeced of your property than a disabled married person. Bluntly, our society seems to be less concerned about the well-being of a single person and his or her money.

A Loving Trust plan is tailored primarily to take care of you and your money. It preserves your property for your use and care by reducing your expenses. By avoiding lawyers and the other costs of a living probate, your Loving Trust planning goes a long way in reducing those costs. Having trustees to implement your instructions also saves expenses; they are legally charged with protecting you and your trust property, and they are liable for any excesses or irregularities as a matter of law.

In chapter 11, "How to Provide for Yourself," we provided two alternatives that you could use as a single person. However, it is likely that you will have to create your own alternative for your disability. Enhance your Loving Trust instructions with your hopes, fears, dreams, and ambitions for your loved ones.

We all become incredibly vulnerable when we are disabled. There is no reason to augment your vulnerability by failing to protect yourself and your loved ones with Loving Trust instructions.

Probate Avoidance

Your Loving Trust planning will avoid probate at your death. Single people can generate significant probate fees. That is why it is most important that you use your Loving Trust planning to avoid all probate fees on your death. The main probate-avoidance gimmick suggested for married people—joint tenancy with right of survivorship—does not work at all for single people. Your Loving Trust plan provides the only effective method by which you can safely avoid probate.

Your Children

In chapter 14, "How to Provide for Your Minor Children," and chapter 15, "How to Distribute Your Children's Property," we provided you with planning alternatives for your children. Each of these chapters discussed several alternatives for caring for and distributing your property to your children and grandchildren. You will want to review each of them before designing your Loving Trust plan.

If you want to leave property to children who are not your own, you would still utilize the alternatives in chapter 15. In your plans for providing for your children, nieces and nephews, or others, you must always give consideration to their ages and experience.

Other Loved Ones

It is our contention that leaving property of any value outright to a loved one is a mistake. It cannot protect them from:

- The claims of their creditors.
- Their disability and resulting need for a living probate.
- The avarice of the many hucksters of the world.
- Their own inexperience or inability to wisely handle their inheritance.

A Loving Trust plan can guide, protect, and teach them. It can pass your wisdom along with your property.

Leaving Property to Charity

In chapter 16, "How to Give to Charity," we explain many different methods for leaving property to charity. Those methods can be made a part of your total Loving Trust plan. Properly structured, leaving property to charity can create federal income, estate, and gift tax benefits in addition to the pleasure you will have by helping your favorite charities.

Federal Estate Tax

If the value of your property is $600,000 or more, it will be subject to federal estate tax. As we discussed in chapter 19, "How to Save Federal Death Tax," it will be very difficult for you to save this federal death tax. The federal government does not give any special estate-tax breaks to single people. Most federal estate-tax planning done by singles deals with sophisticated lifetime gifts, special life insurance trusts, and other complex measures beyond the scope of this book.

We strongly recommend that you read *Protect Your Estate*. We wrote this text primarily with larger estates in mind. It will provide you with estate-tax planning strategies by acquainting you with many of the finer tax-planning points.

Given the difficulty of planning for a single person's federal death taxes, most of our single clients ultimately opted to purchase considerable amounts of additional life insurance to cover their tax liability. In effect, they viewed federal estate tax as a liability that could only be covered or offset by adding more money to their Loving Trust planning.

If you wish to reduce your federal estate tax, you should work closely with a tax attorney and your other advisers in reviewing the available alternatives.

Single people have traditionally been ignored in the planning arena. This neglect may be because of an inability to save meaningful amounts of federal estate tax. We hope that you realize that saving federal estate tax is only one of your many Loving Trust desires. In reviewing your Loving Trust needs, you will want to give particular attention to the following chapters: chapter 11, "How to Provide for Yourself"; chapter 14, "How to Provide for Your Minor Children"; chapter 15, "How to Distribute Your Children's Property"; chapter 16, "How to Give to Charity"; chapter 17, "How to Ultimately Distribute Your Property"; chapter 18, "How to Select Your Trustees."

Chapter Twenty-Two

How to Provide for Your Loved Ones Upon Remarriage

If you have children by a first marriage and you die or become disabled without providing Loving Trust instructions, you may have condemned yourself and your loved ones to potential economic and emotional disaster.

With the national divorce rate so high, it should come as no surprise that second marriages are extraordinarily common. It also should come as no surprise that it is difficult to decide how to provide for loved ones in second marriages because, more often than not, there are children from prior marriages, as well as children from the current marriage. "Yours, mine, and ours" situations mean that tough decisions have to be made, but they are usually postponed due to conflicting emotions and a lack of guidance.

Rather than make a potentially wrong or unfair decision when planning for our loved ones, most of us make no decisions at all. As you can imagine, when there is a death or disability in a second marriage, the problems are often horrendous, and the resulting dissension can tear families apart.

Spouses in a second marriage are often paralyzed in terms of planning because their desires are thwarted by significant planning conflicts. Letting your Loving Trust planning languish because you cannot—or will not—make planning decisions is absolutely the worst thing you can do. Without the protection of a Loving Trust plan, the tragedy of your disability or death can be many times greater than it needs to be. If you have children by a first marriage and you die or become disabled without providing Loving Trust instructions, you may have condemned yourself and your loved ones to potential economic and emotional disaster.

When in doubt, make a planning decision and use a Loving Trust plan. Your Loving Trust plan can always be changed if you change your mind at a later date. Your planning options may not be perfect, but even in their imperfection, they will be far better than the options the probate judge will utilize in rendering his decisions for your loved ones.

There are many proven methods to plan for loved ones in second marriages that are not unlike those we have already covered in part 2. Those thoughts and

210

techniques that we have found particularly relevant to the remarriage problem will be covered in this chapter.

Your "Me" Trust

As we discussed in chapter 11, "How to Provide for Yourself," your Loving Trust planning should present a hierarchy of beneficiaries. This hierarchy can cause emotional complications when you have children by a prior marriage. Will their natural father or mother take care of them following your disability or death? Will your current spouse provide for them? Should you provide for them to the exclusion of your spouse? Should they be treated any differently from their stepbrothers or stepsisters?

These are serious questions that are difficult to answer. You must thoroughly analyze the specific economic and emotional factors in your situation and make those decisions that honestly reflect your thinking.

The needs of most spouses that we have helped in this circumstance fell into two general categories—the breadwinner spouse and the homemaker spouse. Most of our breadwinner spouse clients opted to provide for themselves, their spouses, and their children—regardless of what marriage they were from—in that order. If their current spouses had independent financial means, they frequently placed their children ahead of their spouses on the disability hierarchy. If their children by a prior marriage were adults, they often excluded them in favor of their spouses or their minor children.

The needs of the homemaker spouse clients were significantly different from those of breadwinner spouses. They were always concerned about their children—particularly their minor children—by prior marriages, and generally put their spouse's needs well below their children's.

If you have children from more than one marriage, do you want all your children taken care of equally? Is there a significant difference in their ages? Do you want your younger children provided for first? Will your ex-spouse provide for your first family? Will your spouse provide for your current family? Will your spouse provide for your previous marriage's children? These are practical questions that you must answer when deciding the hierarchy of how you want your loved ones provided for on your disability.

In planning the disability portion of your Loving Trust plan, you must also consider any child support or alimony obligations that you may have. You should provide your trustees with notice of such agreements so those obligations can be continued from your trust funds. In some agreements, payments end upon disability, but in others they do not. In either case, it is important that you alert your trustees so they will be prepared to honor your obligations if it becomes necessary.

You must prepare your trustees to step into your shoes should you become disabled. While disability, in and of itself, engenders significant confusion, its aftermath can be made much worse if there are lawsuits over your property and your obligations.

Explicit instructions are much more important when you have children by a prior marriage.

Settlement Agreements for Divorces

Divorces sometimes create very confusing and unique settlement agreements. There are agreements as to who receives property at what time, and agreements to keep life insurance policies in force. There are even agreements that provide for financial arrangements for the education of the children. The terms of these agreements will greatly affect how you design your Loving Trust plan.

Because of the wide variety and content of settlement agreements, it is impossible for us to deal with their ramifications on even an overview basis. You need to discuss any divorce agreements you may have with your lawyer as part of your Loving Trust design criteria. Failure to coordinate your divorce settlement agreements with your Loving Trust instructions may end up haunting your loved ones. Lack of planning in this area has created many a lawsuit, something that can easily be avoided with a little foresight.

Premarital and Postmarital Agreements

When you marry, your property may become marital property. That means that your spouse may have certain claims to your property on your death. Many states give a surviving spouse substantial rights to a deceased spouse's property.

If both spouses sign a valid contract that sets out the rights each has to the other's property, it can usually override the state's requirements. These contracts can be entered into before marriage and, in some cases, after marriage. Each state has its own requirements as to the content and validity of these premarital and postmarital agreements. These agreements are frequently used in second marriages.

If you have signed one of these agreements, it can substantially affect how you plan for loved ones. Your marital agreement will probably restrict what you receive from your spouse on death and vice versa. It may also affect your federal estate-tax planning in that it may reduce or eliminate your, or your spouse's, unlimited marital deduction and tax-free amounts.

If you have signed such an agreement, be sure to have your lawyer review it as a part of your Loving Trust guidelines. If there are conflicts between your

> **You need to discuss any divorce agreements you may have with your lawyer as part of your Loving Trust design criteria.**

Loving Trust instructions and your marital agreement, they will likely have to be resolved in the courts.

Even if you have signed a marital agreement, it is still possible for you to save federal estate taxes. Working with seasoned professionals will make the task easier, less expensive, and more effective. To facilitate your lawyer's work, you should provide him or her with a copy of it.

Since a marital agreement will restrict what you and your spouse receive from each other on your respective deaths, you very well may want to make a diagram of what your marital agreement says. You can then compare its terms to the alternatives you have selected in your Loving Trust plan. This review will give you a good idea of the conflicts, if any, between the two. Diagramming your marital agreement and filling in "My Checklist for Designing My Loving Trust Plan" (at the end of part 2) should enable you to communicate to your lawyer precisely what your Loving Trust instructions are.

Separate Loving Trust Plans for Separate Planning

When we say that everyone needs Loving Trust planning, we mean exactly that. You and your spouse should each have your own separate Loving Trust plans. Your Loving Trust plans may be identical, but they do not have to be. You and your mate may have different ideas as to how your property is to be used upon your disability. You may each have different feelings as to who should receive your property or how it should be provided for on your death. You may have different beneficiaries, beneficiaries of different ages, or beneficiaries who have widely varying needs. You may also be subject to different divorce settlement agreements.

Separate Loving Trust plans control separate property. Your Loving Trust plan controls only that property that you own in your name. It also controls property that is paid to your own trust plan on death, like life insurance proceeds or death benefits from a retirement plan. Joint tenancy with right of survivorship, life insurance, and death benefits *not payable to your trust* are not controlled by your Loving Trust plan.

In second marriages, we emphasize that separate Loving Trust plans can and should be done. It is likely that you and your spouse have brought separate property into your marriage. The property you have brought into the marriage is yours, and you should plan to do with it as you desire.

You and your spouse may each have different loved ones you wish to care for. This reflects the "yours, mine, and ours" planning requirements that often need to be accomplished when a second marriage involves children from prior marriages as well as from the current marriage. Having different loved ones to plan for dictates that you and your spouse establish your own Loving Trust plan.

You and your spouse should each come to grips with your own situation and design a plan to meet—as closely as possible—all of your separate needs and desires. You may find it easier to make decisions and to determine what you would like to do, knowing that you only have to worry about your Loving Trust planning.

To help you address your own unique circumstances, we will give you a planning idea that has worked well for us over the years. It is an ideal solution to a major second marriage dilemma.

A Gift of Love

Many second marriages involve spouses with children from their previous marriages. Oftentimes the husband's children are with his former wife. He sees them occasionally on visitation days, but their relationship is not especially close. His new wife is often younger than he, and she either desires a family or already has one from her first marriage. In the latter case, her children are usually living with the two of them. She generally views her first husband as an ogre, someone who is irresponsible and not very loving.

There are many instances where an ex-wife and mother has very little property from her first marriage; what she does have may consist of furniture, a car, and personal effects. Rarely does she have much cash or many real assets. In many cases, her first husband is delinquent on his child-support payments. Until her second marriage, she has lived on what she could earn while taking care of her children. Her new husband may have property and a better income than she has been accustomed to having.

A divorced mother's children can be a problem. Those children lost a father and gained a competitor for their mother's affections. They have been the focus of their mother's life ever since the divorce and are not happy with her attempt at refocusing on another man. They generally do not behave kindly to the stranger they must now call "Dad."

The mother's new husband is in a bind; his relationship with his wife's children may not be good. They seem to go out of their way to create tension between him and their mother. He tries to get the children to like and respect him, but the harder he tries, the worse their behavior seems to get. He is afraid that his discipline may trigger significant turmoil between himself and their mother, so he endures their distemper with some distemper of his own.

Meanwhile, the new wife is facing a dilemma. She may know that her husband does not care for her children as much as she does and that there is real competition between him and her children. She is faced with lose-lose situations daily, and can only hope to keep everyone happy.

When such a newly married couple decides to look into Loving Trust planning, it is usually at the wife's insistence. She is probably more insecure with the situation than he is and needs the security that she perceives planning will give her. He goes along with the idea, hoping to establish a little more harmony between them.

When we encountered a couple like this, we knew from experience that the wife's real concern was for her children. She knew that if something happened to her, their real father might not be capable of providing for them—especially if he couldn't even stay current on his child-support payments. She also knew, regardless of his protestations to the contrary, that her current husband wasn't likely to care for them either. She may have observed how poorly the children treated him and how he controlled his anger with only the greatest difficulty. She had no confidence that his feelings would change after her disability or death. She usually became even more agitated when she realized that she didn't have enough property to begin to provide for her children's well-being.

She was in a terrible planning bind and considerable emotional distress when we told her that her ex-husband would more than likely be named as the children's guardian, even if she provided instructions to the contrary.

Given this situation, we explained that a Loving Trust plan, coupled with a loving act, could solve her dilemma. We helped her design her Loving Trust plan to totally take care of her children on her disability or death. We encouraged her to name her current husband as one of its trustees. This, we assured her, would keep her ex-husband from seizing her children's funds. We then encouraged her husband to make a loving act by purchasing a life insurance policy on her life. The policy would be hers to own, and its proceeds would immediately pass on her death to her Loving Trust plan for her children.

Her husband would pay the annual premium on her policy on their anniversary, as his way of saying, "I love you and want to provide a means by which your children will be provided for." So long as they stay married, this loving act could continue. If, however, they should separate or divorce, there would be no requirement that the husband continue the premiums.

Let's now look at the dynamics of the situation. Even if her first husband is named as the guardian of the children, her new husband controls the money as one of his wife's trustees. Her ex-husband would have no way to get any of his children's money for his benefit. This fact alone might deter the children's natural father from seeking their custody. If he does get custody, he will have to interact with the new husband, who will generally go out of his way to make sure that the first husband acts responsibly for the well-being of the children.

The new husband is usually more than content with this arrangement. He is delighted that, for the cost of an insurance policy that provides her with a means to provide for her children, he can make his wife so happy, loving, and secure. He is also happy with being a trustee of the children's trust. He usually believes that he can financially raise the children better than their natural father.

Everyone—the new wife, the new husband, the new wife's children—is protected remarkably well under this Loving Trust arrangement.

When we presented this idea to clients, we ended by explaining why this is a gift of love. Each year on the anniversary of their marriage, the husband—through his love—will make another year's premium payment. It is a token of his love, a reminder that he loves her enough to give her the cash to fuel her Loving Trust planning. Yes, it sounds corny, doesn't it? Yet, not once in the countless times we have presented it was this Loving Trust idea rejected.

A gift of love is not the only method of using a Loving Trust plan in a second marriage. As you have likely realized, there are many different ways to combine the various subtrusts of a trust to meet your every planning objective. By selecting and designing your various subtrusts, you can build a Loving Trust plan that will not only care for you but will also carry your love to others long after you are gone.

The first step in second-marriage Loving Trust planning is to solidify your thinking. Examine your motives in detail and determine what you really want to accomplish. You are going to run into some issues that will be very difficult to resolve. You will worry about fairness and jealousy and all the other very human aspects of planning for loved ones. Reduce your possible solutions to a few key alternatives, then choose the best of the lot. None of them may be perfect, but picking the "best of the worst" is certainly better than not acting at all. Do not insist on perfection, just do the best you can. No one can ask for more than that.

Please keep in mind that each marriage partner can design his or her own Loving Trust plan and that they need not be alike. Each of you can have a Loving Trust plan that best meets your desires and financial situation.

. . . each marriage partner can design his or her own Loving Trust plan and that they need not be alike. Each of you can have a Loving Trust plan that best meets your desires and financial situation.

My Checklist for Designing
My Loving Trust Plan

There are checklists at the ends of chapters 11 through 19 that will quickly enable you to record your planning thoughts. We strongly suggest that you review each of those chapters and fill in each of their checklists before consolidating your desires on this master checklist.

This master checklist for designing your own Loving Trust plan is your Loving Trust blueprint. It will contain almost everything your lawyer needs to prepare your Loving Trust plan quickly and at the lowest cost possible.

Chapter 11: How to Provide for Yourself

This checklist is appropriate for all Loving Trust plans.

( ) 11–1 Take care of me and nobody else.

( ) 11–2 Take care of my needs first and then my spouse's needs.

( ) 11–3 Take care of my needs first, then my spouse's, and then my children's or dependents'.

( ) 11–4 Take care of me, my spouse, and my children based solely on our needs, without any priorities among us.

( ) 11–5 Take care of me and my children based solely on our needs, without any priorities among us.

( ) 11–6 My own motive:

_____

_____

_____

_____

Chapter 12: How to Provide for Your Spouse

You should disregard these alternatives if you do not want to directly provide for your spouse.

( ) 12–1 I want my spouse to have total control over my property.

( ) 12–2 I want my spouse totally taken care of, but I want to limit my spouse's right to leave my property on his or her death.

( ) 12–3 I want my spouse totally taken care of, but I will decide where my property goes on my spouse's death.

( )   12–4 My spouse can have only the income my Pocketbook Trust earns and nothing more; I will say where my property goes on his or her death.

( )   12–5 My spouse will get only whatever my state's laws require that I must leave him or her.

( )   12–6 My own motive:

_____

_____

_____

_____

Chapter 13: How to Provide for Your Family

How to Allocate Between My Pocketbook and Family Trusts

( )   13–1 I want all my property to pass to my spouse in my Pocketbook Trust.

( )   13–2 I want my spouse to receive whatever he or she is entitled to under state law with the balance passing to my Family Trust.

( )   13–3 I want my property equally divided between my Pocketbook and Family Trusts.

( )   13–4 I want _____ percent to pass to my Pocketbook Trust and _____ percent to my Family Trust.

( )   13–5 I want all my property to pass to my spouse in my Family Trust.

( )   13–6 My own motive:

_____

_____

_____

_____

How I Want My Beneficiaries Provided For From My Family Trust

( )   13–7 I want primarily to care for my spouse by providing him or her with as many benefits and as much control as possible.

( )   13–8 I want to provide for my spouse and my children based upon

their respective needs, while giving priority to the needs of
my spouse. I want my children and grandchildren to get what
is left after my spouse's death.

( )   13–9 I want to provide for the respective needs of my spouse and
my children, but if my spouse remarries, I want to provide
only for my children.

( )   13–10 The same as alternative 13–9, except that I want my spouse
taken care of during any period of time that he or she is single.

( )   13–11 I want to provide for the respective needs of my spouse, my
children, and other loved ones, and will set forth my priorities.

( )   13–12 I want to provide for loved ones other than my spouse.

( )   13–13 My own motive:

_____

_____

_____

_____

Chapter 14: How to Provide for Your Minor Children

( )   14–1 All my children are adults. I do not want a Common Trust.

( )   14–2 I want my Common Trust to end when my youngest child is
twenty-one years of age.

( )   14–3 I want my Common Trust to end when my youngest child is
twenty-three or completes college, whichever happens first.

( )   14–4 I want my Common Trust to end when my youngest child is
_____ years of age.

( )   14–5 My own motive:

_____

_____

_____

_____

Chapter 15: How to Distribute Your Children's Property

Advancement Distributions

( ) 15–1 I want my trustees to liberally provide for each of my children.

( ) 15–2 I want my trustees to provide only for the health, education, support, and maintenance of each of my children.

( ) 15–3 My own motive:

_____

_____

_____

_____

Premature Death of a Child

( ) 15–4 I want my child's trust property to pass pursuant to my child's directions.

( ) 15–5 I want my child's trust property to pass to my child's children or, if none, to my other children.

( ) 15–6 My own motive:

_____

_____

_____

_____

Distribution Alternatives

( ) 15–7 I want my property distributed to my children immediately.

( ) 15–8 I want my children to have immediately whatever they want from their Separate Trusts.

( ) 15–9 Make two distributions to my children, one-half at a minimum age, the remainder at another stated age.

( ) 15–10 Make two distributions to my children, the first at a minimum age, or immediately if that age has been met, the second to occur five years from the date of the first distribution.

( ) 15–11 Make four distributions to my children, the first to occur at a minimum age, or immediately if that age has been met, the second through the fourth to occur every five years.

( ) 15–12 Make multiple unequal distributions, the first to occur at a minimum age, or immediately if that age has been met, the others at stated ages.

( ) 15–13 Make no mandatory lifetime distributions to my children, but take care of my children in whatever way they need, whenever they need it from the trust funds.

( ) 15–14 Make entirely different distribution patterns for each of my children.

( ) 15–15 My own motive:

_____

_____

_____

_____

Chapter 16: How to Give to Charity

( ) 16–1 I want to give specific assets to my favorite charities on my death.

( ) 16–2 I want to give cash gifts in specific amounts to my favorite charities on my death.

( ) 16–3 I want to make cash gifts that represent specific percentages of my estate's value to my favorite charities on my death.

( ) 16–4 I want to make cash gifts of specific amounts that cannot exceed a certain percentage of my estate's value to my favorite charities on my death.

( ) 16–5 I want to create a subtrust in my trust that will make gifts in perpetuity to my favorite charities after my death.

( ) 16–6 I want to create a charitable foundation in my Loving Trust planning that will make gifts according to my charitable philosophy to public charities that agree with that philosophy.

( ) 16–7 I want to give my home or farm to charity, but live in it during my life.

( ) 16–8 I want to create a special separate trust for charity to which I can transfer some or all of my assets that will give me a lifetime income.

( ) 16–9 I want to create a special separate trust that will give its income to charity during my life, but which will give its assets to my loved ones on my death.

( )   16–10   I want to purchase life insurance in order to meet my charitable desires.

( )   16–11   My own motive:

_____

_____

_____

_____

Chapter 17: How to Ultimately Distribute Your Property

( )   17–1   I want one-half of my property to pass to my heirs and one-half of my property to pass to my spouse's heirs under my state's laws.

( )   17–2   I want all my property to pass to my heirs under my state's laws.

( )   17–3   I want my property to pass to certain individuals.

( )   17–4   I want all my property to go to charity.

( )   17–5   My own motive:

_____

_____

_____

_____

Chapter 18: How to Select Your Trustees

Naming My Trustees While I Am Alive and Well

( )   18–1   I will act as my sole trustee.

( )   18–2   My spouse and I will act as my co-trustees.

( )   18–3   I will act as a co-trustee along with:

( )   18–4   My own alternative:

_____

_____

_____

_____

Naming My Successor Trustees on My Disability

( )   18–5   The following individuals or institutions will act as my successor trustees in the order I have set out (if I do not name an institution, at least two individual trustees must always serve):

( )   18–6   The following individuals or institutions will _replace all my initial trustees_ and will act in the order I have set out (if I do not name an institution, at least two individual trustees must serve):

( )   18–7   My initial co-trustee must choose a major institutional trustee to serve as successor co-trustee. When my initial co-trustee can no longer serve, this institutional trustee shall continue to serve alone.

Naming My Successor Trustees on My Death

( )   18–8   My disability trustees will continue to serve. They will be replaced by the following individuals or institutions in the order I have set out (if I do not name an institution, at least two individual trustees must serve):

( )   18–9   My disability trustees will be replaced by the following individuals or institutions in the order I have set out (if I do not name an institution, at least two individual trustees must serve):

( )   18–10 My initial co-trustee must select a major institutional trustee to serve as co-trustee. When my initial co-trustee can no longer serve, this institutional trustee can serve alone.

How My Beneficiaries May Terminate My Trustees

( )   18–11 My spouse can terminate any of my successor trustees. After my spouse is no longer a trustee, a majority of my beneficiaries can terminate any of my successor trustees. When all my successor trustees have either been terminated or they are no longer available, my beneficiaries must choose a major institutional trustee.

( ) 18–12 A majority of my beneficiaries can terminate any of my successor trustees. When all my successor trustees have either been terminated or they are no longer available, my beneficiaries must choose a major institutional trustee.

( ) 18–13 My own motive:

_____

_____

_____

_____

Chapter 19: How to Save Federal Death Tax

The Value Of My Estate Is Between $600,000 and $1,200,000

( ) 19–1 I want my first $600,000 to pass to my spouse in my Pocketbook Trust and the remainder to go to my Family Trust.

( ) 19–2 I want my first $600,000 to pass to my Family Trust and the remainder to go to my spouse in my Pocketbook Trust.

( ) 19–3 I want my property equally divided between my Pocketbook and Family Trusts.

( ) 19–4 I want my spouse to receive whatever he or she is entitled to under our state law, with the next $600,000 of my property passing to my Family Trust, and whatever is left—if any— passing to my Pocketbook Trust Two.

The Value Of My Estate Is Over $1,200,000

( ) 19–5 I want to save federal estate tax and thereafter care for my spouse as much as possible with a single Pocketbook Trust.

( ) 19–6 I want to save federal estate tax; I also want to take care of my spouse and to be assured that my children will have one-half of what's left of my property on my spouse's subsequent death.

( ) 19–7 I want to save federal estate tax, while giving as much of my property to my children as possible.

Part Three

HOW TO GET YOUR LOVING TRUST PLAN DONE

Chapter Twenty-Three

How to Find a Loving Trust Lawyer

The only obstacle that stands between your Loving Trust design and getting your Loving Trust plan implemented is finding a lawyer who will write it for you. Time and time again, we have been told by our lecture students and talk-show callers that it is difficult to find a lawyer who will do a Loving Trust plan. Our past experience verifies their exasperation.

However, the number of lawyers who want to prepare Loving Trust plans, or at least who want to attempt to prepare Loving Trust plans, is rapidly growing. Trusts of all types have become a topic of great interest to the public, and lawyers are taking notice. Competition among lawyers has been increasing as their number has been swelling. So has their inclination to extend their legal horizons.

Most lawyers are embroiled in daily conflict. They are under constant pressure to either create or mediate disputes. This constant sparring takes its toll. Many of our colleagues tell us that when their phone rings they often think, "What's gone wrong now?" A Loving Trust practice offers these lawyers a respite from the stress of their litigation practices.

Our Loving Trust lectures invariably generate great excitement among lawyers. The concept offers them an alternative to the traditional way of doing things.

With the help of our suggestions, you can easily find a lawyer to help you with your Loving Trust planning. Many lawyers already have the know-how to draft a basic living trust. If your lawyer does not, you can provide it by using the techniques we describe in this chapter. There is no reason why your lawyer cannot easily and reasonably produce a living trust plan done the Loving Trust way in a very short period of time.

The lawyers you talk with will generally fall into one of five categories:

1. Those who are familiar with the Loving Trust method of planning and

who prepare them for their clients. These lawyers are invariably members of the National Network of Estate Planning Attorneys.

2. Those who are unfamiliar with Loving Trust planning or the National Network of Estate Planning Attorneys but who are familiar with revocable living trusts and are willing to learn about Loving Trust planning techniques.

3. Those who regularly use traditional will planning who would like to expand into Loving Trust planning.

4. Those who have not done a great deal of estate planning but who would like to do so using Loving Trust techniques.

5. Those who are convinced that wills and probate are the *only* way to plan and who dismiss revocable living trusts and Loving Trust planning out of hand.

The first two will meet your Loving Trust needs. The last will not. He or she is the attorney that Dacey and Stock were talking about. Do not waste your time or money on these legal dinosaurs.

Contacting a Lawyer Who Regularly Uses Loving Trust Planning Techniques

We have trained many lawyers nationwide and are in the process of training many more. Our National Network of Estate Planning Attorneys is a national organization of attorneys who are devoted to Loving Trust planning. Members of the Network attend Loving Trust professional seminars, workshops, and have access to numerous practice aids designed to give them the education and tools to accomplish Loving Trust planning.

By using the techniques that follow, you will likely find an attorney who either knows Loving Trust basics or one who wants to know them. If you find a lawyer who wants to know more about the National Network of Estate Planning Attorneys, please see the Authors' Note at the end of this book.

Contacting a Lawyer You Know But Have Not Used

Knowing a lawyer you like will give you a head start in getting your Loving Trust plan prepared. As you know by now, Loving Trust planning is very personal. Your lawyer will need to know what you own, how much you owe, and how all your property is titled. He or she will also be privy to your hopes, fears, dreams, and aspirations for yourself and your loved ones. It is important that you like the lawyer you ultimately select.

If you know a lawyer you like, call and let him or her know that you are

> **Knowing a lawyer you like will give you a head start in getting your Loving Trust plan prepared.**

interested in using his or her services. Tell your friend that you want to help prepare your Loving Trust plan and ask the following questions:

- Would you be interested in helping me put my Loving Trust instructions into a fully funded revocable living trust format?
- Have you read *Loving Trust*?
- Do you have experience in drafting revocable living trusts with Loving Trust instructions?
- Do you have expertise in federal estate-tax planning? (You would ask this only if your estate approximates $600,000 or more.)
- Will you charge for our first meeting? If so, what will your charge be?

Give your friend the opportunity to expand and explain his or her answers. Resist the temptation to ask your questions in machine-gun fashion; take your time. Most lawyers are happy to talk with a potential new client—they want the business. You and your business are a precious commodity to your friend. Let him or her sell you on just how knowledgeable and good he or she is.

We believe that since you are just exploring whether or not you will be using your lawyer friend's services, good taste—and good business—should prevent him or her from charging for the first hour or so of your meeting.

If your friend does charge for an initial consultation, you must make the decision whether or not you are willing to pay for it. Your friend may convince you that he or she is the perfect lawyer for you and that your initial meeting will be so productive it will be worth whatever charge there is.

Whether you decide to proceed or not is up to you. However, you will not have that opportunity unless you first ask the question, "Do you charge for the initial consultation?" More problems are created between lawyers and their clients over miscommunication about fees than in any other area. Make sure you agree on the billing for your first meeting.

Your telephone conversation may not go well. The lawyer could very well become defensive about your Loving Trust requests. He or she may say that it can't be done or that you don't need it; that all you need is a will; that probate is not as bad as it is made out to be, and it isn't that expensive or time-consuming. He or she may even say that probate is different in your state and can be accomplished with streamlined efficiency.

These are responses that we hear about all too often. We believe that they are absolutely wrong. A little bit of probate is usually not all right. That is exactly like a surgeon telling you that a little cancer won't hurt you. If you hear any of these timeworn arguments, politely but firmly end the conversation. You can do better elsewhere. However, if the attorney is not adamantly against the concept but would like to discuss his or her own views, and then suggests that together you can decide the best plan for you, you may want to interview the lawyer. The attorney is showing that he or she is at least open-minded and cares about making the right plan for you.

Another response you may hear is that a Loving Trust is "just an ordinary living trust." Don't fall for this line. There is a world of difference between a bare-bones living trust and a Loving Trust plan. The former has your lawyer's legalese in it; the latter has your complete instructions for your loved ones and includes all of the documents that are necessary to plan for you and your loved ones.

A bare-bones living trust is like a half-finished house, a skeleton of a home that is left half-built with the wind blowing through its unfinished walls. A Loving Trust plan is like the warm homes you see in the magazines during the holiday season. It is full of cheerfulness, good things to eat, and loved ones sharing the goodwill of the holidays. A Loving Trust plan is for loved ones, not hollow hopes and unfinished dreams.

Your friend may want to help you, but admit that he or she is not familiar with Loving Trust planning. The really good lawyers will not attack what they do not know. If the lawyer seems genuinely interested in preparing your Loving Trust plan, tell him or her about the information in this book. You might also suggest that he or she review *The Living Trust Revolution* and *Protect Your Estate*. You might also suggest that your lawyer look into membership in the National Network of Estate Planning Attorneys as explained in the Authors' Note at the end of this book.

Protect Your Estate contains an overview of the process of planning for loved ones. It discusses the legal and tax ramifications of major estate-planning techniques. It is a book written in relatively simple terms that can quickly initiate the nonspecialized professional or interested nonlawyer into major planning concepts.

The Living Trust Revolution explains why a living trust-centered plan is virtually always superior to using a plan based on a will and probate. It once and for all settles the debate as to which type of planning is better. It also explores the reasons why lawyers do not recommend living trust planning all of the time and gives some concrete suggestions as to how a lawyer can change his or her practice from a will-based practice to one based on living trusts using Loving Trust techniques.

It will not take a lot of time or energy for your lawyer to master the information in these books. Most lawyers are intelligent, highly educated, and motivated individuals who are accustomed to studying. Learning the ins and outs of a Loving Trust practice will not be difficult for a lawyer who wants to learn.

Do not waste time; find out as quickly as possible if your friend is interested in a Loving Trust practice. If he or she is unwilling to work with you, thank him or her, ask for a recommendation, and move on. You can either initiate the process with another lawyer friend or utilize the other techniques we describe.

If your lawyer friend accepts the responsibility of preparing your Loving Trust

A Loving Trust plan is for loved ones, not hollow hopes and unfinished dreams.

plan, you should carefully read chapter 24, "How to Work with and Pay Your Lawyer."

Contacting a Lawyer You Have Used

If you already have a lawyer, you should not assume that he or she is a member of the National Network of Estate Planning Attorneys. Ask your attorney if he or she is a member. If not a member, you can find out if your lawyer uses Loving Trust planning techniques and philosophies by following all the steps we have discussed when contacting a lawyer you know but have not used. You should use the same direct approach, and you should ask exactly the same questions as we described in "Contacting a Lawyer You Know But Have Not Used."

Your lawyer may refer you to another partner or associate in his or her firm. If that is your case, you should treat this colleague as if he or she were a complete stranger. You would approach this lawyer in the same manner you would approach a lawyer you don't know.

You Don't Know a Lawyer

We can help you find a member of the National Network of Estate Planning Attorneys or a lawyer who practices using Loving Trust techniques. There are at least four good sources for finding one of these lawyers:

1. Ask friends, relatives, and business associates.
2. Ask your other professional advisers.
3. Contact your bank's trust department.
4. Contact your local Estate Planning Council.

We are confident that you will find either a member of our National Network or a lawyer who uses Loving Trust techniques with one of these methods. As we discuss these methods, we will describe both members of the National Network and those lawyers who are not members but who use Loving Trust planning techniques. Remember that lawyers who are not members of the Network have not been trained as Loving Trust lawyers and do not have access to our special education and practice materials.

Ask Your Friends

Despite the fact that lawyers are far from popular with the public, Loving Trust lawyers usually rank high with their clients. A Loving Trust client generally perceives his or her lawyer as part of a planning team and associates him or her with good thoughts and feelings. Ask your friends if they have either a revocable living trust or a Loving Trust plan. If they do, ask them for the name and telephone number of the lawyer who prepared it.

Most lawyers rely on word-of-mouth advertising. They know that if they do a good job for a client, that client will recommend them to others. A happy client is a good indication that a lawyer has done a good job.

You may have friends, relatives, business associates, and colleagues who have revocable living trusts or Loving Trust planning. Question them as to how they found their lawyer and what they did to check out his or her credentials. Ask them how the lawyer conducted all meetings and on what basis he or she charges. Ask them *how long it took for their trust to be completed.* We emphasize this because too many lawyers take too much time to get their work completed.

Ask Your Advisers

Accountants, financial planners, bankers, and life insurance agents frequently deal with lawyers. They are immersed in the professional community and are usually knowledgeable on who is doing what and how well they are doing it. Most advisers are more than happy to direct you to other professionals with whom they have worked and whom they respect.

We realize that you might not know or work with any of these advisers. If you are in this situation, we suggest that you contact your insurance carriers and ask them for the names of a few of their better insurance agents. You could also ask your friends if they have a top-notch agent that they are happy with. In any case, insurance agents are generous with their time and in most cases should be helpful in assisting you to find the right lawyer.

Don't be surprised if they try to sell you some insurance. That is their job, and the good ones are always on the lookout for new clients. However, do not be put off by this aggressiveness. Take the time to listen to them because they usually have much to say.

If you plan to involve any of your other professional advisers in designing and implementing your Loving Trust plan (we explain how to do this in chapter 26, "How to Get Your Advisers Involved to Save Your Time and Money"), their recommendations can become even more meaningful.

Don't be afraid to ask your advisers whom they would recommend as a good Loving Trust lawyer. Your advisers are there to help you; they will be flattered and will usually go to great lengths to help you find just the right lawyer.

Contact a Trust Officer

Almost every city or town in the United States has a bank with a trust department. Larger cities also have trust companies. By law, trust departments, trust companies, and their employees cannot prepare trust documents. These institutional trustees administer trust documents that are prepared by lawyers engaged in the private practice of the law.

Before a trust department will accept the trusteeship of any trust, its officers will review the actual trust document to see if it meets minimum standards of clarity and legality. Some trusts are rejected because they are legally defective, others because their instructions are too vague or unclear.

Because trust officers review trust documents, they are in constant contact with lawyers who prepare them. Some trust officers have the sole task of calling on lawyers and selling them on the idea of using the trust department as the trustee for the trusts they draft. Trust departments often provide assistance to lawyers who wish to prepare trusts but are insecure with their talents.

Contact the trust departments of your local banks or your local trust companies and make an appointment with one of their trust officers. Share this book with them and ask for a list of lawyers who have such a practice; it is likely that you will be given several names. If you ask, it is also likely that your trust officer will help you set up an appointment with your first choice.

If your bank has a trust department, ask your personal banker for an introduction. He or she will be glad to accommodate you. If your bank does not have a trust department, set aside a few hours and go trust-department shopping. If you arrive at their reception desk, the receptionist will usually arrange for you to meet with a trust officer without a prior appointment.

Remember, you are a potential client for that trust department and the officer you meet with. He or she will want to explain to you why you might wish to choose that trust department as a trustee in your Loving Trust plan.

You will not be charged for this referral service. Trust departments provide much information as a public service. They are a wonderful source of Loving Trust lawyer recommendations. In our opinion, they are the best and most professional source of Loving Trust expertise.

Contact an Estate Planning Council

Most major cities have an Estate Planning Council. Members of the Estate Planning Council include lawyers, accountants, life insurance agents, and financial planners. These professionals meet on a regular basis to discuss trends in estate planning, new laws, and new ideas. They are the professionals who spend much of their time planning estates.

Look in your telephone book to find the phone number of the Estate Planning Council in your area. If you cannot find the number in the phone book, call your local bank's trust department for the number or for information on how you can contact officers or members of your local Estate Planning Council. Once you have located a member or an officer, you should be able to get a list of lawyers who are members. You can then begin the process of contacting its lawyer members.

Meeting a Lawyer You Do Not Know

Once you have the names of lawyers who prepare revocable living trusts or Loving Trust plans, you need to make contact with them. We are advocates of the direct approach. Call the lawyer. This may not be as easy as it sounds. Lawyers are often unable to take calls and may not be able to return your call right away. You may not receive a return call at all unless you leave the proper message.

When a lawyer sees a telephone message from someone whose name does not look familiar, he or she may very well put your call slip on the bottom of the stack assuming that you may be selling something. If you are unable to make contact, leave a message that you are interested in using his or her services and would appreciate a prompt call back. Most lawyers want new clients. When they see your "I'm a potential new client" message, they will likely put your slip on top of their stack.

When you talk with the lawyer, mention who gave you his or her name and state your business. Ask the questions and use the techniques that we described in "Contacting a Lawyer You Know But Have Not Used." If you feel good about your conversation, set an appointment; if not, cut the conversation short with a polite but firm "Thank you" and go to the next name on your list.

Many lawyers leave instructions with their secretaries as to how new clients are to be handled. If this is the case, listen to the secretary and follow his or her procedure. You can take the opportunity to ask about how the lawyer works, the charge for the initial meeting, and any other information you are offered. Secretaries often are better at explaining office procedures than their lawyer bosses. If you still want to talk to the lawyer, insist on it.

Not all lawyers will promptly return your telephone call. If a lawyer, or his or her secretary, does not call you back within a day and a half, go to the next name on your list. This is not the person you want to prepare your Loving Trust plan. Lawyers who are not prompt in returning their phone calls are usually not prompt in getting their work out.

Confirm in Writing

Neither you nor the lawyer wants to start off on the wrong foot. A great way to do so is for either of you to miss the time or day of the first meeting. Communications can go awry; confirm your appointment in writing. It is doubtful that the lawyer's office will do so.

Here is a sample letter for you to use:

> **Lawyers who are not prompt in returning their phone calls are usually not prompt in getting their work out.**

[Date]
[Address]
Dear [Lawyer's Name]:

I look forward to meeting with you at your office on [date of first meeting] at [time of first meeting]. It is my understanding that there will be no charge for this meeting and that it will take between one and two hours.

The purpose of our first meeting is to discuss the design and preparation of my Loving Trust planning. I am enclosing a copy of *Loving Trust*, as well as my completed *My Checklist for Designing My Loving Trust Plan* and *My Personal Information Checklist*. My spouse will be attending our meeting.

If there are any changes, or if any of my statements are not consistent with your understanding, please contact me at your earliest convenience.

Sincerely yours,

> . . . you are employing the lawyer as your adviser. Advisers offer advice and make recommendations. They do not give orders.

Your objective is to find a lawyer you like and who is familiar with Loving Trust planning. Start the relationship with the attitude that you are employing the lawyer as your adviser. Advisers offer advice and make recommendations. They do not give orders. This letter should help you do just that.

We once hired a lawyer to represent us on some legal matters. He was expensive and very well-known. He was also egotistical. We had many disagreements with him over his recommendations, and he always put his recommendations in terms of what we *had* to do. On one occasion, when he stood up and said, "You must do the following things," we finally decided we had had enough. "You're fired! Now, what do we *have* to do?" Our legal "adviser" got the point. His job was to advise us; we would make the decisions. Advisers are supposed to advise; clients are supposed to make decisions.

You must now prepare for your meeting so that it will be as productive as possible.

Chapter Twenty-Four

How to Work with and Pay Your Lawyer

If you wish to reduce your lawyer's fees, you should take the initiative to do as much of your Loving Trust design as you possibly can.

If you wish to reduce your lawyer's fees, you should take the initiative to do as much of your Loving Trust design as you possibly can. You will not want your lawyer to waste his or her time—and your money—on nonlegal matters.

You need to be organized so that you can quickly communicate your Loving Trust instructions to your lawyer. If you do a good job of this, your next meeting should result in a signed Loving Trust plan. You can, in a matter of weeks, have your Loving Trust plan in hand. You are the catalyst that will make your Loving Trust planning possible. How you work with your lawyer will also have a significant impact on the amount of his or her fee.

The First Meeting

Your first meeting with your lawyer is critical. You will need to cover much ground in ascertaining:

- whether to hire him or her
- how much he or she will charge
- whether you wish to modify or embellish your Loving Trust instructions
- when the lawyer's work will be completed

Your first meeting should take between one and two hours. Many people are surprised at this. You might expect it to be longer, but if you follow some of the simple procedures that we will explain, you can get your Loving Trust business efficiently communicated in this time. Please remember that the less time you spend with the lawyer, the lower your fee will be.

You should do most of the spadework so that your lawyer can concentrate on drafting your Loving Trust documents without having to waste time on information gathering and other ministerial functions. Your advance work will make it easier for you to accomplish the objectives of the first meeting and will facilitate your lawyer's grasp of what you want done.

What to Bring to the First Meeting

Bring this book with you. It will help you to make your points and give you confidence when making them. It will also give your lawyer the opportunity to see where you got your ideas so that he or she can better understand what you want accomplished. The book will give you and the lawyer a frame of reference to begin the meeting and will help set the tone of your meeting.

Make sure you bring copies of "My Checklist for Designing My Loving Trust Plan" (you will find this on page 217) and "My Personal Information Checklist" (you will find this at the end of the book). They include key family and financial information that your lawyer will need to know to quickly understand your planning situation. They will also allow him or her to affirm or correct your Loving Trust design. You should have sent copies of both of these checklists with your confirmation letter to give the lawyer a head start in preparing for your meeting.

You should also, if at all possible, bring your spouse. If you don't, you will waste a great deal of time and create unneeded conflict.

We have met too many times with people to discuss a Loving Trust design in the absence of the spouse. The result of such a meeting was that the husband or wife confidently made all the design decisions and assured us that "My wife or husband will love it!" Based on these assurances, we prepared the Loving Trust planning exactly as the person designed it. At the next meeting, when we met to review and sign the trust, everything went wrong. The excluded spouse was usually belligerent and made us go through the "hows" and "whys" of the first meeting all over again. The excluded spouse had no idea what was going on and was suspicious of us and his or her spouse. We spent twice as long as was necessary because we had to repeat ground that had already been covered. Because the excluded spouse was generally hostile, the ambience was ruined, and a fun exercise was turned into a chore.

Bring your spouse to the initial meeting with the lawyer. The only exception to this strict rule is when you do not want your spouse to know about your planning. If that is your situation, make no pretense of telling your lawyer that you are speaking for your spouse.

Interviewing the Lawyer

We use the phrase "interviewing the lawyer" because that is what you ought to be doing in the initial stages of your first meeting. The interviewing process begins as soon as you walk into the lawyer's office. How the reception room is kept up, the attitude of the receptionist, and the manner in which you are greeted are indications of what the lawyer is going to be like.

A dirty or shoddy reception room can be a sign that your lawyer is not very considerate of other people's feelings. If the receptionist or secretary who greets you is discourteous or uncaring, it is almost a sure thing that you will find the same attitude in the lawyer.

You should have to wait no longer than ten or fifteen minutes before you are ushered into the lawyer's office. If the wait approaches the fifteen-minute mark, you should inquire into the reason for the delay. If you cannot get a reasonable response or commitment as to when the lawyer will be ready to meet with you, it is time to leave.

Lawyers are busy and are not always in control of their calendars. However, you should not endure unreasonable delays or unfriendly treatment. Do not forget that you are hiring the lawyer; he or she is not hiring you.

The lawyer's demeanor should reflect courtesy and care. A convivial greeting may mean that you have found a person who is not under the gun and who has the time and the state of mind to concentrate on you and your Loving Trust plan. Regardless of whether he or she is busy or not, you have every right to expect that you will have his or her undivided attention during the course of your meeting.

There should be a minimum amount of time devoted to pleasantries about weather or hobbies, or "How about those Mets?" You are there for a purpose, and so is the lawyer. You have outlined that purpose on the telephone and in your letter confirming the appointment. Use the time wisely, and politely stick to the business at hand.

How the Lawyer Charges

Your first order of business should be to confirm how the lawyer is charging for your meeting. We do not believe that you should be charged for the first meeting or, at the very least, for the first hour or so of that meeting. You need to size one another up so that you can each decide whether you wish to work together.

You should also generally discuss the lawyer's billing procedure. Does the lawyer bill hourly, or does he or she have a set fee? There are very few situations where unexpected circumstances increase the number of hours needed to fully complete a Loving Trust plan. A fair fee should be quoted before the work begins, and you should have the opportunity to say "No, thank you" if it is more than you feel is reasonable or than you can afford.

If the lawyer normally bills hourly, we would suggest that you ask the lawyer to alter the normal billing procedure and quote a fee for your Loving Trust planning. If the lawyer insists on hourly billing, you should ask for a close approximation of the time he or she expects to devote to it and, of course, the hourly rate.

Drafting Loving Trust documents is not like a lawsuit where a lawyer has no control over the time it will involve. A lawyer should know the time it will take to prepare, explain, and get Loving Trust documents signed. If that is not the case, you should extend your "Thank you, but no thank you," and find another lawyer.

One of the complaints that lawyers frequently hear these days is that they charge too much for pushing buttons on their computers; that they do not prepare documents, their machines do. Many people believe that computers do most of a lawyer's work; that the lawyer relies on boilerplate legal documents that are programmed into word processors; and that the lawyer does very little legal thinking. This is not an accurate picture.

We used to give our clients a tour of our word processing center. This was where our clients' Loving Trust documents were produced. Our clients were somewhat taken aback when we actually admitted we used computers. They acted impressed, but we knew they were thinking: I suspected you guys had it made, now I know it. You just have a nonlawyer operator push a button and out comes a document. You sell paper by the pound and charge us full price, but your computers do all the work!

Knowing what they were thinking, we would say, "Every word in those computers is reviewed constantly by our lawyers. We are always updating and improving what we do. Can you imagine the time it has taken us to create all that legal boilerplate so that the computers can spit it back out? If we had to draft your Loving Trust documents from scratch and by hand—if we had to re-create all the words, phrases, and research just for your Loving Trust plan—your fee would be enormous. By using computers and word processors, we can spread the high costs of research and drafting over all our clients. They allow us to charge you far less than your Loving Trust planning is worth. Our technology allows us to spend more time with you, rather than on ministerial production functions. By using modern technology, we can give you your Loving Trust planning quickly and at a very fair price."

Don't complain when you see computers in your lawyer's office—rejoice. By having this type of technology, you can get a better Loving Trust plan at a lower cost. Drafting Loving Trust documents with word processors is much more efficient and accurate than doing it by hand. Your lawyer can tailor his or her boilerplate to your Loving Trust needs, and eliminate wasted time on those aspects of a Loving Trust plan that do not have to be tailored for every client. Technology allows your lawyer to do a good job for you at a fair price and allows the lawyer to make a profit. There is nothing wrong with that. If your lawyer insists on reinventing the wheel, you're going to end up paying for its research and development.

Once you have discussed your lawyer's billing philosophy and method, do not expect that he or she will be able to quote you an exact fee at this juncture. In

> **Don't complain when you see computers in your lawyer's office— rejoice. By having this type of technology, you can get a better Loving Trust plan at a lower cost.**

order to proceed, you still have to discuss your design parameters and make the commitment.

Getting Your Loving Trust Planning Completed

Now is the time that your preparation will pay off. You should give your lawyer "My Checklist for Designing My Loving Trust Plan" and "My Personal Information Checklist." Explain to your lawyer that you want the Loving Trust plan described in "My Checklist for Designing My Loving Trust Plan."

Go over each of your checklists with your lawyer, emphasizing any information you think is particularly helpful to your lawyer's understanding of your Loving Trust. Ask any questions that you have with regard to your Loving Trust planning or trusts in general. This is the time for you to ask the lawyer *all* your questions.

Once your lawyer has reviewed the information in "My Checklist for Designing My Loving Trust Plan" and "My Personal Information Checklist," he or she should bring to your attention any opportunities or problems that he or she has spotted. Because you have given your lawyer complete information about your family, the design of your Loving Trust plan, and the property you own, he or she should be able to concentrate on the legal and tax implications of what you want to do and on the property you have to do it with. These are your lawyer's primary functions.

At this juncture of the first meeting, you and your lawyer should have an excellent idea of how your Loving Trust planning is designed, the elements it consists of, and what needs to be done to prepare your Loving Trust documents. Now it is time for the moment of truth—actually hiring the lawyer to prepare your Loving Trust plan.

The Fees and the Commitment

When you and your lawyer have agreed upon the terms of your Loving Trust planning you should ask your lawyer how much it will cost. Your lawyer should know, based on the information you have provided, the amount of work required to draft your Loving Trust documents and thus should be able to quote a fee. As we stated earlier, get a fee quote if possible. If he or she insists on hourly billing, get a range, with a promise that the Loving Trust planning will not exceed the top end.

If the fee staggers you, ask the lawyer why it is so high. See if you can find out from the lawyer why the fee is higher than you expected. It may be that you and your lawyer can work out a fee that is acceptable to both of you. Don't be afraid to question the fee and discuss it. Your lawyer is as interested in having you happy with the fee as you are.

Should you and the lawyer not be able to agree on a reasonable fee, thank the lawyer for meeting with you and find another lawyer who will do the same work at a lower cost. It is no sin to decline a service that you feel costs more than you can afford or are willing to pay.

Once you have agreed upon the fee, you need to ask an additional question: "When will my Loving Trust plan be done and ready to sign?" No Loving Trust plan ought to take more than three weeks—or a month at the outside—to be completed. They are not that difficult to do if a lawyer is organized and has not overcommitted his or her time. If your lawyer cannot get your Loving Trust plan done in three weeks and set up a meeting for you shortly thereafter, you have the wrong lawyer. Except for vacation, illness, or other unavoidable delay, there is no excuse for taking longer than this to complete your work.

If you and your lawyer can agree on a deadline for completing your Loving Trust plan, you should also agree on the lawyer's retainer. Your lawyer has to commit people and other resources to the preparation of your Loving Trust plan. By requiring a retainer, your lawyer is assured that you have made a commitment too.

Your lawyer may not ask for a retainer; many do not. Whether your lawyer asks for a retainer or not, we believe that you ought to pay for your Loving Trust planning—in full—when it is completed to your satisfaction.

It is imperative that you and your lawyer schedule your next meeting before you leave his or her office. If you do not make a subsequent appointment at that time, you are asking for Murphy and procrastination to stall your Loving Trust planning. Keep the momentum going; set deadlines.

Unless you have a real need or desire to see a draft of your Loving Trust documents, make it clear to your lawyer that you do not want to see "draft agreements" prior to your next meeting. When your lawyer sends you a "draft" of your Loving Trust plan, he or she is giving you a homework assignment—in effect, asking you to review it. Most of our clients were not interested in homework, and you may not be either. You are not a lawyer, and you ought not have the responsibility for reviewing your lawyer's legal work if you do not want to. Your lawyer has all the information needed to successfully draft your Loving Trust plan. If your lawyer needs more information, he or she can call you. You will want your lawyer to review your entire Loving Trust document with you at the next meeting. You will then have the opportunity to ask your questions and to point out errors.

Confirm Your Agreement in Writing

You should confirm your agreement in writing within a few days after your meeting. It will put the burden on your lawyer to keep the commitments he or she made.

We have included a sample letter for you to pattern your letter after. It is well worth your time to write and send it. The letter is designed to protect both you and your lawyer from any misunderstanding that may have taken place as a result of your first meeting:

[Date]

[Heading]

Dear [Lawyer's Name]:

I enjoyed meeting with you and look forward to working with you on my Loving Trust planning.

This letter is to confirm those agreements that we made in our meeting. For a total fee of _____, you are going to prepare my Loving Trust planning based on "My Checklist for Designing My Loving Trust Plan" that I discussed and left with you. On [date and time of day agreed at last meeting] I will meet with you in your office to review and sign my Loving Trust documents.

If this is not your understanding, please get back to me as soon as possible.

Sincerely yours,

The Last Meeting

We have deliberately chosen to call this second or follow-up meeting the last meeting. Except in extraordinary circumstances, no more than two meetings are necessary to discuss, agree to, and sign Loving Trust documents. If you have completely filled in and presented "My Checklist for Designing My Loving Trust Plan" and "My Personal Information Checklist," two meetings are all that are needed to get the job done. Two meetings also conserve your lawyer's time and keep fees to a minimum.

Your last meeting should take no longer than two or three hours. It is likely to be somewhat longer than your first meeting because it will be devoted to reviewing your finished Loving Trust documents. Your lawyer should take you through the entire document, answer your questions, and make needed corrections at that time. You shouldn't leave without signing your Loving Trust documents.

Don't forget to bring your spouse to your last meeting. You may also wish to invite your individual trustees to attend. The learning experience will be invaluable and will make them much better trustees. They can ask questions and become real participants.

You should also consider inviting your other advisers to this meeting. In chapter 26, "How to Get Your Advisers Involved to Save Your Time and Money," we discuss just that.

Many times we have had last meetings where an insurance agent, accountant, or other adviser attended. These meetings were invariably more successful because of the adviser's participation. Whether other advisers attend or not is up to you, but you should allow them the opportunity to attend if you, and they, think it would be helpful.

Reviewing and Signing Your Loving Trust Documents

Your lawyer should go through your Loving Trust planning with you. The review ought not to be a word-for-word reading of the document. Your lawyer should explain each paragraph in simple and easy-to-understand terms. As your lawyer reaches each part of your Loving Trust plan that presents one of your design alternatives, your lawyer should refer to "My Checklist for Designing My Loving Trust Plan."

You should also look at "My Loving Trust Diagram." As your lawyer explains each subtrust, you can refer to the diagram and begin to become comfortable with how your Loving Trust plan is put together.

As you are taken through your Loving Trust planning, do not hesitate to ask questions. Some of its legal phrases and terms may confuse you or be foreign to you. It is perfectly all right to ask questions about these confusing aspects of your Loving Trust plan.

As you and your lawyer review your Loving Trust plan, mistakes may be found. These can be typographical errors or substantive errors that change the meaning of your Loving Trust plan. Such errors, in this day of fast and efficient technology, can be corrected while you are in the lawyer's office.

After you and your lawyer have reviewed your Loving Trust documents, and you are comfortable with what they say, you should sign them.

You should sign a minimum of three Loving Trust plans. Unlike a will, which should have only one original, a Loving Trust plan can have many duplicate originals. For your protection, you should have an original Loving Trust plan, so should your lawyer and your trustees. Who gets originals is up to you, but remember, you can have as many duplicate originals as you want.

After you and your lawyer have reviewed your Loving Trust documents, and you are comfortable with what they say, you should sign them.

You will also sign a "Pour-Over Will" and "Durable Special Powers of Attorney." Do not worry about these, they are just "fail-safe" mechanisms to make absolutely sure your property is put into your trust if you neglect to do so while you are alive and healthy. We will discuss these documents at length in chapter 25, "How to Get Property into Your Loving Trust Plan."

Finishing the Last Meeting

Once you have reviewed and signed your living trust and the other documents related to it, there are still a few more matters to take care of. The first is a discussion you will have with your lawyer with regard to putting property into your Loving Trust plan. Chapter 25, "How to Get Property into Your Loving Trust Plan," is devoted to explaining just how that is done.

Your lawyer can help you put your property into your Loving Trust plan. Your lawyer should review "My Personal Information Checklist" and point out any problem areas that may arise in doing this. He or she can answer any questions you may have about the procedure you must follow. You can either totally rely upon your lawyer to put your property into your Loving Trust plan, or you can involve him or her only on a limited basis.

The last order of your last-meeting business is to pay your lawyer. As we previously mentioned, your commitment is to write a check for the services you received. You should also give him or her a sincere "Thank you." This is just as important as being prompt in your payment. Your lawyer will very much appreciate your "Thanks." Many lawyers work for more than money, and this is especially true of Loving Trust lawyers.

If the Law Changes

You should ask your lawyer what happens if there is a subsequent change in the law that affects your Loving Trust planning. We are strong advocates of the position that by taking you on as a client, your lawyer should also take the responsibility for contacting you if there is a change in the law that affects your Loving Trust planning.

There have been very few changes in trust law as compared to other legal areas. While changes in trust law are uncommon, changes in the federal estate-tax laws have been more frequent. Even so, those changes have largely affected those who have large estates; they have not had such a far-reaching impact on the great majority of the population as to be a burden to most lawyers.

Your lawyer should contact you if there is a change in the law that affects your Loving Trust planning. He or she should also explain how it affects your trust, what needs to be done to make it current, and what the charge will be to get the amendment done. We have included a sample letter for you to use for this purpose.

> [Date]
>
> [Heading]
>
> Dear [Lawyer's Name]:
>
> I would like to thank you once again for preparing my Loving Trust plan. As you can imagine, I am vitally concerned that my Loving Trust planning is kept up-to-date with changes in the laws. While I recognize that I have a responsibility to apprise you of changes in my life that may affect my Loving Trust planning, I want to make sure that you will notify me whenever you believe a change in the law will affect my Loving Trust planning.
>
> I will rely on you to keep me informed as to changes in the laws and with respect to your recommendations as well.
>
> I understand that any changes I make in my Loving Trust planning will not be covered by my original fee and will be subject to a fee arrangement that we will agree on.
>
> Sincerely yours,

Original Documents

When you leave your lawyer's office, take your original Pour-Over Will, your living trust, and all your other original documents with you. Your lawyer can keep duplicate originals or copies of all the documents that he or she needs. There is no reason whatsoever to leave your original documents with the lawyer. You should keep them in your possession.

Since there will be several originals of most documents, and since they will be spread among several people, there is no reason to take special precautions to protect them. Keep them where you keep all your important papers. Do not put all of them in a safe-deposit box. If you die or become disabled, safe-deposit boxes can be difficult for other members of your family to get into.

You will have one original of your Pour-Over Will. Since there is only one original will, you should keep it in a safe place. If you have named an institutional trustee, it is likely that the institution will store a complete set of your documents, including your Pour-Over Will, in its trust vault, free of charge.

Make sure to tell your trustees and your beneficiaries where your original documents can be found. If anything happens to you, there should always be

Make sure to tell your trustees and your beneficiaries where your original documents can be found.

someone who knows where to look for your important papers. These precautions may seem a little silly, but the old saying that "an ounce of prevention is worth a pound of cure" certainly applies here.

Tune-ups

Our world is built around change. Circumstances change, people change, laws change. We cannot prevent change from occurring in our lives.

When changes occur that may affect your Loving Trust planning, it is quite simple to change or amend your Loving Trust planning to adapt to those changes. Unlike a will, a Loving Trust plan is made to readily accept change. Your lawyer can make such a change easily and quickly by preparing an amendment to your Loving Trust document.

In most cases, a short letter to your lawyer explaining the change will enable the lawyer to draft it and send it back to you in a short period of time. There is generally no reason for a formal visit unless you want to redesign your Loving Trust planning on a massive scale. And, unless you have had major changes in your life, there is no reason for follow-up or regular visits.

If you take the time and make the effort to locate a good Loving Trust lawyer, and if you adequately prepare for your meetings with him or her, two meetings should suffice to create a Loving Trust plan that will serve your and your loved ones' needs for a long time to come.

Chapter Twenty-Five

How to Get Property into Your Loving Trust Plan

Property that you own in your name, joint tenancy property, property owned in tenancy in common, and life insurance and retirement plan proceeds that name someone other than your Loving Trust as primary beneficiary will not be controlled by your Loving Trust plan. To make your Loving Trust plan work, you must get your property into it.

When we talk about getting your property into your Loving Trust plan, we are really talking about putting your assets in the name of the revocable living trust that is the foundation of your Loving Trust plan. A Loving Trust plan, as you now know, is much more than a simple boilerplate revocable living trust. It is a plan that not only includes a revocable living trust that contains your instructions for you and your loved ones, but it also includes other documents that help ensure that your property will be used for your benefit while you are alive and for the benefit of your loved ones and charities after you have passed away.

You have several choices as to how you can get your property into your Loving Trust plan. One choice is to do nothing and let the probate court do it. That choice is not acceptable to most of us. A Loving Trust plan is supposed to *avoid* probate, so letting the probate court control how your property is put into your Loving Trust plan is self-defeating.

Another choice is for you to put property into your Loving Trust plan solely through your own efforts. That is what the traditional how-to books tell you to do. They give you a great number of forms to help you be your own lawyer. Norman F. Dacey, in *How to Avoid Probate!*, includes more than 550 pages of forms, and there is a coupon in the back to order even more! Most of these forms are written in complicated legalese that even most lawyers would find confusing. It is no wonder that most do-it-yourself legal forms invariably do not work.

Putting your property into your Loving Trust plan is easy only if you know

247

what you are doing. Anyone who tells you differently doesn't have any idea of the legal problems and complexities that can arise if you don't do the job right.

If you have property in joint tenancy with right of survivorship, property in tenancy in common, life insurance, a retirement plan, a business, investments, or other types of property, you are talking about a potential nightmare if you attempt to transfer it into your Loving Trust without help. Good old Murphy and his law will be knocking at your door for sure.

Let's put this into perspective. In probate, the court-appointed agent almost always retains a lawyer to do the work. Probate takes a great deal of time but not always because some lawyer is dragging his or her feet. Many times the probate process is longer than it ought to be because of the difficulty in finding exactly what property is owned and where the title to the property is.

Think about what you own. You are lucky if you can find it, let alone its title. Imagine how hard it will be for someone else to do it when you are not able to help.

When you put property into your living trust, you are, in effect, probating your own estate. It is a whole lot easier and cheaper to do your own probate while you are alive and well than it is to have someone else do it after you are disabled or dead. The trick to putting property into your Loving Trust is to get it done *quickly* and *correctly* at the lowest possible cost.

> The trick to putting property into your Loving Trust is to get it done *quickly* and *correctly* at the lowest possible cost.

Make Someone Accountable

A Dacey or Stock trust may end up invalid because a do-it-yourselfer chose the wrong form, signed in the wrong spot, or made some other mistake. Sometimes, the do-it-yourself form is valid, but is incorrectly utilized. In either case, what was supposed to happen—avoiding probate—didn't, because Murphy took over.

Who suffers from all of these mistakes? Not the author of the do-it-yourself book. The author sold the book and is on to other projects. Not Murphy. He has triumphed once again and is stalking more victims. The only ones who suffer are the do-it-yourselfers and their loved ones. What recourse is there if do-it-your-selfers make a mistake that costs a lot of money? If they are alive but disabled, we suppose they could sue themselves, and if they are dead, their loved ones could sue the estate for that mistake.

Ridiculous? Of course it is. Since our do-it-yourselfer wanted to save a few dollars by practicing law, using the "on-the-job training" method advocated by do-it-yourself authors, he or she could cost loved ones a great deal of heartache and money. Often those loved ones would be better off if the do-it-yourselfer had left a cheap will. Had an equally incompetent lawyer done the same bad job, the lawyer could be sued for malpractice and be held accountable.

We know of a lawyer who once was asked to do a favor for a neighbor. The neighbor owned a summer home in the mountains with two of his brothers-in-law. The neighbor liked one brother-in-law; the other "deadbeat" he disliked intensely.

The neighbor wanted to give his third of the summer home to the brother-in-law he liked. So what did the lawyer do? A deed was prepared, signed, and recorded giving the neighbor's third of the summer home to the deadbeat. Our story has a good ending: The lawyer and his malpractice insurance company straightened it out and compensated the neighbor for the lawyer's mistake.

The task the lawyer was given was simple and done as a favor, but the lawyer was held accountable and paid for his error.

The best way to put property into your living trust is to use other people to do it for you. Use your advisers' expertise. Let them take the responsibility, the accountability, and the liability for putting your property into your living trust. You do not have to work hard if you do this, *you just have to work smart.*

Work Smart, Not Hard

We have shown you how to design your own Loving Trust plan and how to get it prepared at the lowest possible cost. Our techniques for putting property in your Loving Trust will also keep your costs down. By working smart on the front end, you can let others do the hard work at little or no cost to you. Even if you have to pay to get some of the work done, it will be cheaper than trying to do it yourself or not doing it at all. Not putting your property into your trust, or not putting it in correctly, will cost you and your loved ones far more than paying a few dollars to get it done right.

Fill In "My Personal Information Checklist"

At the end of this book you will find "My Personal Information Checklist." Be careful to list all your property as you fill it in. Do not worry about things that you own that are of little value. You can lump them together in the category we call "Other Personal Property." Concern yourself with your valuable property. Your residence(s), your business, investments, collections, jewelry, and other valuable property should be included in your checklist.

Locate the Titles to Your Property

Locate the titles to the property you have listed. For every type of property, there is a method of identifying who owns it. The word "title" is a sort of general, catchall term used to describe how property is owned. The term "evidence of title" is the actual document that shows title. For example, a car title is the piece of paper you look at to decide who owns a particular car. The document itself is the evidence of title. The name on the car title determines the car's ownership. Like a car title, there is some document or other evidence that identifies how most property is owned. If the document that evidences title cannot be found, neither you nor your lawyer will be able to determine the ownership.

Cowboy movies show a great example of the use of title. Remember the ones where some outlaws steal a herd of steers and then try to sell them? Someone always says, "How do I know you own 'em?" The outlaws don't have their own brand or a bill of sale, of course, and the fight is on.

Ascertaining the title to your real estate, cars, and investments can be easy. If you have real estate, your deed is your title. Read the deed and you know whose name your real estate is in. For a car or other licensed vehicle, like a boat or a truck, look at your title. It works the same as a deed. Whoever's name is on the title is the owner. For stocks, your stock certificate is your title. For bonds, the bond itself is the title.

To locate the title to most of your property, you need only remember one thing:

> Your title to property is whatever document or documents you received when
> you bought the property and would need if you were to sell it.

If you made investments in partnerships, real estate trusts, or other more exotic property, you signed the documents when you made your investment. These documents are your evidence of title. If you handle your investments through stockbrokers and they hold your investments, then your brokerage account is your evidence of title. Whatever you signed to set up the account is what you need to ascertain your ownership.

There are some types of property that are sold without legal documents passing hands. Let's use your bicycle as an example. When you sell it, you either get cash or a check. No one asks about title. If you buy a bike from a store, however, you are given a bill of sale, called a receipt. That is your title to your bike. If you later sell your bike, you really should give the buyer a bill of sale. Almost all personal property like bikes, clothes, and furniture are bought and sold using a bill of sale. That is what is used to transfer them from one person to another.

The same is true of collections, such as artwork or stamps, and most other forms of personal property. Sometimes you keep the bill of sale (receipt), sometimes you do not. If you do not, then your canceled check is your receipt and your proof of title to the property. If you pay cash, then "possession is nine-tenths of the law." The fact that you have the property in your possession means you probably own it.

To determine title to the property you possess but for which you do not have a receipt or a canceled check, you need to look to who paid for it. If you paid for it out of your money, it is yours. If the money came from a joint account, then the property is owned jointly.

Bank accounts, savings accounts, certificates of deposit, and other cash investments are created by signing a signature card or other document establishing the account. Whatever you signed to set up the account is your evidence of title to that account.

Life insurance policies, disability policies, and retirement plans differ from most types of property when you are looking for the particulars of ownership. You will need to locate your life insurance policies and disability policies, along with the application you originally signed and any changes in the policies, called endorsements. It is on the application—not the policy—that you will find who owns it and who will receive the proceeds.

You must find the beneficiary designations for your insurance policies and your retirement plans. They are needed so that the proceeds can be directed into your trust.

To help you locate the title to your property, each category of property in "My Personal Information Checklist" explains what document is your evidence of title. For real estate, as an example, it is a deed. For a partnership, it is usually the partnership agreement. It has spaces for you to mark whose name your property is in. You will mark one of the following categories of ownership:

- Your Name Alone
- Your Spouse's Name Alone
- Joint Tenancy with Right of Survivorship (this includes Tenancy by the Entirety Property)
- Tenancy in Common
- Community Property
- Don't know

By reading the various titles to your property, you should have little trouble figuring out who legally owns what. If you cannot, don't worry about it. Bring to your lawyer the documents that you think show title and get help. There is no reason for you to agonize over title. It takes three years of law school and a few years of experience for a lawyer to begin to understand title. Do not expect to be an instant expert. It takes a lot of training to understand the intricacies of property ownership. This is a major point that traditional do-it-yourself authors neglect to tell their unfortunate readers.

Your other advisers can be of great assistance in locating title to your property. If you cannot find the deed to your house or to your investment properties, contact the broker or lawyer who handled the purchase for you, the bank who provided the mortgage money, or the title company that helped close the sale. One or the other will likely have the deed or a copy of it. For stock or bond

> It takes three years of law school and a few years of experience for a lawyer to begin to understand title. Do not expect to be an instant expert.

investments, contact the broker who sold them to you. For life insurance, contact your life insurance agent. For your group insurance, go to your personnel department or benefits office.

If you devote a little thought to how you acquired your property, you should be able to think of someone who can help you. Don't be shy in asking your advisers to do this. They will likely not mind doing it and will save you time and money. Please remember to work smart, not hard.

Know the Name of Your Trust

Your trust will have its own "legal" name that will appear on the titles to property contained in it. The legal name of your trust must state the names of your trustees, your name as its maker, and the date the trust was signed. For example, a trust created by Franklin H. Cosbie, whose trustees are Franklin and his wife, Gretchen, would have as its name:

> Franklin H. Cosbie and Gretchen E. Cosbie, trustees, or their successors in trust, under the Franklin H. Cosbie Living Trust, and any amendments thereto, dated _____, 19__.

That's quite a name, and will take some getting used to. Like anything else, after you use it for a while, it won't seem so bad. Using the proper name of your trust is vital when you are putting property into your trust. Both you and your advisers must know your trust's legal name.

The proper name of your trust will appear in your trust itself if your lawyer uses our approach. If, for some reason, the name of your trust does not appear in your trust document, ask your lawyer to write it down for you.

Property in Joint Tenancy with Your Spouse

As you locate your titles, you may find that you have property in joint tenancy with right of survivorship, or tenancy by the entirety, with your spouse. Joint tenancy, as we made clear earlier in this book, is not a good way to hold title to property.

Joint tenancy is a very complex method of owning property, even though it may not seem so on its face. You will be making a major mistake if you attempt to change your joint tenancy property to some other form of ownership by yourself. You should not make any attempt to transfer property held in joint tenancy without consulting with your lawyer.

Joint tenancy property offers special problems that can have far-reaching effects if improperly transferred to your Loving Trust. Before it is put into your trust, you must either put it into your name, your spouse's name, or in tenancy in common. Which of these alternatives is best for you is based on your age, your spouse's age, the nature of the property, and what it is worth. The quality of your marriage and other personal considerations also weigh heavily on how this property is to be titled.

A few minutes with a Loving Trust lawyer will go a long way in determining how your joint property should be transferred into your trust. Failure to correctly transfer this property can result in unfavorable tax results.

Community Property

In some community property states, you and your spouse will find it quite easy to create your own Loving Trust plans and put your community property in them. However, in community property states like California, there are hidden traps for those who stumble along without proper advice. In California, use of a joint trust for you and your spouse eliminates most of the problems that arise with regard to property transfers.

Willy-nilly transfers of community property can create havoc when funding a Loving Trust. A Loving Trust lawyer can quickly advise you how to properly transfer your community property to your Loving Trust plan.

If you live in a community property state and you have property in joint tenancy with your spouse, there are some potentially devastating income-tax results that can occur upon either of your deaths. It is especially important for you to discuss with your lawyer how title to this property should be changed, and this is true whether or not you use a Loving Trust plan.

Joint Tenancy Among Nonspouses

Property held in joint tenancy between nonspouses definitely needs to be examined by a lawyer. We have seldom, if ever, seen a situation where nonspouses owned property in joint tenancy and it accomplished their objectives, or where its owners fully understood the consequences. Once property is in joint tenancy between nonspouses, transferring it out can create gift taxes and other unexpected consequences. Worse yet, there may be lingering gift-tax problems from when the property was originally put in joint tenancy! Real problems arise when nonspouses hold property in joint tenancy, and we strongly recommend that you ask your lawyer how he or she is going to straighten them out.

Homestead Property

Some states have special laws regarding primary residences that protect them from creditors and that may reduce property taxes. This property is called homestead property. You should ask your lawyer to advise you as to the effects of transferring this property into your trust.

Let Your Fingers Do the Walking

Once you know what you own and where the titles are, you can decide which advisers will transfer what property into your trust. You need only contact them and tell them what you want done.

Rather than give you 550 pages of Dacey-like forms, we will show you how all your property can easily, quickly, and inexpensively be put into your trust by professionals who know what they are doing and *who will be accountable for their actions*.

We have included sample letters for you to use that will put the burden on your advisers and other people to transfer property into your trust. You should use these letters, or ones like them, if you expect to get your property into your trust and have a chance to hold accountable the professional who does it. Always keep for your files a copy of the letter you write. If you leave a good paper trail, you will not get lost or ambushed by fast-talking professionals.

Your Lawyer

The professional with whom the transferring process begins is your lawyer. He or she will have the expertise to advise you on the best and most efficient methods of transferring your property to your trust.

Generally, the more property you have and the more valuable it is, the more you need to rely on your lawyer to help transfer it into your trust. If you have modest amounts of property, you will be able to rely more heavily on others for help. In either case, you should discuss the transferring process with your lawyer. Taking a little extra time with your lawyer to discuss any transferring pitfalls and opportunities will certainly save you time, money, and aggravation.

In most situations, there is no need to have your lawyer make every transfer of property into your Loving Trust. Lawyers are better and more efficient at transferring some types of property than others. They are particularly skilled at transferring real estate. For example, getting your residence, or any other real estate, out of joint tenancy and into your trust is a perfect use of a lawyer's talents.

Community property transfers should also be left to your lawyer, because of the income tax ramifications. Putting valuable personal property into your trust—jewelry, artwork, collections, and the like—is old hat to a lawyer. Closely held business interests, such as family corporations, partnerships, and sole proprietorships, should be transferred by your lawyer. In addition, copyrights, patents, and other rights to receive income, like accounts or notes receivable, are best transferred by your lawyer.

Your lawyer will also know about different devices used to transfer property into a trust. For example, some states have adopted a law called the Uniform Probate Code. The Uniform Probate Code is a liberal probate law that is intended

> . . . the more property you have and the more valuable it is, the more you need to rely on your lawyer to help transfer it into your trust.

to make probate easier and cheaper to do. Whether it has or not is very questionable, but among its by-products are some simple methods for putting property into a trust.

One such method for transferring some types of property into a trust is a payable on death (POD) designation. It is a device that allows you to have a beneficiary designation for many kinds of property. Under a POD, the title can remain in your name. Upon your death, however, the property automatically passes to your trust. A POD is simple and effective. Ask your lawyer if your state allows you to use it.

A useful device for transferring real estate into a Loving Trust is called an unrecorded deed. Some states allow you to complete a deed that effectively transfers your real estate into your trust even though you do not record it. Your trustee can record it on your death or disability. The effect is to avoid probate and avoid the sometimes inconvenient process of actually recording the deed. If you have a substantial amount of real estate, an unrecorded deed can eliminate some of the hassles of putting real estate in a trust. This is a transfer method that you should ask your lawyer about.

There are many methods for transferring property into your trust. Your lawyer has the expertise to determine which is best for you. Ask your lawyer which property he or she should transfer and which property your other advisers can transfer.

Life and disability insurance proceeds, bank accounts, brokerage accounts, and retirement plan proceeds are some types of property that can be transferred into your trust by your other advisers. We will explain how this is done in the sections that follow. By working together as a team, you, your lawyer, and your other advisers can properly and quickly transfer your property into your trust at the lowest possible cost.

After you and your lawyer have an understanding of what property he or she will be transferring into your trust, ask your lawyer how much it will cost. Most lawyers will charge hourly for this work. This is a fair approach because there is no way, in most cases, for your lawyer to know in advance how long it will take to get the job done.

Your lawyer should be able to estimate how many hours it will take to transfer your property into your trust. Use his or her estimate as your cost benchmark and tell your lawyer to contact you if it appears that this estimate will be exceeded.

If your lawyer has paralegals, the name given to highly trained nonlegal professionals who work for lawyers, then ask your lawyer if his or her paralegals can do the work. Legal secretaries can also be used to transfer property into a trust, and you should ask your lawyer if that is possible in your case. Ideally, you want secretaries or paralegals to do all the transfer work and your lawyer to review what they have done. This takes far less of your lawyer's expensive time and uses your lawyer's skills in the most efficient manner. The billing rate of secretaries and paralegals is usually far less than your lawyer's.

When you retain your lawyer to transfer all or some of your property to your trust, you should confirm your understanding in writing.

[Date]

[Heading]

Dear [Lawyer's Name]:

In our meeting on [Date], we agreed that you would transfer property into my trust. We agreed that you would charge on an hourly basis and that you anticipate spending no more than _____ hours. Should the time you need exceed this number of hours, you will contact me before proceeding. It is my understanding that you will use paralegals and secretaries as much as possible to make the transfers, and that you will be involved primarily in the supervision and review of the transfers.

The property that you will transfer to my trust will be all the property listed on *My Personal Information Checklist*, with which I furnished you, except the following property, which my other advisers will transfer for me.

We both recognize that transfers to my trust should be accomplished as soon as possible to avoid any problems should I become disabled or die; time is of the essence.

Sincerely yours,

Much of your property can be transferred by other people. Many of them will do so at no cost or at significantly less cost than your lawyer.

Your Insurance Agent

One of the best, if not the best, of your inexpensive advisers is your insurance agent. For the most part, insurance agents work on a commission. While the amount of commissions varies, depending on what you buy and how much you spend, insurance agents usually earn every dime that they get. Once you buy a product through them, they will continue to service that product free of charge.

You need to contact the insurance agent who sold you your life or disability insurance policies. Tell your agent that you want to change the beneficiary of your insurance to your trust and that you want him or her to do it.

Your agent should furnish you with Change of Beneficiary forms that he or she has already filled in. If they are blank, ask your agent to complete them before signing.

Most insurance companies require that a primary beneficiary and a contingent beneficiary be named on a beneficiary designation. The primary beneficiary will be your living trust. The contingent beneficiary can be anyone you want. Your contingent beneficiary will receive the insurance proceeds only if you revoke or cancel your Loving Trust plan and forget to change your primary beneficiary.

Here is a form letter that you can send to your insurance agent.

[Date]

[Heading]

RE: Change of Beneficiary Designation for [Your Name]

Dear [Your Insurance Agent's Name]:

Pursuant to our conversation of [Date], this letter is to confirm changing the beneficiary designation of the following [Life Insurance] [Disability] policies:

Insured Name of Company   Policy Number

Please change the primary beneficiary of each of the policies to: _____, trustees, or their successors in trust, under the _____ Living Trust, and any amendments thereto, dated _____, 19___.

I am relying on you, as my agent, to perform all the appropriate steps to assure that my beneficiary designations are changed properly. Please notify me in writing when you have completed the changes.

Sincerely yours,

In most cases, your agent will be kind enough to change the beneficiary designation of all your policies, whether he or she sold them to you or not. However, if he or she declines to do so, you should seriously consider changing agents. If you do not have an insurance agent, contact the local representative of the insurance company who issued the policy and explain what you need done. You should confirm your conversation in writing.

[Date]

[Heading]

RE: Change of Beneficiary Designation for [Your Name]

Dear [Name of Person with Whom You Spoke]:

Pursuant to our conversation of [Date], I wish to change the beneficiary designations of the following policy(ies):

Insured Policy Number

Please send me a Change of Beneficiary designation for each policy, as soon as possible, as I am doing personal planning for me and my family. Thank you for your prompt attention to this matter.

Sincerely,

If you have any questions about the beneficiary designations you receive from the insurance company, call and have them explained to you. Life insurance companies are in a people-oriented business, and it has been our experience that they go overboard to be courteous and kind. They will help you as best they can to solve any problems or answer any questions you may have concerning your beneficiary designations.

Some life insurance companies are very particular about how they allow a beneficiary designation naming a trust to read. They have determined their own rules and may reject your beneficiary designation. If this happens to you, take the path of least resistance and use their suggested language. The result will be the same and you will be spared the aggravation of taking on the company's red-tape bureaucracy.

You would be wise to have your lawyer quickly review these changes. This will assure you that the beneficiary forms have been completed correctly and that your lawyer will stand behind them in the event of an error.

For employer group policies, you will need to seek out the proper person in your company's personnel or benefits office. This person will have the proper forms for you to sign. If your company benefits representative is unsure about what to do, you should have him or her talk with either your life insurance agent or your lawyer. You can also request that your company's insurance agent contact you. You can be sure that he or she will know about what you want, and how to accomplish it.

Whether you use your company benefits representative or the company's insurance agent to change the beneficiary of your company insurance policies, confirm the change in writing. Here is a form letter that you can use to confirm your request:

[Date]

[Heading]

RE: Change of Beneficiary Designation for [Your Name]

> **If you have any questions about the beneficiary designations you receive from the insurance company, call and have them explained to you.**

Dear [Company Representative or Your Company's Insurance Agent]:

I wish to change the beneficiary designation of the following policy(ies) that I have as an employee of [Company Name]:

Type of Policy   Policy Number

Please change the primary beneficiary of each of the policies to: _____, trustees, or their successors in trust, under the _____ Living Trust, and any amendments thereto, dated _____, 19___.

Since I am doing Loving Trust planning, it is very important that these changes are made as quickly as possible. I am relying on you to do so. If you have any questions, please do not hesitate to contact me at your earliest convenience.

Thank you for your prompt attention to this matter.

Sincerely,

Avoid completing any change of beneficiary designation forms yourself. If all else fails, let your lawyer do them. If you provide your lawyer with the proper forms, he or she will have no difficulty in completing them for you. Your objective should always be to have a professional make the change so, if there is a mistake, you will have someone who is accountable to make you or your loved ones whole.

Your Stockbroker

Ask your stockbroker to change the name of your stocks and bonds into the name of your trust. For good customers, there is usually no charge or a nominal charge. If you're a light trader, or a nontrader, you will be charged a fee for each certificate you have. These fees are usually far less than a lawyer would charge.

To change the name on your stocks, bonds, or other securities, your stockbroker will need your original certificates. Make certain you are given a written receipt for these certificates. Once endorsed by you, they may well be negotiable and easily stolen. To protect yourself and to hold your stockbroker accountable, do not leave any securities with your stockbroker without a written, signed receipt.

If you own stocks, bonds, mutual funds, money market funds, or any other investments through an account with a stock brokerage firm, changing the name of the account to the name of your trust will have the effect of putting everything in that account in the name of your trust. Accounts like this are called

> **Your objective should always be to have a professional make [a] change so, if there is a mistake, you will have someone who is accountable to make you or your loved ones whole.**

259

"Street Name" accounts. There is no charge that we know of for changing a street account name. It can be done with a few entries into the stockbroker's computer.

As always, confirm the change of account name or the change of the certificates themselves in writing. Make your stockbroker accountable exactly as you have your lawyer and your insurance agent. Here are two form letters for you to use. The first is for actual stock certificates or bonds. The second is for a change in the name of your account.

[Date]

[Heading]

RE: Name Change of Securities for [Your Name]

Dear [Name of Stockbroker]:

On [Date], I left certain securities with you so that you can transfer the ownership from me to the name of my trust. I have attached a copy of the receipt that you gave me, setting forth the securities that I left with you.

Please change the name on each of the certificates to: _____, trustees, or their successors in trust, under the _____ Living Trust, and any amendments thereto, date _____, 19___.

I am relying on you to make these transfers accurately and as soon as possible, as I am doing personal planning for me and my family. It is my understanding that you will charge me _____ for each certificate changed.

Please notify me in writing when you have completed the changes.

Sincerely yours,

For a change of account name only, use the following letter:

[Date]

[Heading]

RE: Change of Account Name for [Your Name]

Dear [Name of Stockbroker]:

On [Date], I requested you to change account number _____, which is currently in the name of [Current Account Name], to the name of my trust. The account name should now read: _____, trustees, or their successors in trust, under the _____ Living Trust, and any amendments thereto, dated _____, 19___.

I am relying on you to make this change in account name accurately and as soon as possible, as I am doing personal planning for me and my family. It is my understanding that there is no charge for this name change.

Please notify me in writing when you have completed the change.

Sincerely yours,

Tax shelters, limited partnerships, and other investments that you have made through your stockbroker can also be changed into the name of your trust by your stockbroker. Your stockbroker will either know how to do it or whom to contact to make the change. If you cannot locate the broker who sold you these investments, look at your investment information and write the promoter directly. You will be instructed by the promoter in how to accomplish a name change. Once again, you need to use a letter to assure that the proper change of name will be made.

[Date]

[Heading]

Re: [Name of Investment]

Dear [Name of Promoter]:

On [Date], I telephoned you with regard to changing the name of my investment in [Name of Investment] to the name of my trust. Enclosed are copies of the documents I signed when I purchased the investment.

The name of my trust is: _____, trustees, or their successors in trust, under the _____ Living Trust, and any amendments thereto, dated _____, 19___.

Please change the name of my investment from my name to the name of my trust and send me any documents that I must sign to make the transfer complete. I would appreciate your making this change as soon as possible, as I am doing personal planning for me and my family. Thank you for your prompt attention to this matter.

Sincerely yours,

If you have an IRA or Keogh plan with your stockbroker, or if you have purchased life insurance through your stockbroker, your broker can arrange to change your beneficiary designations. You should use the following letters to request and confirm that your stockbroker has the forms necessary to change your beneficiaries.

[Date]

[Heading]

RE: Change of Beneficiary Designation for [Your Name]

Dear [Name of Stockbroker]:

This letter is to confirm changing the beneficiary designation of the following life insurance policies:

Insured Name of Company   Policy Number

Please change the primary beneficiary of each of the policies to: _____, trustees, or their successors in trust, under the _____ Living Trust, and any amendments thereto, dated _____, 19___.

I am relying on you to take all appropriate steps to assure that my beneficiary designations are properly changed. Please notify me in writing when you have completed the changes.

Sincerely yours,

The form letter to use for changing the beneficiary for an IRA or Keogh plan:

[Date]

[Heading]

RE: Change of Beneficiary Designation for [Name of Retirement Plan and Account Number]

Dear [Name of Stockbroker]:

This letter is to confirm changing the beneficiary designation for [Name of Retirement Plan and Account Number].

Please change the primary beneficiary to: _____, trustees, or their successors in trust, under the _____ Living Trust, and any amendments thereto, dated _____, 19___.

I am relying on you to take all appropriate steps to assure that my beneficiary designations are changed properly. Please notify me in writing when you have completed the changes.

Sincerely yours,

Stockbrokers are the most competent people in the world to transfer securities into your trust. When directed properly, they can do this work better, faster, and cheaper than either you or your lawyer could ever hope to.

Your Banker

You may bank at a bank, save at a savings and loan, or get credit at a credit union. No matter what kind of financial institution you use, there will be someone there who can help you transfer your accounts to your trust. Contact your customer service representative and explain that you would like to transfer all your accounts to your trust. The customer service representative can provide the proper forms to make the changes and can help you fill them in.

You can be of great help in this process by providing as much information as possible for each of your accounts, including the account number and the statement the bank or savings and loan sends you regarding the account's status. With this information, the service representative can determine the type of account you have and the best method for changing its name to that of your trust. The changes in the names of these accounts can be made quickly and without a lot of red tape.

A frequently asked question with regard to changing checking accounts to the name of a trust is whether or not the checks themselves have to have the name of the trust on them. *They do not.* The checks can remain in the same name as you have now, regardless of whose name is on the signature card. No one has to know by reading your checks that you have a trust.

It is common for a relative of an older person to want to be able to sign checks on the older person's account. The solution used by most people is to put the account in joint tenancy. Since joint tenancy is a terrible way to own property, the alternative is to name the relative as a co-trustee with an older person. Each trustee can then be given the authority to sign checks. The older person still owns the account, which is now in the name of his or her trust. The relative and the older person can each sign checks on the account as trustees of the trust. When the older person dies or becomes disabled, the account is controlled by the trust. It does not pass to the relative by operation of law as it does with joint tenancy.

When you change the name of your accounts into the name of your trust, you should confirm the changes in writing. Here is a form letter for you to use:

[Date]

[Heading]

RE: Change of Name of Accounts for [Your Name]

Dear [Name of Customer Service Representative]:

This letter is to confirm changing the name of the following accounts to the name of my trust:

Current Name on Account   Type of Account   Account Number

Please change the name of each account to: _____, trustees, or their successors in trust, under the _____ Living Trust, and any amendments thereto, dated _____, 19___.

I am relying on you to take all appropriate steps to assure that my accounts are properly changed. Please notify me in writing when you have completed the changes.

Sincerely yours,

If you have an IRA or other retirement plan at your bank or other financial institution, then your customer service representative can also help you change the beneficiary designation of the plan to your trust. The service representative will provide the proper forms and will, in most cases, be happy to fill in the forms for you. To protect yourself and your loved ones in case of an error, again confirm in writing the change of beneficiary designation.

[Date]

[Heading]

RE: Change of Beneficiary Designation for [Name of Retirement Plan and Account Number]

Dear [Name of Customer Service Representative]:

This letter is to confirm changing the beneficiary designation for [Name of Retirement Plan and Account Number] to my trust.

Please change the primary beneficiary of my plans to: _____, trustees, or their successors in trust, under the _____ Living Trust, and any amendments thereto, dated _____ , 19___.

I am relying on you to take all appropriate steps to assure that my beneficiary designations are changed properly. Please notify me in writing when you have completed the changes.

Sincerely yours,

Your banker should be very familiar with living trusts. Bankers work with trusts on a daily basis. If, for some reason, you have any problems with changing the name of your accounts and your financial institution has a trust department, ask to see a trust officer. A trust officer can intervene and help you to get the job done.

A Special Word About Retirement Plans

Some types of retirement plan beneficiary designations need special treatment if you want to name your trust as the beneficiary. Congress requires that for some retirement plans your spouse must approve changing your beneficiary designation. Each plan has its own kind of Spousal Consent Form to accomplish this.

If you have any doubt about the meaning of spousal consent, or if you do not understand it, the trustee of your retirement plan can explain it to you. If you are not completely satisfied with the trustee's explanation, ask your lawyer, accountant, or insurance agent; these people should have no problem explaining it to you.

There are complex income and estate-tax rules that govern retirement plans and Individual Retirement Accounts (IRAs). The tax effects of changing the beneficiary designations vary, depending on many factors. Before making any beneficiary changes to these plans, you should *always* consult with a competent tax adviser.

When They Ask to See Your Loving Trust Plan

Your Loving Trust plan is your private plan to provide for you and your loved ones. You can choose to show it to whom you want, and you can choose who will not see it. That is your choice.

Because trusts of all types are mysterious to many people, they tend to become cautious when dealing with a trustee. They have no idea why they should be cautious, but they are. They are comfortable dealing with an individual, a corporation, or a partnership, but they are seldom comfortable dealing with a trust through its trustees.

As you put property into your trust and work with it, people in the business world are going to ask, or even demand, to see a copy of your trust. Since your trust is private, and since it may be quite lengthy, it will not be very convenient to let others read or keep a copy of it. There are some excellent alternatives to showing your trust to every person who is nervous about doing business with it.

Some states allow an affidavit of trust. This is a one-page document that will satisfy everyone that your trust is "legal" without having to read it. You should check with your lawyer to see if your state provides for a trust affidavit.

In most instances, people doing business with your trust will be interested in seeing or knowing only a few things about it. They will want to know if it is really your trust, that you are one of its trustees, that you have the authority to act on its behalf, and that it is valid. By giving them copies of the following parts of your

265

trust, you will satisfy their needs without giving them your entire Loving Trust plan:

- The title page, which shows your name as the maker and the names of your trustees.
- The signature pages, which show that your trust is valid.
- The Trustees Powers article of your trust, which describes the powers of the trustees.

This information should suffice for all purposes. There is no reason to show any other part of your Loving Trust plan to anybody. Your trust is a private document and should be kept that way.

There is a technique called a Nominee Partnership, which is a very effective device that is used to eliminate the need to tell anyone you even have a Loving Trust plan. It is a legal method to disguise your trust as a partnership, so nervous Nellies will not question you to death. We have written about how a nominee partnership works in *Protect Your Estate* and in our *A Loving Trust Compendium* for lawyers.

If you would like to keep your trust totally confidential, we strongly suggest that you discuss this technique with your lawyer.

Your Loving Trust planning has nothing to do with your creditors or what you owe them.

Your Debts

Your Loving Trust planning has nothing to do with your creditors or what you owe them. You will still be liable for your debts whether you establish a Loving Trust plan or not. A living trust is not used to avoid your creditors while you are alive; it is used to avoid probate, provide for loved ones, and protect the property you leave to your loved ones from *their* creditors.

When you put your property into your trust, you do not have to put in your debts too. The law is very kind to your creditors, so transferring your property to your Loving Trust will not adversely affect their rights; you will still owe them whatever you owe them. In most cases, you do not have to notify your creditors that you are putting your property into your trust.

There is one instance where you may have to be somewhat careful. When you transfer mortgaged real estate to your trust, you should notify the mortgage holder. Sometimes they get upset when they see their collateral change hands, even if it is to a living trust. Ask your lawyer before you make the transfer whether or not you should notify your mortgage holder. When in doubt, notify your lender. There is almost always no problem in making the transfer, and your notification can eliminate any misunderstandings that may arise.

What If You Do Not Put All Your Property into Your Loving Trust?

Some people are not very diligent about putting their property into their trusts. For some it is just too much of a hassle. Some people initially fund their trust and then neglect to keep it current by failing to put their new acquisitions into it. Other people just plain forget about putting some of their assets in it.

There are two methods to help ensure that your trust will still control your property if you become disabled or die, even if you didn't manage to put all of your property into it. These "fail-safe" devices have helped many people throughout the years. You need both of them to protect you and your loved ones.

Durable Special Power of Attorney

Your lawyer should provide you with a Durable Special Power of Attorney as part of your Loving Trust plan. A Durable Special Power of Attorney allows you to give others the power to transfer your property into your trust if you become disabled and are unable to do it yourself. This is where the "durable" comes from; the power survives your disability. For example, if you have a stroke that totally incapacitates you, and you have not transferred all your property into your trust, those people to whom you have given such a power can transfer your property into your trust for you. Durable Special Powers of Attorney are very effective and are valid almost everywhere.

Make sure that your Durable Special Power of Attorney is really "special." "Special" means that whoever you name can only transfer your property into your trust; they cannot sell, take, use, or give it to anyone. They can only put it in your trust, so that it can be administered pursuant to your Loving Trust instructions.

Some lawyers draft Durable Powers of Attorney that are general powers of attorney. *Do not sign one of these.* Limit the power of the people you name to one thing: the ability to transfer your property to your trust. Granting the holder any more power means you have lost control over your property. A general power of attorney, even if done in the guise of a Durable Power of Attorney, is dangerous and should be avoided.

Since Durable Special Powers of Attorney are limited to one function, you can give them to many people, although some states restrict them to relatives. Generally, the more you give out, the better chance there is that someone will always be available to transfer your property into your trust if you are disabled. Give one to your lawyer and one to your accountant. If you are close to your insurance agent, give one to him or her. Hand them out to relatives and to the trustees you name in your trust.

> A Durable Special Power of Attorney allows you to give others the power to transfer your property into your trust if you become disabled and are unable to do it yourself.

Durable Special Powers of Attorney, when limited to transferring your property into your trust, can only help you; they cannot hurt you. They are fail-safe devices to prevent probate on property you neglected to put in your trust.

Pour-Over Will

As much as we dislike wills, for every trust there must be a short, single-purpose, "fail-safe" will. For safety's sake, a special kind of will, called a "Pour-Over Will," must be signed so that property that you neglect to put in the name of your trust will end up in it after your death.

A Pour-Over Will simply says:

> I leave any property owned by me at my death, and not already in my trust, to my trust. Please have my executor put it in my trust.

Property in your name at your death is subject to probate. If you have not left a will leaving this property somewhere, it passes to your heirs as decided by the law of your state. Since you want your Loving Trust instructions to control all of your property after you die, you must provide that any property not in the name of your trust gets there through your Pour-Over Will. That's where it gets its name—any assets you forgot to put in your trust are poured over into it after your death.

Most states have a small-estate probate exemption. That means that if you do not put a small amount of property into your trust, this property will not have to go through the probate process. Say that you die with $10,000 worth of property that you forgot to transfer to your trust. In some states, this property can be transferred into your trust if you have a Pour-Over Will, without a formal probate proceeding. Thus you can have the best of all worlds: the ability to forget a little bit of property and the opportunity to avoid probate. The amount of this small-estate exemption changes from state to state. Ask your lawyer what the amount is in your state.

It is always best to put all your property into your trust while you are alive and well. However, by using a Durable Special Power of Attorney and a Pour-Over Will, you can be doubly assured that you and your loved ones will still be able to take advantage of your Loving Trust instructions.

Your trust controls only the property that is in it. Putting your property into it may not be easy if you attempt to do so by yourself. By using our techniques, you can quickly and correctly get your property into your trust through utilizing the services of other people. By working smart, you can keep the time and dollar costs of doing so to an absolute minimum. You can also assure yourself that if mistakes are made, someone other than you or your loved ones will pay to correct them.

Chapter Twenty-Six

How to Get Your Advisers Involved to Save Your Time and Money

By properly using your advisers in the implementation of your Loving Trust planning, you should be able to save time and money and end up with a superior Loving Trust product.

We certainly advocate a "team" approach when designing a Loving Trust plan. Unfortunately, the public often views more than one professional as too many people on a single shovel. Sometimes this is true, but just as often it is not. Knowing how and when to use each of your advisers in the Loving Trust process is the key to saving time and money.

You May Want to Use Other Advisers

Reading this book will make you knowledgeable. It will not make you a certified Loving Trust specialist. It is very likely that you will have many questions that we have not raised or answered. We cannot anticipate and write about every conceivable method of designing and implementing your Loving Trust planning. We can only give you general principles, examples, and solutions.

If you have a relatively simple design for your Loving Trust plan and you understand its basics, you will only need a lawyer to answer a few of your questions, to draft your trust, and to help you put property into it. If you have a lot of questions, you may need to talk with your life insurance agent or accountant. You may also wish to talk with stockbrokers or financial planners, or you may want to seek the services of your bank's trust department before you meet with your lawyer. By receiving this "coaching" prior to meeting with your lawyer, you may be able to better communicate your desires.

Different advisers offer different planning perspectives. Professional advisers

> Knowing how and when to use each of your advisers in the Loving Trust process is the key to saving time and money.

269

have a tendency to present a limited number of planning strategies to their clients. This is not done out of laziness or incompetence. It is the product of their education, experience, and background. By asking questions of all your advisers, you will elicit different opinions and get the benefit of many points of view. This will allow you to expand your horizons and give you greater insight into the Loving Trust alternatives that are best for you.

Lawyers do not have a monopoly on teaching trust law and estate planning. They are not your only source of information when it comes to designing your Loving Trust plan. Lawyers are the only advisers who can render legal advice, but other advisers can help in the planning process.

Professional advisers other than lawyers can often be profitably consulted in the design and implementation of your Loving Trust plan. In our experience, many nonlawyer advisers have a very strong working knowledge of trusts and are better at explaining and recommending trust-planning strategies than many lawyers. Remember, professional advisers who are not lawyers cannot give you legal advice, but they can share their knowledge and better prepare you for meeting with your lawyer.

Before we go on, we would like to emphasize that no matter how knowledgeable your nonlegal advisers may be, do not allow them to draft your Loving Trust documents. Only lawyers may draft the legal documents that are found in Loving Trust plans. Anyone else who does it, other than yourself, is breaking the law. Drafting legal documents without a license is a crime in every state. Doing it yourself is not a crime; it's just criminal.

Because the concept of the revocable living trust is becoming more and more popular, there are several businesses that sell revocable living trusts and other estate-planning documents directly to people in an attempt to avoid the traditional attorney-client relationship. Whatever you do, *do not fall prey to these businesses.* It is imperative that you use a lawyer of your choice, as well as other professional advisers, to help you in your planning. We strongly believe that these businesses are doing a disservice, and should be avoided at all costs.

> . . . no matter how knowledgeable your nonlegal advisers may be, do not allow them to draft your Loving Trust documents.

Which Advisers to Involve

There are a number of professionals available to help you with the process of designing your Loving Trust planning. These are basically the same advisers who can help you put your property into your trust. They are your:

- Life insurance agents
- Trust officer
- Stockbroker
- Financial planner
- Accountant

They each have a specific professional function and perspective, and if properly utilized, can offer you much help in the design of your Loving Trust plan.

Your Life Insurance Agent

Loving Trust plans work better when they have real-dollar fuel in them. Insurance proceeds represent that real-dollar fuel that will provide the cash it takes to support and care for your loved ones in the case of your untimely disability or death. It is the most inexpensive and most effective method of getting real-dollar fuel into your Loving Trust planning that we know of. It would be wise for you to involve your life insurance agent in designing your Loving Trust plan.

Many life insurance agents have had formal training in Loving Trust planning techniques, trusts in general, or estate planning. Life insurance companies have traditionally offered excellent training programs in these areas for years. In addition, national organizations, like the American College of Life Underwriters, offer extensive courses to life insurance professionals on all aspects of trust and estate planning. Those life insurance agents who have graduated from the American College are allowed to use the letters "CLU" (Chartered Life Underwriter) after their names, indicating that they have graduated from a thorough insurance and planning curriculum.

Many life insurance agents do not have a CLU designation yet have expertise in Loving Trust techniques. You should ask your agent what training he or she has had in the areas of Loving Trust planning, trusts in general, and estate planning. You may be pleasantly surprised at just how much expertise your agent has.

A number of life insurance companies offer their agents a service known as advanced underwriting. Advanced underwriters are highly trained home-office employees whose sole function is to aid agents with clients having tough life insurance, tax, and other planning problems. If your agent does not know the answers to your questions, it may be that he or she represents a company with a strong advanced underwriting department that can be utilized to answer them and to help you design and implement your Loving Trust plan. Your agent should make these home-office experts available to you at no additional cost.

You should interview your life insurance agent as much as you would your lawyer. It would be helpful if you could work with an agent who has some expertise in Loving Trust planning or who has access to insurance company home-office experts who do. Your life insurance agent should be very much a part of your Loving Trust advisory team.

The more knowledgeable your life insurance agent is about Loving Trust planning techniques, the more likely it is that you will receive the correct answer to your questions and planning concerns for your loved ones. And the more likely it will be that your insurance portfolio will fit your family's needs.

Trying to be your own insurance agent is as dangerous as trying to be your own lawyer. In an effort to reduce the cost of life insurance, many life insurance companies have started to sell directly to the consumer through magazine and newspaper advertisements, without using a trained life insurance agent. Life insurance, like the law, is complicated. Because there are so many different types of policies and so many companies, it is almost impossible to know what policy and company is best for any given situation. Using an agent may mean you will pay slightly more for your life insurance, but the service and advice you will get will more than make up for the extra cost. Life insurance agents are one of the better advisory bargains.

You should contact your agent early in the design stage of your Loving Trust planning. When you meet with your agent, tell him or her exactly what you are doing and that you would like him or her to help you design your Loving Trust planning.

It is likely that your life insurance agent will ask for some personal information. By giving him or her good information, you will make it easier for your agent to help you. Give him or her a copy of "My Personal Information Checklist." If you are uncomfortable doing so, you should start searching for another agent.

Your agent should be able to explain how a Loving Trust plan works and how it can be used to provide for you and your loved ones. He or she should also have a working knowledge of the federal estate tax and how it may affect you and your family.

By far the most important input your life-insurance agent can give you—other than the amount and type of life insurance that you need—is his or her ideas on providing for loved ones. We have given seminars to many top life-insurance agents all over the country. Their greatest strength, other than knowing their products, is their feeling for and knowledge of people. Life insurance agents are people-oriented.

Your life-insurance agent should be familiar with the Loving Trust concept. It will help if the two of you are talking the same language. If you have to bring your agent up-to-speed, it will not delay your progress a great deal. Life-insurance agents are used to studying; it will not take long for him or her to understand the concepts in this book.

We teach select members of the life-insurance industry and have been impressed with their Loving Trust commitments. We encourage you to have a life-insurance agent as one of your key advisers.

For the price of buying insurance protection, which you likely have or need anyway, you can enlist this knowledgeable adviser on your Loving Trust team. If you do not have an agent you are comfortable with, take the time to interview others. Find one you like who knows what he or she is doing. Together, you can design a Loving Trust plan that meets your needs and specifications and that has the proper amount of real-dollar fuel to make it work.

Your Trust Officer

Trust companies and banks with trust departments are wonderful sources of Loving Trust advice. Trust officers are well versed in trust law and in the day-to-day practicalities of how they work. They are competent to answer almost all of your Loving Trust questions.

Trust officers offer a different design perspective. Where a life-insurance agent will encourage planning for loved ones and will emphasize the love in your Loving Trust planning, trust officers will view your Loving Trust planning more from a business or operational perspective. They will be more concerned with complexity of administration, investment strategy, and liability issues. They will dwell on trust mechanics.

Many, if not most, trust officers are lawyers. If they are not lawyers, they will still have had considerable training in the creation and operation of trusts. Trust departments usually have large staffs that contain many trust-specialist experts. If the person you talk to cannot answer your questions, he or she should be able to seek out fellow employees who will surely be able to.

Trust officers are in the business of operating and administering trusts. They want your business, which is why they will be more than willing to meet with you to discuss your Loving Trust thoughts without charge. Trust officers want you to name their institution as a trustee. You represent new business to the trust officer and his or her financial institution.

Trust departments and trust companies charge by taking a percentage of the value of the property they administer as their annual fee. This percentage is usually less than 2 percent, making them a real bargain in the marketplace. They would not charge this fee until your Loving Trust planning activated on either your disability or death, or if you choose to have them be your trustee to manage your property now.

If you would like to discuss your situation with a trust officer, you should contact your bank or local trust company to set up an appointment. If your bank does not have a trust department, find the names of those that do. You do not have to bank at an institution in order to use their trust department's services. Institutional trustees offer a unique public service. They are staffed with professional people who will treat you both politely and kindly.

When you meet with a trust officer, please keep in mind that trust officers have many trusts to administer and that they have a limited amount of time. Prepare for the meeting by writing down the questions you wish to ask. Explain that you are in the process of designing a Loving Trust plan and that you are considering naming a financial institution as one of its trustees. Be sure to bring your copy of this book; again, you need to be talking the same language. The trust officer must be familiar with your Loving Trust goals to be an effective adviser.

A trust officer can be of service to you in several ways. He or she can help you understand how a Loving Trust plan works and what you can do to provide for loved ones. The trust officer can answer legal and nonlegal questions concerning trust law and your Loving Trust planning. He or she can offer invaluable experience in how a Loving Trust operates and how it can be administered. A trust officer can help you locate the Loving Trust lawyers in your community. Finally, a trust officer can help you transfer many types of property into your Loving Trust.

Traditionally, there is no fee for these implementation services. They are rendered as both a public service and as an inducement to you to name their bank as one of your trustees. When designing your Loving Trust plan, do not overlook the valuable services of a trust officer.

> **When designing your Loving Trust plan, do not overlook the valuable services of a trust officer.**

Your Financial Planner

There is a great deal of confusion as to what a financial planner is and what one does. We do not expect the confusion to dissipate until this relatively new breed of adviser is somehow licensed and controlled. Lack of licensing has made the selection and use of those who hold themselves out as financial planners somewhat risky.

Generally, financial planners analyze and make recommendations about almost every aspect of their clients' financial lives. Some of the services that they provide include family budgeting, choosing and managing investments, ways and means of building wealth, and estate planning. Financial planners come from all walks of life; they may be accountants, life-insurance agents, lawyers, or even people who just believe they have expertise or experience in finances.

There are institutions that teach and offer certificates to people who desire to be financial planners. Once a financial planner has graduated from the American College, for example, he or she may use the designation ChFC (Chartered Financial Consultant). A financial planner may also belong to professional associations such as the International Association of Financial Planners.

You must be very careful in selecting a financial planner. Even those recommended by friends or other advisers should be subject to your most careful scrutiny. Make sure that anyone you are considering is certified or chartered and that he or she has the background and experience to assist you. Always ask for a résumé and a list of references. Do not hire anyone until you have thoroughly checked his or her references.

Once you have gone through the preliminaries of establishing his or her credentials, you should immediately inquire how that financial planner charges for his or her services.

Financial planners generally charge for their services in one of three ways. Some charge solely on a fee or hourly basis, much like a lawyer or an accountant. You should ask what the fee is and how it is determined. Your first consultation should be at no charge.

Other financial planners receive their compensation from commissions generated by the investment products they sell. These include life insurance, stocks, bonds, and investments of all types. These planners make money only if you buy, so they would like your business only if you are a buyer, not a looker. It is not uncommon for these types of financial planners to charge a minimal fee for the preparation of your master financial plan. This plan will have suggestions as to what investments you ought to make and sometimes even the amount of life insurance you need. The financial planner will then offer to sell you the products that your plan suggests you need.

Some financial planners charge both a fee and take commissions. Many of them will offset their fee by the commissions they earn, in effect giving you a fee rebate if you buy their products.

A financial planner who is well-versed in Loving Trust planning may very well save you money by being able to answer those nonlegal questions that you would otherwise ask your lawyer.

If you have a financial planner who is up-to-date on Loving Trust planning, it will greatly facilitate your ability to quickly and successfully complete your Loving Trust planning. If you do not have a financial planner, there is no need to hire one just for Loving Trust planning.

Like an insurance agent, your financial planner can help you create and design your Loving Trust planning. Even though oriented to the financial side of planning, good financial planners are people-oriented. It is not by accident that some of the better financial planners are also members of the life-insurance profession.

Your Stockbroker

Many brokerage firms offer free seminars concerning "Estate Planning." This topic encompasses wills and trusts, as well as related investment areas including life insurance. These seminars can prove to be the perfect opportunity to have many of your Loving Trust questions answered. Local lawyers are frequently the guest speakers at these seminars. They will offer their views on estate planning, trust planning, probate avoidance, and related planning areas. While not all the lawyers may understand the Loving Trust approach, you should be able to ask meaningful questions of them if you attend such a gathering. This will allow you to receive some "free" legal advice and facilitate your understanding.

The lawyers and other speakers who conduct these seminars are compensated by the sponsoring brokerage firm. They are free to you. They, just like the brokerage firm, hope to attract clients from the audience. These seminars may be a good place for you to find a lawyer.

Stockbrokers sometimes provide financial planning services for their clients. Their knowledge of Loving Trust planning goes well with their overall financial acumen. The larger brokerage firms sometimes have lawyers on their staffs who can assist the broker and his or her client with Loving Trust design.

The services offered by stockbrokers are usually not free unless you are a very good client. Fees vary. Sometimes they are hourly and sometimes they are set at a predetermined amount. Make sure you know in detail what services are provided by your stockbroker and how much they cost before agreeing to an engagement.

Unless you know your broker well, do not lean too heavily on him or her for guidance in the design of your Loving Trust plan. He or she has other things to do in order to make a living.

Your Accountant

If we could realistically do it, we would require that all our clients have an accountant. An accountant's objectivity, knowledge, and skills are very useful when confronting some of the financial problems that life has to offer. We have always encouraged our clients' accountants to get involved with us early in the Loving Trust process.

Accountants invariably charge by the hour, and their rates are usually very reasonable for the service they provide. The hourly rate charged by all but the most sophisticated accountants is usually well below that charged by lawyers.

Accountants understand the need for proper Loving Trust planning. They have been advocates of probate avoidance and providing for loved ones for many years. They have traditionally been major advocates of Loving Trust planning.

An accountant is invaluable in the Loving Trust process. This is because he or she usually knows more about his or her client than the clients know about themselves. If you have an accountant, you are far more likely to have more contact with him or her than with all your other advisers combined.

If you are single and you are worth in excess of $600,000 or if you and your spouse have property worth more than $600,000, we strongly suggest that you have an accountant as one of your Loving Trust advisers. Accountants are usually well versed in the federal estate-tax aspects of Loving Trust planning and can be very helpful in federal estate-tax planning. We are confident that they are competent in this area because we wrote an American Institute of Certified Public Accountants' course on *Estate and Gift Taxation*. Having a professional to "run the numbers" will help you save time and money in the Loving Trust process.

Your accountant can help you and your lawyer transfer property to your Loving Trust. Many times we have had clients' accountants work with us in locating title to property and making sure it was transferred into our clients' Loving Trusts. Accountants are used to keeping good records, and they keep track of your transactions in great detail. They are invaluable when it comes to knowing the specifics of your financial life.

You do not always need a full team to design and implement your Loving Trust plan. You and your lawyer can do it very successfully together. We have found, however, that by using other advisers, you can make the process of designing and implementing your Loving Trust planning much more efficient— and a great deal more fun. By properly using your various advisers' talents, you can also keep your time and dollar outlays to an absolute minimum.

Authors' Note

Because of the overwhelming response to *Loving Trust* from both the public and our professional colleagues, we have created the National Network of Estate Planning Attorneys to assist lawyers in learning and implementing Loving Trust techniques.

The National Network of Estate Planning Attorneys is for lawyers only. It was created to provide an educational and practice resource that enables conscientious lawyers to quickly learn and implement Loving Trust techniques in their practices. It provides highly professional seminars, course work, reference material, and practice aids that will assist attorneys to quickly adapt their professional practices so that they can provide sophisticated Loving Trust techniques to their clients.

If you know of any attorneys who would like to learn more about establishing a professional Loving Trust practice, they can do so by calling 1–800–638–8681.

My Personal Information Checklist

Date of Preparation _____

Business Address _____

MY:

Full Legal Name _____

Nickname _____

Home Address _____

Home Phone (_____) _____

Birth Date _____

Occupation/Title _____

Business Address _____

Business Phone (_____) _____

MY SPOUSE'S:

Full Legal Name _____

Nickname _____

Birth Date _____

Occupation/Title _____

Business Address _____

Business Phone (_____) _____

MY CHILDREN:

Full Legal Name _____

Birth Date _____

MY SPOUSE'S CHILDREN (if different from mine):

Full Legal Name _____

Birth Date _____

MY OTHER DEPENDENTS:

(Friends or relatives who depend on me for all or part of their support.)

Name _____

Relationship _____

QUESTIONS ABOUT YOU AND YOUR FAMILY:

You should fully brief your attorney on the following matters:

1. Do you have a child with a learning disability?
2. Do any of your children receive government support or benefits?
3. Do you have adopted children?
4. Do any of your children have special educational, medical, or physical needs?
5. Are any of your children institutionalized?
6. Are you or your spouse receiving social security or disability benefits?
7. Do you wish to disinherit any of your children, grandchildren, or other relatives?
8. Whom do you wish to be the primary guardians of your children?
9. Whom do you wish to be the contingent guardians?
10. Have you been divorced?
11. Are you making payments pursuant to a divorce or property settlement agreement?
12. Have you been widowed?
13. On what date were you married?
14. In what states have you lived while married to your current spouse? During what periods of time did you reside there?
15. Have you or your spouse ever filed federal gift-tax returns?
16. Have you or your spouse completed previous will, trust, or estate planning?
17. Did you and your spouse ever sign a pre- or post-marriage contract?

HOW MY PROPERTY IS OWNED

This checklist is designed to help you list all the property you own and how it is titled. You may own more property than can be listed on this checklist. If so, use extra sheets of paper to list your additional property.

Immediately after the title heading for each kind of property is a brief explanation of what document or documents you will need as evidence of title to your property. Remember, having these documents is essential in transferring property to your Loving Trust. By collecting this documentation yourself, you will save substantial professional fees.

How you own your property is extremely important for purposes of properly designing and implementing your Loving Trust plan. For each property category, there is a column titled "How It's Owned." When filling in this column, use the following abbreviations:

For prperty owned in your name alone, use	MINE
For property in your spouse's name alone, use	SPOUSE
For property in joint tenancy with your spouse, use	JTS
For property in joint tenancy with someone other than your spouse, use	JTO
For property in tenancy in common with your spouse, use	TCS
For property in tenancy in common with someone other than your spouse, use	TCO
For community property, use	CP
If you can't determined how the property is owned, use	?

Cash Accounts

[Evidence of title: signature card or the document you signed to set up the account.]

How It's Owned _____

Checking Account:

Institution where located _____

Account Number _____

Savings Account:

Institution where located _____

Account Number _____

Certificate of Deposit:

Institution where located _____

Account Number _____

Money Market:

Institution where located _____

Account Number _____

Life Insurance and Annuities

[Evidence of title: the policy itself, including all endorsements and amendments, and the original application you signed.]

How It's Owned _____

Name of Insured _____

Company Issuing Policy _____

Type of Policy _____

(Is the policy whole life, universal life, single premium life, an endowment policy, an annuity, group term life, or some other type of policy? If you cannot tell, either call your insurance agent or bring the policy to your attorney for review.)

Policy Number _____

Primary Beneficiary _____

Contingent Beneficiary _____

Disability Insurance

[Evidence of title: the policy itself and the application you signed.]

How It's Owned _____

Name of Insured _____

Company Issuing Policy _____

Policy Number _____

Beneficiary _____

(If you cannot find a beneficiary designation, either call your insurance representative or bring the policy to your attorney for review.)

MY PERSONAL INFORMATION CHECKLIST

Retirement Plans

[Evidence of title: summary plan description, documents you signed to set up the plan, account statement, beneficiary designation.]

How It's Owned _____

IRA:

Primary Beneficiary _____

Contingent Beneficiary _____

PROFIT-SHARING PLAN

Primary Beneficiary _____

Contingent Beneficiary _____

PENSION PLAN

Primary Beneficiary _____

Contingent Beneficiary _____

OTHER TYPES OF RETIREMENT PLANS

Type of Plan _____

Primary Beneficiary _____

Contingent Beneficiary _____

Publicly Traded Stocks, Bonds, and Other Securities

[Evidence of title: Stock certificate, bond instrument, the documents you signed to set up a street account or a copy of the statement, documents you signed when purchasing the security.]

How It's Owned _____

STOCKS:

Name of Company _____

Number of Shares _____

Certificate Number _____

BONDS:

Name of Company _____

Face Amount _____

Identifying Number _____

OTHER SECURITIES:

Name of Company _____

Amount _____

Identifying Number _____
STREET NAME ACCOUNT:

Name of Brokerage Firm _____

Account Number _____

Non-Publicly Traded Investments, Tax Shelters*

*Includes limited partnerships, REITs, and all other investments where you are not an active participant.

[Evidence of title: documents you signed to purchase each investment or tax shelter.]

How It's Owned _____

Name of Investment _____

Name of Broker or Promoter _____

Type of Investment or Shelter _____

Notes, Contracts, and Other Receivables

[Evidence of title: promissory note, written contract, or other documents creating right to receive payment.]

How It's Owned _____

Person/Company Who Owes You _____

Face Amount of Obligation _____

Due Date _____

Real Estate, Including Your Residence

[Evidence of title: deed or land contract (do not use mortgage or tax assessment).]

How It's Owned _____

Address or Description of Property _____

My Own Business

[Evidence of title: stock certificate, partnership agreement, or any other documents that you believe created your business entity.]

How It's Owned _____

CORPORATION:

Name of Corporation _____

Type of Stock (Common or Preferred) _____

Certificate Number _____

Number of Shares _____

PARTNERSHIP:

Name of Partnership _____

General or Limited Partnership _____

Percentage Owned _____

SOLE PROPRIETORSHIP

(Since a sole proprietorship has no actual title to it, you must list all bank accounts and property owned in the name of the business for the purpose of determining title. If property used in the sole proprietorship is in your name, list it in this section rather than elsewhere.)

Name of Business_____

*Tangible Personal Property**

*Tangible personal property includes motor vehicles, boats, jewelry, collections, antiques, furs, and all other nonbusiness personal property.

[Evidence of title: Registration or title issued by your state, bill of sale, receipt, canceled check, or source of cash to purchase property, gift tax return, or inheritance tax return if you received property by gift or inheritance.]

How It's Owned _____

Description of Property _____

*Other Property**

*Other Property is any property that you have that does not fit into any listed category. For example, patents, royalties, and mineral interests, such as oil and gas, could be listed here.

[Evidence of title: documents you signed to purchase the property, documents you received when you received the property, or any other document you have that shows you own the property.]

How It's Owned _____

Brief description of property _____

Index